How to do social researc

Methods Lab

Series editors: Rebecca Coleman and Kat Jungnickel

The *Methods Lab* series is committed to leading-edge critical and creative research practices in and beyond academia. It aims to be a publishing platform that supports a wide range of approaches to studying and intervening in the social world. Through repurposing and borrowing from inside and outside the academy, it stretches the walls of disciplinary scholarship.

How to do social research with...

Edited by
Rebecca Coleman, Kat Jungnickel and Nirmal Puwar

Goldsmiths
Press

Printed and bound by Short Run Press Limited, UK
Distribution by the MIT Press
Cambridge, Massachusetts, USA and London, England

A CIP record for this book is available from the British Library

ISBN 978-1-913380-42-7 (pbk)
ISBN 978-1-913380-40-3 (ebk)

www.gold.ac.uk/goldsmiths-press

This book is dedicated to the administrative and professional staff who are no longer in the Sociology Department at Goldsmiths but supported the infrastructure of learning and research before the restructure of Goldsmiths, which began in 2019. Their sound professionalism and kindness are missed daily. Here we would like to name especially Violet Fearon, Chloe Nast and Clare Lewis.

Contents

Figures

Contributors

MARGARITA ARAGON is a Lecturer in Sociology in the Department of Psychosocial Studies, Birkbeck, University of London. Her research is primarily concerned with examining the intersections of race, gender and disability in their historical and contemporary iterations.

LES BACK teaches sociology at the University of Glasgow, and before that at Goldsmiths, University of London. His writing spans the sociology of urban life, youth, racism, right-wing extremism, music and popular culture and sport. More recently, he has been exploring the relationship between sociology and music through his teaching, but also by interviewing sociologists who are practising musicians. This interest emerges from his own life because throughout his long sociological career he has had a shadow life as a journeyman guitarist performing with the black British blues singer Earl Green amongst others.

MICHAELA BENSON is Professor in Public Sociology at Lancaster University. She is particularly known for her research on migration, citizenship and belonging, notably through her work on Britain's relationship to its emigrants and overseas citizens at moments of major political transformation including Brexit and decolonisation. She has published several academic monographs including *The British in Rural France* (2011, Manchester University Press), and *Lifestyle Migration and Colonial Traces in Malaysia and Panama* (co-authored with Karen O'Reilly; 2018, Palgrave). In recent years, she has developed her sociological practice to include podcasting, producing and presenting the series *Brexit Brits Abroad* (2017–2020) and *Who Do We Think We Are?* (2021–present).

AOIFE CAMPBELL-FRANKS is an early career researcher at the University of Dundee. Her research is concerned with the construction of disability within state discourses as well as exploring the ways in which disabled people navigate and resist ableist housing policy.

REBECCA COLEMAN is Professor in the Bristol Digital Futures Institute (BDFI) and the School of Sociology, Politics and International Studies, at the University of Bristol. She did her PhD in the Sociology Department at Goldsmiths, University of London and later worked there and co-directed the Methods Lab. Her research explores digital media and culture, temporality and interdisciplinary, participatory methods. Recent publications include *Glitterworlds: The Future Politics of a Ubiquitous Thing* (2020, Goldsmiths Press), 'Feminist New Materialist Practice: The Mattering of Method' (co-edited, 2019, *MAI: Feminism and Visual Culture*), and 'Futures in Question: Theories, Methods, Practices' (co-edited, 2017, *Sociological Review*).

FAY DENNIS is a Wellcome Trust Research Fellow in the Sociology Department at Goldsmiths, University of London. Her work explores the sociomaterial entanglements of illicit drug use. Fay has been conducting research in this field for over a decade and has become particularly interested in the contingency of drug effects determined not by the substance but as situated enactments of drug-body-worlds. In this area, Fay has been experimenting with different methodologies for attuning to these practices and processes. Her current project, funded by a Wellcome Trust University Award (2022–2027), continues this work in relation to post-pandemic changes in substance use treatment.

MONICA GRECO is Professor of Sociology at Goldsmiths, University of London, and a Fellow of the Alexander von Humboldt-Stiftung. Her research engages with the history, philosophy and contemporary practices of psychosomatic medicine with the aim of probing and expanding contemporary imaginaries of health. Monica's publications include the monograph *Illness as a Work of Thought* (1998, Routledge) and a special issue of the BMJ journal *Medical Humanities* on the topic of 'Biopolitics and Psychosomatics' (2019), as well as numerous articles in peer-reviewed journals.

KIRAN GREWAL is a Reader in Sociology at Goldsmiths where she convenes the MA in Human Rights, Culture and Social Justice and co-directs the Unit for Global Justice. Kiran's current research focuses on the social justice struggles of marginalised and/or subaltern groups in Sri Lanka and what they can contribute to decolonial theory and practice. She is the lead investigator on a British Academy-funded project, titled 'Building New Critical Democratic Communities in Sri Lanka: The

Role of Traditional Arts and Ritual! For more information, please see https://decolonial.org.

MICHAEL GUGGENHEIM is a Reader in the Sociology Department at Goldsmiths, University of London. He researches food, disasters, environmental experts and change of use of buildings, and he is interested in expanding the methods repertoire of sociology.

YASMIN GUNARATNAM has an expertise in qualitative, artistic and participatory research methods. Her publications include *Researching Race and Ethnicity: Methods, Knowledge and Power* (2003, Sage), *Death and the Migrant* (2013, Bloomsbury Academic) and the co-authored book *Go Home? The Politics of Immigration Controversies* (2017, Manchester University Press). Yasmin is a sociologist in the School for Education, Communication and Society, Kings College (University of London).

CATHERINE HAHN is an artist and social researcher. She is a Lecturer in History of Art and Administrator of the Studio 3 Gallery, University of Kent. Previously she taught at Goldsmiths in the Visual Cultures and Sociology Departments. Catherine researches art's role in society, in particular the museum as a community resource. Catherine uses drawing to investigate the institutional conditions of art. For the past three years, she has been a researcher with the Global Gender and Cultures of Equality project, GlobalGRACE (Goldsmiths), exploring how equalities are made in the arts sector in South Africa and the UK.

KATALIN HALÁSZ is a Leverhulme Early Career Research Fellow at Brunel University. She uses arts-based research methods to explore the affective lived relations and embodied experience of race and gender. She has staged a number of participatory and multimedia performances in the UK, Denmark, Germany, USA, Brazil, Bolivia and South Africa, and has curated exhibitions in London. She is on the board of the *International Visual Sociology Association* and on the editorial board of *Qualitative Research*. More on her artful sociological research can be found here: www.katalinhalasz.com/

ELLA HARRIS is currently a Leverhulme Early Career Fellow at Birkbeck, University of London, Department of Geography. Her work explores 'crisis cultures' and uses interactive documentary as an experimental method.

EMMA JACKSON is an urban sociologist and ethnographer. She is Senior Lecturer and Convenor of the MA Sociology (Urban Studies) Programme in the Sociology Department at Goldsmiths, University of London. Her research and writing explore the relationship between everyday practices of belonging, the production of spaces and places in cities, and relations of class, multiculture and urban change. She is also an editor of *The Sociological Review* and a trustee of the IJURR Foundation.

KAT JUNGNICKEL is a Reader in Sociology, Director of the Methods Lab and Principal Investigator on the European Research Council-funded project 'Politics of Patents' at Goldsmiths. Her research explores mobilities, gender, technology cultures, DIY/making practices, and visual and inventive methods. Recent publications include: (ed.) *Failurists: When things go awry* (with Lammes, Hjorth and Rae; 2023, Institute of Network Cultures), (ed.) *Transmissions: Critical Tactics for Making and Communicating Research* (2020, The MIT Press), and *Creative Practice Ethnographies* (with Hjorth, Harris and Coombs; 2019, Rowman & Littlefield).

SOBIA AHMAD KAKER is currently Lecturer in Criminology at the Department of Sociology, University of Essex and is a member of the advisory board at Karachi Urban Lab (Pakistan). She is an interdisciplinary urban studies scholar whose research focuses on the 'lived' aspects of uncertainty and insecurity in Pakistani and other global south cities. She is interested in studying the ways in which urban residents and governors navigate everyday uncertainty and insecurity, and how social and spatial processes of crime and security governance impact urban sociopolitical relations. Sobia adopts an ethnographic and contextual approach to her work.

PHOEBE KISUBI MBASALAKI is a Lecturer in Sociology at the University of Essex. Prior to that, she was a Post-Doctoral Research Fellow on the GlobalGRACE project (www.globalgrace.net) working between the African Gender Institute (AGI), the Centre for Theatre, Dance and Performance Studies (CTDPS), University of Cape Town and the NGO Sex Workers Advocacy and Educational Task Force (SWEAT). She was also a Lecturer on the Gender Studies programme at the AGI, University of Cape Town. Her research interests lie in critical race, class, gender, sexuality, creative activism, public health as well as decolonial thought and praxis.

CAROLINE KNOWLES is Global Professorial Fellow at Queen Mary, University of London and the Director of the British Academy's Urban Infrastructures of Well-Being Programme. She is an urban sociologist who writes about globalisation – particularly circulations of people (as migrants), objects and materials. Her most recent book, *Serious Money: Walking Plutocratic London* is published by Penguin (2022). Other recent books include *Flip-Flop: A Journey through Globalisation's Backroads* (2014, Pluto Press; www.flipfloptrail.com) and *Hong Kong: Migrant Lives, Landscapes and Journeys*, with Douglas Harper (2009, University of Chicago Press).

VIK LOVEDAY is a Senior Lecturer in the Sociology Department at Goldsmiths, University of London, whose work is concerned with the analysis of contemporary UK universities, including issues related to governance, precarity and inequalities. Aside from work on Higher Education, Vik is also interested in cultural memory and identity, and is currently conducting research on perceptions of public art and architecture in 'post-communist' contexts.

SARA MATCHETT is an Associate Professor and the Director of the Centre for Theatre, Dance and Performance Studies (CTDPS) at the University of Cape Town. She is the Co-Founder and Artistic Director of The Mothertongue Project women's arts collective. She is also an Associate Teacher of Fitzmaurice Voicework® and the African Regional Co-ordinator of the Fitzmaurice Institute. Her teaching profile centres on practical and academic courses and her research explores breath as a catalyst for generating images for performance making. Her particular interests are in embodied practices that focus on presencing, co-sensing, collaborating and co-generating as a way of transforming egosystems to ecosystems.

MARIAM MOTAMEDI-FRASER is a Reader in Sociology at Goldsmiths. Her research focuses on the animal sciences, with a special interest in the concept of species. She is the author of *Dog Politics: Species Stories and the Animal Sciences* (2024, Manchester University Press). Mariam teaches an undergraduate module called 'Thinking Animals' and an MA module called 'The Ethics and Politics of Animals'. Monk is an unflappable black Labrador. In the eight years that Mariam and Monk have lived and worked together, he has challenged many of her own and her students' preconceptions and assumptions about dogs, and about human–animal relationships.

SEVASTI-MELISSA NOLAS is an academic, writer and accidental archivist, who teaches Sociology at Goldsmiths, University of London. She researches childhood, youth and family life from children's and young people's perspectives using group work and visual methods and is best known for her work on children's participation and childhood publics, and thinking about the things that matter to children from the child's perspective. She is Director of the Childhood Publics Research Programme and the Children's Photography Archive, and co-edits the journal *entanglements: experiments in multimodal ethnography.*

NIRMAL PUWAR has been an academic at Goldsmiths, University of London since 2003. She is a British Academy Innovative Fellow. Her book *Space Invaders* (2004, Berg Publishers) generated a framework for considering the conditions of inclusion within institutions. She experiments with a range of research methods. She co-founded the Methods Lab to mutate relations within and beyond the walls of the academy and is Co-Director of the Centre for Feminist Research. *Live Methods*, co-edited with Les Back (2012, Wiley-Blackwell), is one of 18 collections she has co-edited. As a Writer-As-Resident she has been writing a book titled *ONE MILE WALK: Walking Along with...* (2024, Punctum Press) with a focus on decompositions and recompositions. Creative academic writing and artistic collaboration sits at the heart of this project.

ALEX RHYS-TAYLOR is a Senior Lecturer in Sociology at Goldsmiths. His research is focused on the ephemeral micro-interactions that comprise everyday life in the city. He has written extensively about the social life of smells and flavours in social processes, often through the prism of food objects such as mangoes, eels and fried chicken. His current research is an effort to understand changes to etiquette and notions of civic virtue in the post-pandemic global city.

KATHERINE ROBINSON is a Lecturer in Sociology and Convenor of the MA in Sociology at Goldsmiths, University of London. She is an ethnographer whose research explores issues in urban public space and everyday practices in organisations, from international non-governmental organisations (NGOs) to public libraries in South London and Berlin.

LOUISE RONDEL is an early career researcher in Sociology at Goldsmiths, University of London and teaches sociology and criminology. Working across urban sociology and critical beauty studies, her research interests include beauty work, urban spaces, materials, infrastructures, bodies, water and questions of social and environmental justice. Louise also co-curates 'Infrastructural Explorations', a series of interactive walking workshops which invite participants to critically engage with the impacts of infrastructure on the urban landscape.

MARSHA ROSENGARTEN is Professor in Sociology and Co-Director of the Centre for Invention and Social Process in the Sociology Department at Goldsmiths, University of London. She is the author of *HIV Interventions: Biomedicine and the Traffic in Information and Flesh* (2009, University of Washington Press), co-author with Mike Michael of *Innovation and Biomedicine: Ethics, Evidence and Expectation in HIV* (2013, Springer) and co-editor with Alex Wilkie and Martin Savransky of *Speculative Research: The Lure of Possible Futures* (2017, Routledge). Recent publications focus on biomedical research within the field of HIV, Ebola and Covid-19.

MONICA SASSATELLI is Associate Professor at the University of Bologna, Department of the Arts and Senior Lecturer at Goldsmiths, University of London, Sociology Department. Her research and teaching concentrate on cultural events and institutions, cultural policies and creative industries, more recently with a focus on visual arts. She is also interested in methodological innovation, particularly the use of drawings and comics in social research. Recent publications include, on Europe, 'Europe's cosmopolitan identity: Images of unity in diversity in the Euro' (in F. Mangiapane and T. Migliore [eds], *Images of Europe*, 2021, Springer); on comics in sociology, 'Show and tell' (*Sociologica*, 15(1), 2021).

MARTIN SAVRANSKY is Senior Lecturer and Convenor of the MA in Ecology, Culture and Society in the Sociology Department at Goldsmiths, University of London. His work combines philosophy and the social sciences, post-colonial thought and the environmental humanities, to activate speculative methodologies of life on unstable ecological terrain. He is the author of *Around the Day in Eighty Worlds: Politics of the Pluriverse*

(2021, Duke University Press) and *The Adventure of Relevance: An Ethics of Social Inquiry* (2016, Palgrave Macmillan), and Co-Editor of *After Progress* (2022, Sage) and *Speculative Research: The Lure of Possible Futures* (2017, Routledge, 2017).

CHRISTOS VARVANTAKIS has a background in social anthropology and sociology and currently works as Co-Director of the Children's Photography Archive C.I.C. His research focuses on the intersections of childhood and youth, politics, archives and urban cultures, as well as on qualitative, visual and multimodal research methodologies. He is Co-Editor of the journal *entanglements: experiments in multimodal ethnography* and Head of Programming at the Athens Ethnographic Film Festival – Ethnofest.

Acknowledgements

This collection includes contributions from people who are or have been based in the Sociology Department at Goldsmiths. It acknowledges and records a vast body of intellectual creativity; as a catalogue of how methods have been compiled, as well as how they have been compiling us. The book has been produced over a long and difficult time, including the beginning of the Covid-19 pandemic, as well as an exhausting period of mass industrial action. The university sector in the UK has been under pressure from intersecting crises in the wake of austerity, Brexit, culture wars, increased cost of living and energy shortages, as well as hostile political views on higher education. The arts, humanities and social sciences in particular are feeling these forces. Many universities and departments, including our own, have been restructured as a result. We would like to acknowledge here at least two important points that arise from this situation.

The first is that the writing of this book has been conducted in conditions of political struggle; amidst structures of feelings of destruction and depletion. We would like to thank all the contributors to the book for sticking with the collection. Many of the people who were based in the Sociology Department when we began the book no longer work here. This book captures a moment in time by showcasing the remarkable range of skills, interests and talent in one place. The fact that so many people leapt at the opportunity to make this book together, despite what was happening around us, also signals the strength of support, care and commitment that underpins the uniqueness of our department.

People are infrastructure and institutional changes and histories are part and parcel of our research environments. We would therefore like to show our gratitude to and solidarity with the departmental professional services who kept the life and interlinked atmospheres of learning, teaching and research alive for so long. Violet Fearon, the Undergraduate Programmes Co-ordinator has been a calm steady anchor, through choppy times, for staff and students, for over 22 years. Violet was at the centre of the Sociology Department, sitting on the ninth floor of the Warmington Tower, which features on the cover of this book. Chloe Nast, the Research Administrator, was a holding station during trying times. Clare Lewis and Claire Jarman made managing the department feel smooth when we are sure it was anything but. All left in the most difficult of circumstances during the restructuring process. We would also like to acknowledge and thank colleagues in the Sociology Department, past and present, who do not have chapters in the book, for being crucial parts of a supportive, vibrant and inventive research culture. Thank you to Louise Rondel for her calm, organised good humour whilst compiling, formatting and copy-editing the manuscript and to Clare Hamman for valuable assistance with the proofs and index. Thanks also to Paul Chokran for the original artwork and design for the book cover, adapted by Goldsmiths Press.

The second point is that we think methodological innovation is necessary in conditions of dramatic change and crisis. We strive to build on, adapt, reinvigorate and make new methods to adequately relate to our social worlds. As we explore in the Introduction, the Methods Lab, located in the Sociology Department, has been a key space through which interdisciplinary methodological inventiveness has been fostered at Goldsmiths. It aims to re-route the walls of the academy in the generation of mutating methods to work on problems and issues at hand. The Methods Lab was co-founded by Les Back and Nirmal Puwar in 2004 and co-directed until 2017 by Nirmal and Mariam Motimedi Fraser when Kat Jungnickel and Rebecca Coleman took over. The idea for this book has a long germination, with one starting point being an event, organised in 2015 by Rebecca and Noortje Marres, called 'How to do sociology with…', where members of staff and students gave short, videoed presentations on the 'things' with which they did their research. This event morphed into a series of exploratory practice-based workshops led by early career researchers, many of whom have chapters in the book, and ran alongside other practice research workshops led by Kat. At the same time, Nirmal, Sobia Ahmad Kaker and Rebecca organised workshops on writing, which started at the House of the Illustration in Kings Cross, where we experimented with writing about research differently. The discussions and exercises from here provided inspiration for how many of us wrote the chapters for this book, during various lockdowns. Influenced by creative non-fiction writing methods, Nirmal led online collective writing workshops and gave us different prompts to encourage us to consider particular, and often overlooked, aspects of our research process. There are, also, much earlier starting points for and routes to this collection in the Sociology Department and we see this catalogue of ideas and practices as contributing to the long-standing tradition of teaching and research on, around and for methods.

Introduction: How to do social research with...

Rebecca Coleman, Kat Jungnickel and Nirmal Puwar

How to do social research with... is a book that focuses on the relations involved in the doing of critical, creative and interdisciplinary research with a range of unusual and unexpected things and people. But what does this mean and what does it involve? What does this book contribute to an array of interest in and enthusiasm for methodology and method across the social sciences? What does it do that is different?

In this Introduction, we address these questions. Our opening sentence posits a number of different entry points.

Doing Critical, Creative and Interdisciplinary Social Research *with* a Range of Unusual and Unexpected *Things and People*

At the core of the book is an attempt to explore what is involved in doing research *with* a range of relationships and unusual *things*. The contributions to this book examine how research is done with a variety of things – *objects*, such as chillies and bowling balls; *media*, such as i-docs, documents and podcasts; *materials*, such as wax and plastic; *practices*, such as knitting, archiving through crowdsourcing, activism; and what we might call *living entities*, with, for instance, a dog, plants or ghosts, feelings and human participants. (This list is not exhaustive; a point we return to below.) Focusing on doing research *with* things, people and other living entities highlights *relationships*, as the 'with' functions to alert us to the relations through which research is, and must be, conducted. The collection therefore places these things, people and relationships at the centre of analysis, with authors considering, among other issues: when, where, why and how they have been doing research *with* them; and how they build on, reconfigure and/or do something other than what established methods do. We try to concentrate on the things, people and relationships that are central to doing research, but are sometimes – often – overlooked in reflections and reports.

Given the histories of knowledge making, it is important to consider the ethical responsibilities of researchers – us – in designing and carrying out research, and in what our attention is drawn towards. In her work on decolonising methodologies and methods, Linda Tuhiwai Smith (2021, first published in 1999) focuses on the long history of the exploitation of indigenous peoples in the construction of research; indeed, she details how research based on scientific principles has depended upon colonial relations where indigenous peoples have systematically been dehumanised and treated as objects of fascination, dissection and knowledge. Tuhiwai Smith argues that research methodologies must be fundamentally revised so as to 'disrupt the relationships between researchers (mainly non-indigenous) and researched (indigenous), between a colonising institution of knowledge and colonised peoples whose own knowledge was subjugated, between institutions and communities, and between and within indigenous communities themselves' (2021, p. x). Such research involves a shift from seeing research as about outputs and outcomes (data, publications, acclaim for researchers, for example) to emphasising process. Tuhiwai Smith notes, '[i]n many projects the process is far more important than the outcome. Processes are expected to be respectful, to enable people, to heal and to educate. They are expected to lead one small step further towards self-determination' (2021, p. 115).

What becomes clear with such an understanding of methodologies and methods is that our understanding of what has agency in our research must encompass the people and non-human entities that have been sidelined and objectified as sources of extraction. This argument complicates the list of 'things' we have outlined so far. Traditionally, things have been understood as inert and at the whim of people. In this book, we explore how different kinds of living and non-living things, alongside our practices, lie at the core of the ways in which research is done – we do research with and through them. What Tuhiwai Smith's work, among others, shows us is how certain people have been designated and treated as things and how their words, images, objects and land have been extracted by researchers. To decolonise methods, it is necessary for certain people to be treated and heard as active agents. We must not overlook people in our move to consider objects, media, materials, practices and non-human entities.

What we try to do in this book is draw attention to the plethora of relationships involved in research as well as to the ways in which research is and might be ethically shaped and crafted with and through them. Indeed, Donna Haraway (2016) notes that, 'it matters what stories we tell to tell other stories with; it matters what knots knot knots, what thoughts think thoughts, what descriptions describe descriptions, what ties tie ties. It matters what stories make worlds, what worlds make stories' (2016, p. 12). This book begins from the premise that both people and things matter to doing research and that the specifics of these people and things – what they are and do – are central to the research relationship. Of course, relationships and things are forged together. Extractive research relationships have been constituted with specific things, such as scribes, imperial archives, tape recorders, surveys and cameras.

Doing Critical, Creative and Interdisciplinary Social Research with a Range of *Unusual and Unexpected* Things and People

In focusing on the things and people with which research is done, our attention has been drawn to the *unusual* and *unexpected*. By 'unusual' and 'unexpected' we mean, first, to foreground the often-overlooked diversity of things and people with and through which research is done. That is, we see the distinctiveness of the collection lying partly in its attention to the things and people that are not always reflected upon or understood as part of the research process in methods texts – from recalcitrance to insider anxiety to outrageous propositions to performative experiments. Second, the collection also draws attention to the unusual and unexpected, weird and wonderful things and relations, through which research is done – from sewing to infrastructures to WhatsApp soapies to body mapping. In this sense, we aim not only to elevate the overlooked but also to expand the repertoire of social research methods themselves.

All of the contributors to the book work and/or study – or at some point have done so – in the Sociology Department, Goldsmiths, University of London, a department that has long sought to provide spaces for methodological experimentation and the expansion of the sociological imagination, within and beyond the walls of the academy. Multiple research centres and units at Goldsmiths have been generating methods-related questions, such as the Centre for Urban and Community Research (CUCR), the Unit for Global Justice and the Centre for Invention and Social Practice (CSISP), which produced the collection that dwelled on 'Intimacy in Research' (Fraser and Puwar, 2008). A key nexus of work with methods in the department has been the Methods Lab, a research unit established in 2004 to consolidate and build on this history in the department of expertise in developing research methods and teaching social research. Since then, members of the department have experimented with different modes of knowledge making, including curating, which has become a central strand of the work of the Methods Lab: exhibitions have been produced on campus, with the Kingsway Corridor in the Richard Hoggart Building re-purposed for exhibitions from the Sociology Department on multiple occasions since 2006, and installations in international galleries, museums and in unusual places, such as Coventry Cathedral. There has also been a sustained focus on placing practice at the centre of research and troubling boundaries between theory/method/practice as well as between disciplines. Partly as a result of such initiatives, researchers are working in interdisciplinary ways that might produce and/or share knowledge, understanding and data in untypical ways, producing new methods and means of communicating research and shedding light on the value of, and continuing need for, more established methodologies and methods.

Doing *Critical, Creative and Interdisciplinary Social Research* with a Range of Unusual and Unexpected Things and People

The terms *critical, creative* and *interdisciplinary social research* can be over-used and somewhat empty. What we mean by them here is something quite specific. We see this collection as advancing critical and creative approaches to social research relationships both in working *with* people and things and in focusing our attention on them.

Taking the term 'critical', part of what we understand the book to concentrate on is methodology and method themselves. In this sense, methods are not only what produce data on which we turn our critical faculties, but methods are themselves worthy of our critical appreciation. Here, then, just as we might critically analyse a text or argument, or data (e.g., interview extracts, ethnographic fieldnotes, responses to a questionnaire, statistics from a survey, a photograph or video produced in a focus group), we might also critically analyse the methodologies and methods via which data are generated. As with the critical analysis of texts, arguments and data, a critical analysis of methodologies and methods involves close and careful examination and evaluation aimed not so much at criticising as exploring, unpacking and appreciating the strengths and limits of an approach, why and how it was developed and deployed, and what it does. 'Critical', then, is about cultivating a sensitive comprehension of methods and methodologies. Here we are building on a plurality of schools of thought on the ethics and reflexive process of research making.

Our understanding of 'creative' in one sense refers to the wonderous relations, weird things and specific people with which/whom research is done. Here, we can identify a creative approach to doing research, in as much as creative refers to being imaginative, inspired and inventive. C.W. Mills (1959) states that the sociological imagination, when enraptured by a topic, tends to 'roam' across disciplines, finding insight in the most unlikely of places. Speaking of the discipline of sociology in the 1950s, he remarks on how the sociological imagination is found in literature, for example, rather than in sociology books. Historically, social sciences have consisted of a heterodoxy of methods, including the visual, even if these methods are not centred in methods textbooks. The visual data portraits of W.E.B. Du Bois (2018), as well as Mass Observation and the activities run by the Sociological Society in the 1930s at Le Play House (Scott, 2018), being cases in point. Writing about geography, Harriet Hawkins clusters 'creative' methods with 'experimental' and 'artful' ones and highlights the importance of 'creative practice' 'including visual art, image-making, creative-writing, performance techniques' to contemporary social research methods (2015, p. 248). More specifically, she argues that such creative practice has become important as geographers and other social researchers aim to 'engage, research and re-present the sensory experiences, emotions, affective atmospheres and flows of life', 'grasp the messy, unfinished and contingent' aspects of social life and knowledge production, and enrol 'non-specialist audiences in geographical causes' through 'the participatory and communicative potential of these practices together with their ability to constitute new and engaged "publics"' (2015, p. 248).

Les Back (2012), in outlining the contours of 'live methods' in sociology, refers to the need for social researchers 'to develop forms of attentiveness that can admit the fleeting, distributed, multiple, sensory, emotional and kinaesthetic aspects of sociality' (2012, p. 28). He argues for an extension to

the range, texture and quality of what passes as academic representational practice and writing. I want to argue for a more literary sensibility inside the research vocation but also for the extensions of sociological form through the embrace of multi-media (sound, image and text).

(Back, 2012, p. 28)

Creative practice for Back is a kind of 'artfulness'; 'being wily or bringing a *bit of craftiness into the craft*' (2012, p. 34, emphasis in original). For this collection, some of us came together during online writing retreats to allow ourselves to write from the middle of our research happenings, to take a close-up view of what we have been up to in our research. We tried to create space for writing on research processes in creative ways, away from the usual strictures of authoritative social science writing genres. Working with creative non-fiction, as a way into our research encounters and imaginations, we wrote to a number of writing prompts, including one on 'I was surprised by...'.

Taking inspiration from such understandings of 'critical' and 'creative' methods, we also seek to develop interdisciplinary methods along the lines proposed by Celia Lury (2012), who argues that interdisciplinary methods are 'interactions *across* and *between* disciplines' (2012, p. 1, emphases in original), where the interaction aims not for disciplines to be integrated or blended together, nor for disciplines to disappear. 'Instead', she proposes, 'interdisciplinarity emerges through *interferences* between disciplines and between disciplines and other forms of knowledge' (2012, p. 1, emphasis in original).

While we have noted above that the contributors to this book are in some way attached to the discipline of sociology, this is not sociology as it is traditionally practised (it is unusual and unexpected), and contributors take their inspiration for their methods from the interferences between many disciplines and fields, and other knowledges and practices – this is most evident in chapters on, for example, collaging, comics, curating, drawing, music and performance, but also a guiding principle for all of the contributions. Another definition of creativity, then, is the resourcefulness that comes from roaming across and taking inspiration from other disciplines and practices, and in so doing making something new, or making something anew. That the title of the book is focused on social research rather than sociology is intended to build on such an understanding of interdisciplinarity.

Doing Critical, Creative and Interdisciplinary Social Research with a Range of Unusual and Unexpected Things and People

Our final word of note – *doing* – might, at first glance, seem to be an innocuous word. However, as with our other words, we see it as pointing to something specific – the hands-on and often messy issues involved in carrying out social research. As with the words 'things' and 'people', we think that this aspect of social research can often be smoothed out and cleaned up in written accounts of research, where discussion of methodology and methods is often perfunctory and descriptive. The liveliness of sociality and the things that are involved in making social research data are often not included. In keeping with contributors' interests in methodological innovation and craftiness, we asked them to emphasise their practical experience of methods, to lead the reader through what they did, why and how, and to reflect on their cases and scenarios, including their limits and surprises. Our aim was to open up what can be overlooked in the accounts of doing social research and make the trials, mess and surprises central to the discussion, as well as to highlight how doing critical, creative and interdisciplinary social research involves experimenting, failing, learning and trying again, often resulting in a raft of unusual and unexpected insightful happenings.

Overall, what we hope to convey in this introduction and collection is that methods are important and exciting. They are involved in constituting and organising the social world we study, and are central to making particular social realities (Law *et al.*, 2011). Methods are not boring. Neither are they neutral or insignificant. Insight too often occurs in the unexpected and messy life of methods with everyday and unusual things and settings. The range of ways of doing social science in this book are heterogeneous and inspired by different theoretical and methodological traditions. While each author understands methodology and method differently, what they share is a conviction that methods are active relationships in the social worlds at stake in a research project. As a group, we aim to share this potential inventiveness and creativity in doing research. We hope this collection inspires readers to experiment with their own practice and keep adding to the toolbox and library of the many things you can do social research with and alongside.

References

Back, L. (2012) 'Live sociology: Social research and its futures', *Sociological Review*, 60(1_suppl.), pp. 18–39.

Du Bois, W.E.B. (2018) *Visual Data Portraits: Visualising Black America*. New York: Princeton Architectural Press.

Fraser, M. and Puwar, N. (2008) Special Issue on 'Intimacy in Research', *History of the Human Sciences*, 21(4).

Haraway, D. (2016) *Staying with the Trouble: Making Kin in the Chthulucene*. Durham, NC: Duke University Press.

Hawkins, H. (2015) 'Creative geographic methods: Knowing, representing, intervening. On composing place and page', *Cultural Geographies*, 22(2), pp. 247–268.

Law, J., Savage, M. and Ruppert, E. (2011) 'The double social life of methods', CRESC Working Paper No. 95, pp. 1–18. Available at: www.open.ac.uk/researchprojects/iccm/files/iccm/Law%20Savage%20Ruppert.pdf

Lury, C. (2012) 'Introduction: Activating the present of interdisciplinary methods', in Lury, C. (ed.) *Routledge Handbook of Interdisciplinary Methodologies*. London: Routledge, pp. 1–25.

Mills, C.W. (1959, reprinted 2000) *The Sociological Imagination*. Oxford: Oxford University Press.

Scott, J. (2018) *British Social Theory: Recovering Lost Traditions Before 1950*. London: Sage.

Tuhiwai Smith, L. (2021) *Decolonizing Methodologies: Research and Indigenous Peoples*. Third edition. London: Zed Books.

1

How to do social research with... activism

Kiran Grewal

Introduction

There have been many conversations recently on how to make the university accountable for its privilege (colonial and other) and responsive and relevant to today's challenges. As social researchers we are increasingly asked how our work acknowledges and addresses historic injustices, exclusions and silences and what contribution we make to creating different futures. For some scholars this has meant openly identifying as activist researchers (Hale, 2006). For others it has involved defending space for critical reflection separate from action in order to imagine alternatives (Brown and Halley, 2002).

This positioning of 'action' versus 'thought' has established an unhelpful, reductive binary with some of us assumed to be 'doing' and others 'theorising' (Osterweil, 2013). In reality, many of us are trying to do *both* in the face of institutional barriers that seek to maintain the divide. The call to 'decolonise' or 'liberate' our knowledge production practices requires all social researchers to be at least a little bit activist. Wherever we position ourselves in the 'thought'/'action' continuum, we all need to critically reflect on how we produce knowledge and what our research contributes to the world around us. In this chapter I reflect on how I have tried to integrate some of this 'activist' spirit into my own research praxis.

Alternative Critical Communities: Examples from Sri Lanka

I first visited the eastern Sri Lankan town of Batticaloa in 2012 as a weekend break from a research project I was working on in the capital, Colombo. A feminist activist and artist friend had asked me to visit and meet her network and her husband, an academic at the local university and a community theatre activist. I was eager for an excuse to leave Colombo where my life revolved around the university, meetings with bureaucrats and wandering the beautiful, over-privileged suburbs of the rich. I wanted to see Sri Lanka outside of this bubble and I was keen to visit a town famous for its particularly lively local activist scene.

While I have gone on to write about it (Grewal, 2017), I never intended to make Batticaloa a 'research site'. Rather, over the next three years it became a site of refuge from the frustrations of my actual research project and a site of inspiration and energy, drawn from the wonderful activists who became my friends. It was only in 2017 that I first went to Batticaloa as a 'researcher'.

This was a turning point in my research trajectory. Up until then I had worked primarily with law and formal institutions. But I was increasingly frustrated by the limits of my analysis. What interested me most was not what 'experts' or legal documents had to say, but how ordinary people understood and made use of human rights. I felt that exploring this could bypass the stale debates that continue to dominate the field of human rights. Whether arguing that human rights were emancipatory or oppressive, too much academic work seemed over-generalised and inattentive to the perspectives of the very subjects in question: the victims of injustice, marginalisation and violence. I wanted to document the underexplored 'everyday life' of human rights. However, I struggled to think of ways to access the 'subaltern' perspectives I felt were important but also not accessible via any conventional research method.

At the same time I began to realise that, quite organically, my engagements in Batticaloa had become a form of ethnographic research. I had learnt a lot about how different marginalised communities and individuals thought about rights and justice even if I had not directed discussion on those topics. I had just been a participant in a range of activities: *kooth-thu*[1] and *parai*[2] rehearsals and performances, art exhibitions, community discussion forums, film screenings, book fairs, protests and one large

---

[1] A form of traditional Tamil community theatre, usually retelling stories from Hindu epics.
[2] A form of drumming associated with the Tamil Paraiyar community, traditionally performed at funerals.

community arts festival. This participation had come with responsibilities. All present were expected to contribute what they could and I was rightly asked to do the same. This involved everything from helping community groups to identify and use human rights laws in their negotiations with local authorities to advocating to government departments about the benefits of investing in certain community activities. Meanwhile my feminist activist friends put me on the spot in one meeting, asking me to feed back to them what I thought of their group and its activities, given that I had followed them around for so many years (!). The 'everyday life' of human rights in Batticaloa was not an object of study but something I was actively being asked to co-create.

This was the ultimate gesture of welcome. I didn't have to search for ways to make my research encounter reciprocal: my friends demanded I come prepared to offer something, whether by explaining concepts, documenting their work or using the social capital of 'international academic' to add weight to their work. But it also went beyond ensuring I was not engaged in the 'extractive' research various indigenous scholars have powerfully named and critiqued (Gaudry, 2011). We all concluded that there was something uniquely valuable in academic–activist–community collaboration. This was exciting but also raised important questions.

If research is a joint venture, how does that affect the questions we ask, methods we deploy, theories we use and outputs we produce? How do we address issues of power and inequality, the risks of diverging interests and interpretations, the danger of epistemic injustice and the reality that some things may always be lost in translation? I do not have answers but will share two examples of my own efforts at consciously doing social research with activism.

Essay Books: Translation and Co-Production

As I was finishing the academic book referred to above, I sent copies to my Sri Lankan collaborators. I asked them to confirm they were happy with what I had included and how, to point out inaccuracies and let me know what they thought of my analysis before it was published. Presenting back my perceptions and analysis of Sri Lanka – a place I felt I still only superficially knew – to people whose lived reality I was commenting on was daunting. I felt extremely anxious I would be called a fraud, told I had completely misunderstood everything, that I had nothing remotely relevant or useful to say. It was a huge relief when I received generally positive responses, even as I worried that my friends were just being kind. It was even more gratifying when some told me that my descriptions and analysis allowed them to see their own situation and work in a different light.

However, the more I thought about what it meant to be an ethical researcher, the more issues arose. The reality was that only those who had a certain level of academic English could in fact access my work. But I also couldn't just send a short summary of 'key points'. In sending my writing to collaborators, I wasn't just checking for factual accuracy but looking to start a conversation: on how my analysis of their reality resonated or not with their own, whether the observations of an outsider contributed anything new or useful, what they thought about my conclusions and where my research should go next. This required that they have access to my analysis and an understanding of my theory in order to speak back to it.

Meanwhile, because of my friends' insistence, I had been trying to document our conversations and activities in less formally academic ways. Contributing short articles to magazines and online blogs, many of my pieces had also been translated into Tamil and provided the starting point for further discussions whenever I was next in Batticaloa. It meant that I had accumulated a lot of short articles and my own journal entries reflecting on events I had attended and linking them to theory I was reading. During 2017, we came up with the idea of turning these pieces into a set of small books. This would provide more accessible ways for me to present back my research and analysis while at the same time offering an introduction to certain theoretical concepts and contributing to the activist work my friends were doing around challenging dominant discourses of caste, class, gender and ethnicity.

The essays were a pleasure to produce, offering a chance to speak more personally, freed from some of the constraints of academic convention. They allowed me to link the theory I was reading with the situation before me. More importantly, I had an opportunity to try and explain those links to others in a way that opened up possibilities: whether valorising their work, linking them beyond their immediate context or posing questions that might provoke reflection. By publishing and disseminating the books as widely as we could we also sought to expand our community network.

At the same time, I had to develop new skills. I had to make my writing less formal and more conversational: something that took a lot of rewriting and some fairly robust constructive criticism from non-academic friends. I also had to justify why I thought particular theoretical insights mattered, making me think hard about how to explain difficult concepts in a way that made them practically relevant.

Accessibility also required that we translate the essays into the local languages: Sinhala and Tamil. This was tricky as not many people were well versed in the theorists I was citing. The friends who took on this task did crash courses in subaltern and political theory, watching every YouTube talk they could find, reading and discussing with me the texts I had referred to and coming back to me with their versions of what they thought I was trying to say. Their translations added new dimensions and the essay books became co-productions.[3]

So too, the theory took on new life. We were less concerned with working out the 'true meaning' of this or that theorist than with presenting theory in a way that was meaningful to those reading. We acknowledged that the further the interpreter was from the academic discipline, the less likely they were to know the implicit, contextual background the theorist was drawing on. But rather than seeing this as a limitation, we saw it as liberating – freeing certain concepts to circulate and animate new ideas and conversations but also to develop, change and be enriched in the process.

The Feminist House

Alongside cultivating different writing practices, we have also experimented with creating alternate spaces for engaging with and making theory. Over many years my activist friends had cultivated a practice of regular informal discussions in people's homes or public spaces. The topics varied greatly and were a space for sharing personal experiences, discussing and analysing power and strategising practical responses. What I could add to this was theory, concepts and examples from elsewhere.

[3] Copies of the essay books can be downloaded here: https://decolonial.org/.

Some of the best discussions were with young women where we collectively reflected on when we became aware of our gender, how gender affected our lives and how this could be responded to politically and practically. We spoke of shared issues as well as different pressures related to sexuality, religion, communal and family norms, post-war politics and economics. These spaces provided us all with insights into different lived experiences and led to deep friendships. They also offered opportunities to discuss concepts and theories that could then help to develop analyses.

We became increasingly conscious that there was a demand for these discussions but a lack of space. Very few activists' homes could accommodate large groups and many live in extended families. There was also a need for a refuge, where people could have time and space away from the pressures of daily life to think and discuss. I was reminded of Gayatri Spivak's (2004) distinction between the critical education offered to the world's elite versus the narrow education given to the world's poor: producing good workers and consumers and discouraging broader questioning. Theorising requires a certain luxury of time and space as well as access to ideas.

An opportunity opened up when a group of us received two research grants in 2019. These included a fieldwork budget to cover accommodation costs for the team. Using this we rented the top floor of a house on Batticaloa lagoon: a lovely place with large balconies that still cost less than the expected hotel budget. Keeping our furniture to a minimum – mattresses on the floor, mats to sit on – we now had a nice big open space to host discussions, welcome other activists and researchers and create a little library.

It became a haven over the next two years until Covid-19 unfortunately meant we had to give up the lease. We cultivated it as a space of retreat from normal life, encouraging people – particularly women – to come, debrief about their lives and work, read, work on their own projects or simply relax, chat, eat, dance, sing, sleep, have fun. We tried to model different relationships of care, solidarity and responsibility, to explore how to debate and disagree respectfully and without violence. We also tried to regularly name and address the hierarchies and inequalities that we inevitably brought with us into that space without allowing them to fracture us. This was in turn aided by the discussion of concepts, ideas, theories.

When one friend turned up with a book on fascism, it launched a crash course in critical theory conducted over a week. We produced a list of terms and concepts that people wanted to understand – from hegemony to post-structuralism. Every morning was spent preparing: madly reading up, often on theory I also had only superficially read and understood in some distant student past. Every afternoon people would drift in from 4pm, some coming straight from work, some with children in tow, some turning up having heard about our discussion through word of mouth. While some had undergraduate degrees, others had barely finished school. None of them were 'scholars'. The discussions would last a few hours, conducted in Tamil and English, usually ending with a simple shared meal. We tested the parameters of concepts, discussed the contexts within which they were first named and theorised, pushed them beyond their origins, experimented with applying them to make sense of something topical, reinvented them in ways that felt useful, abandoned those that didn't resonate.

While the gathering wasn't big (maybe 10–15 people on any given day), it is important to convey the diversity of people who made use of and contributed to this space: from across different class, caste, ethnic and religious backgrounds. In a highly stratified and ethnically divided society, this was no small achievement – largely made possible by my activist friends' tireless efforts at cultivating alternate forms of community. In participating in this process, I offered the few valuable assets I have: my access to information, training in concepts and analysis and ability to share these with others and contribute to building spaces for reflection, exchange and debate. In turn I gained exciting new conversation partners and co-theorists who constantly enrich my own thinking while also offering me a community and a home.

Conclusion

So why does any of this matter? Perhaps it doesn't. These spaces and contributions may be of minor significance, really only meaningful to the handful of us directly involved. I am okay with this. In making a claim for social research with activism I have no desire to reproduce some form of elite intellectual vanguardism. As social researchers we have no more important a role to play than others in changing the world. But nor do I believe we have none. Rather, like Shannon Speed (2008), I see myself as part of a community engaged in struggle, each of us bringing whatever resources we have and playing whatever part we can. The examples I have offered here are not meant to be exemplary. Many criticisms can be levelled at my approach and thinking; as this is work in progress, I would genuinely welcome the feedback. It is also worth noting that the approaches and forms our research takes and the relationship to activism (however conceived) will and should vary greatly from researcher to researcher. But it is hoped that these examples suggest ways in which social research can be done with activism and some of the pleasures to be had in the process.

Postscript – As usual I sent this chapter to my friends in Sri Lanka for their feedback. Having read it carefully, Hasanah called me early one morning with a list of suggestions and reflections. She pointed out that the chapter didn't fully convey the emotional bonds we have established and in particular noted a very important detail I had omitted. From 2015 on I no longer travelled alone to Sri Lanka but with a small addition who has been present in every activity described above. Being a single mother doing fieldwork has been incredibly challenging and only possible thanks to the generosity and support I have received from my Batticaloa community. It has also forged deeper relationships as research collaborators have watched my struggles, helped in the parenting of my child and cared for both of us. This too has shaped the research. Yet it was only through sharing my writing – and others taking the time to thoughtfully respond – that I was even made aware of this. I wanted to note this separately rather than integrating Hasanah's feedback into the text to show both the limits of (at least my own!) critical self-reflexivity and the immense value of treating research as a collaborative process.

References

Brown, W. and Halley, J. (2002) Left Legalism, Left Critique. Durham, NC: Duke University Press.

Gaudry, A.J.P. (2011) 'Insurgent research', Wicazo Sa Review, 26(1), pp. 113–136.

Grewal, K.K. (2017) The Socio Political Practice of Human Rights: Between the Universal and the Particular. Abingdon: Routledge.

Hale, C.R. (2006) 'Activist research v. cultural critique: Indigenous land rights and contradictions of politically engaged anthropology', *Cultural Anthropology*, 21(1), pp. 96–120.

Osterweil, M. (2013) 'Rethinking public anthropology through epistemic politics and theoretical practice', *Cultural Anthropology*, 28(4), pp. 598–620.

Speed, S. (2008) 'Forged in dialogue: Toward a critically engaged activist research', in Hale, C. (ed.) *Engaging Contradictions: Theory, Politics, and Methods of Activist Scholarship*. Berkeley, Los Angeles, London: University of California Press, pp. 213–236.

Spivak, G.C. (2004) 'Writing wrongs', *South Atlantic Quarterly*, 103(2–3), pp. 523–581.

2

How to do social research with... archiving through crowdsourcing

Sevasti-Melissa Nolas and Christos Varvantakis

Introduction

In our chapter, we reflect on doing social research by crowdsourcing materials for an archive. Crowds have occupied an ambivalent position in public and sociological imaginations – at once demonised as problems and venerated as problem solvers (Wexler, 2011). Crowdsourcing itself emerged from marketing practices and has since been taken up in various research contexts (Keating and Furberg, 2013). In this chapter we approach crowds and crowdsourcing as neither problems nor solutions but as de facto valuable interlocutors, a public (Warner, 2002) who can engage and grow our epistemic imaginations through contributing to the building of an archive. We play around with the notion of the archive and with practices of archiving through crowdsourcing as these relate to the creation of an open access online archive of *earliest political memories.*

Our case study is drawn from the European Research Council-funded 'ERC Connectors Study (2014–2019),'[1] a multimodal ethnographic study which explored the relationship between childhood and public life with 45 six-to-nine-year old interlocutors in Athens, Hyderabad and London, during which we focused specifically on children's encounters, experiences and engagement with politics broadly defined.[2] In the study, we wanted to consider the earlier times in the life course during which 'the political' might be encountered, the shape it takes, the meanings it acquires, the practices it emerges through and out of. Over a period of three years, we carried out research with younger children aged six at the time we first met

[1]European Research Council Starting Grant 335514 to Nolas.
[2]A full list of project publications can be found here: https://childhoodpublics.org/dissemination/writing/academic-articles/

them, and all from very different family backgrounds. This involved multimodal ethnographic research: we asked children to take photographs of 'things that mattered to them', we walked together around their neighbourhoods and cities, and we spent much time playing and chatting in the repeat visits to their family homes.

The question of earliest political memories was invented in a moment of necessity before the study started (see next section); it was not written into the study design though it became integral to it. The archive of earliest political memories materialised towards the end of the study, as the problem of what to do with the rich data we had collected presented itself. We have written this chapter in a way that honours this unexpected and emergent element in our research, and in this sense, we take you through that process. We write at an historical moment in which archives are becoming increasingly more public and participatory, and in which social researchers are increasingly being required to archive their data, as well as to engage publics in their research. As such, this is a time when very plausibly a social researcher may inadvertently become an archivist, as we did. It is also a time during which calls are being made to democratise archives, and crowdsourcing provides one way in which archive making may be made accessible to a wider public.

'Let Us Not Begin at the Beginning, Nor Even at the Archive'[3]: It Did Not Begin as Archiving

In our research, we had not set out to create an archive of earliest political memories. Asking about earliest political memories was originally devised in response to a crisis. We tell the story of this crisis in different voices, starting with Melissa occupying the 'I' position before moving to a 'we' position that better captures our collaborative relationship since March 2014 (see also Nolas and Varvantakis, 2019).

In February 2013, when seven and a half months pregnant, I (Melissa) received the welcome news that a Starting Grant proposal submitted to the European Research Council (ERC) had been shortlisted. The interview was to be held sometime towards the end of May 2013. My baby was due

[3]Derrida, 1995, p. 9.

sometime in the beginning of April (if he so chose to be on time). In prepa-ration for the interview and before any formal instructions from the funder, I asked previous award holders at my institution about their interviews – what and how they prepared. All spoke about PowerPoint Presentations. I rallied myself to write what I felt to be a compelling visual pitch about why it was important to fund a piece of research on younger children's political participation, at the same time as my energy levels and concen-tration dwindled. Two weeks before my due date, another email from the ERC landed in my inbox with interview format instructions; **'PowerPoint or video presentations are not allowed'** (original emphasis).

In a state of panic, and with little energy or time left to create anything from scratch, I found myself thinking of other, powerful ways to convey the validity and importance of researching the political with younger children. How might I convince what I imagined would be a panel with at least a handful of sceptics, in a short space of time, that childhood and the politi-cal could go together? I thought of my own encounters with 'the political' that permeated my childhood. Growing up in Athens in the 1980s there was always a sense of 'something happening', if not actually happening. Political conversations, verbal sparring between different family members and intergenerational teasing about political identifications were a stable backdrop to weekly Sunday family lunches. At the time, I didn't under-stand the content of these discussions, but I knew their rhythm and their affects intimately, knowing very well the performance of 'falling out' and 'making up' at different points in the Sunday lunch proceedings.

I engaged in a proto-crowdsourcing experiment, emailing friends and family to find out if memories like these – that showed how early on in our lives political experiences find us – were salient for others too. The responses were fascinating both in terms of the range of experiences shared, what counted as 'political', and the different orientations that con-tributors had towards those memories and experiences (humorous, sad, ambivalent, allegorical, and in some cases no memories of a political nature, however defined, at such a young age). Armed with the confidence that these responses gave me, I headed off to Brussels for my interview post-partum.

When we (Melissa and Christos) met in 2014 on the now funded ERC 'Connectors Study' project, poring over the 'little stories' of earliest political memories that Melissa had collected, we started to think of the question of earliest political memory as an imaginative way to capture the attention of *adult audiences* and to recruit them into contemporary children's worlds, the subject of our research, by reminding them of their own 'earliest political memories'. One of the challenges we faced from the outset – not so much from within our own interdisciplinary field of childhood studies, but beyond it in our 'parent' disciplines (sociology, anthropology, political science, social psychology) as well as in the public sphere – was a romantic figure of the child: as innocent, close to nature, in need of protection (in retrospect, perhaps also the prevailing idea of politics as 'dirty' and 'contaminating'). How to create a 'crack' (Holloway, 2010) then, in such sticky figurations of the child, to open even the tiniest of spaces to meaningfully occupy our adult interlocutors' senses, for enough time to fold them into a conversation about children's political lives?

'Earliest political memories' became a cypher (Kraftl, 2015) through which to make the 'political child' audible and resonant to new audiences (funder, colleagues, research participants, 'the public'), those now perhaps living in 'a different country'. Memory is 'a cornerstone of identity' (Andrews, 2014, p. 3) and 'the creative refashioning of the self' (Lambek and Antze, 1996, p. xx, quoted in Carsten, 2005, p. 5). It is also a 'causeway' between the social and the intimate, the private and the public, the personal and the political. We appealed to autobiographical memory and engaged in another crowdsourcing activity, asking adult people to think back to when they first remembered anything that they would consider then or now political; and we tried the question out informally, with friends, acquaintances and colleagues. The question was arresting, often putting our interlocutors into a ruminative space: 'you made me think...', we heard more than once as eyes glazed off into pasts of varying distances from the present. On some rarer occasions, when mentioning the topic of the research, earliest political memories were offered up to us unprompted, with excitement, a depositor finally finding their archive: 'Oh, how interesting, I remember when I was eight...'.

Memory Fever for Sure, but Still Not Archiving...

These conversations propelled us to continue, and we experimented further, extending this proto-crowdsourcing activity into the research. We started to formalise the collection of these memories through biographic interviews with the parents of the children in the study; this helped us to contextualise 'the political' in the study of children's everyday lives, as that circulated within the confines of their homes (Nolas *et al.*, 2017). Then in June 2016, we launched our crowdsourcing experiment on Twitter and Facebook where we asked members of the public to contribute their 'earliest political memories' through an online submission form we had created on the study blog. The initial 70-odd submissions we received were then shared with a designer[4] who created illustrations for each of the memories collected; memories and their illustrations were then, after a period, blogged and posted on the study Twitter feed at a rate of one a day. These memories landed in subscribers' inboxes and timelines over a period of four months. These 'little stories' found a highly receptive audience if online submissions to the blog, re-tweets and Twitter thread conversations are anything to go by. The crowdsourcing experiment was launched just after the UK referendum on European membership in June 2016 and the re-blogging activity of the collected memories took place through the run up to the U.S. presidential elections and the event itself in November 2016. While we cannot be sure what created this resonance, it would not be outlandish to suggest that these illustrated little stories captured a historical moment and facilitated the 'filtering of the present through ideas about the past' (Sutton, 1998, p. ix).

We really like this notion of 'filtering' the present through ideas of the past; the idea of a memory as a filter. But it also made us realise that perhaps earliest *political* memories are not part of the usual, everyday repertoire that lives are filtered through – earliest memories, perhaps seeped in stories of attachment and loss, but less so stories about politics. Childhoods – our age group – are not entirely typical starting points for narratives of political identity. So perhaps our question afforded our interlocutors a different way of remembering themselves and then constructing themselves and their experiences in the present. These earliest political memories also served another function in our research: it created publics around the study, and recruited adults into contemporary children's political lives.

Towards the end of the study, we extended our crowdsourcing activity to in-person settings when we staged exhibitions in the study cities.[5]

[4]Nat Al-Tahhan website: https://natalt.co.uk/about-nat
[5]https://childhoodpublics.org/events/in-common-childrens-photo-stories-of-public-life/

Earliest political memory #63

Watching children of about my age (9 at the time) pick
through a huge rubbish pile for scraps of food, whilst
adults used the other side of the same rubbish pile as a
toilet, outside the Taj Mahal complex in India. Going
inside to the complex, I recall being told the value of each
gemstone in the Taj Mahal by a tourguide and asking
why they didn't just sell the gemstone to pay for the food
for those clearly struggling to eat outside.

Tags:
Themes: Poverty Wealth
Locations: India
Decades: 1990s
Ages: 28
Genders: Female
Ethnicities: Mixed South
Asian White
Occupations: Unknown

Download original

Figure 2.1 Example of an 'earliest political memory' collected through
crowdsourcing and illustrated by Nat Al-Tahhan.

The exhibition itself became a crowdsourcing exercise for new memories,
donated by visitors – members of the public. At these week-long exhibition
events, we asked for contributions of 'earliest political memories' which
attendees wrote down on small A5 cards and which we displayed on exhibition props, such as a 'washing line' and a tree, at the venues we used.
These further earliest political memories were digitised and subsequently
published on the blog and Twitter feed, therefore extending the daily

digests for a further period. Taken together, crowdsourced and exhibition-collected memories, with varying degrees of demographic and contextual data on the memory donors, now include about 200 little stories that are publicly accessible in a digital online archive.[6]

And So, to the Archive (at Last): Archiving from Below

As the project end date began to loom on the horizon, the question of what to do with these rich and enrapturing records started to emerge. The fizz that 'earliest political memories' had generated left us with a feeling of obligation: leaving them as memories unfolded on a blogroll, jpegs and doc files on computer drives would probably commit them to digital obscurity. Surely, we could do better than that? It was in this way that the idea of collating them into an openly accessible online archive emerged.[7]

Born digital archives are those archives where the records have been natively created in digital format. The born digital archives represent a spanner to the logics of order and provenance that underscore traditional concepts and practices of 'the archive' as 'the guardian or keeper of the juridical evidence of government agencies' (Cook, 2013, p. 106). Jarrett M. Drake (2016) sees the boom of 'born digital' archival collections as a disruption to the hierarchies and exclusions of state administration and a key vehicle for decolonising the archive (Ranade, 2018, p. 86). At the same time, the turn to 'community' in archival studies scholarship in the early 2000s reflected concern with the politics of representation and collective memory and ethical issues of control, status, power and post/neo-colonialism in the mediation of the cultural record (Cook, 2013).

In many ways, these preoccupations with collective and emancipatory archival practices sit well with a long left-leaning tradition in cultural studies committed to documenting history from below, represented by the likes of Stuart Hall, Richard Hoggart and Raymond Williams, as well as with more contemporary feminist thought and practice in and around archives (Bruce-Jones, 2020; Moore *et al.*, 2017; Puwar, 2021). In our own work, we understood the memories we crowdsourced as 'little stories' that

[6]https://childhoodpublics.org/archives/earliest-political-memories/
[7]https://childhoodpublics.org/archives/earliest-political-memories/

were particularly valuable in the face of grand historiographic narratives of the political changes to which those memories referred. As social scientists, we attended to every single one of the stories we heard and read, and we realised that these stories, each one in itself as well as a sum of their parts, were a form of personal historiography, invaluable in that they melded together history, memory and affect. We were also conscious that the people who were submitting their memories to us (either in discussions, in interviews, via the online submission form on the blog or during the exhibitions) were sharing their present selves' understandings of what constitutes the 'political', by deciding (defining) today what counted as political in their childhoods.

In terms of the archive itself, this was an unintended but no less participatory outcome of the study. Our archive was constructed processually over time. As mentioned, we had not intended to create an archive of such small bits of personal histories and views on the *political* (indeed, we never intended to pose the question in the first place). Nor had we intended to do this through crowdsourcing. But realising the value that this question held for us and our interlocutors, near and far, kept us asking that question. As such, the process of crowdsourcing earliest political memories for an archive-yet-to-be at the time of collection was entangled with the process of 'continuing to pose the question.' And 'continuing to pose the question' was never separate from creating the space for reflection, by asking that question of parents in the study, and the public. In this sense, an archive was grown organically, its resulting categories, the very navigational devices of the archive, the outcome of this bottom-up, crowdsourced, process. The proliferation of these little stories coalesced into and eventually gave shape to an archive.

Conclusion

Researching with archives exercises our epistemic imagination: the past may well be a different country, but so might the future. Archives allow us to play with temporality in our thinking, encouraging us to simultaneously think backwards (from the present to the past) as well as forwards (from the present to futures yet to come); in archives we both find and lose ourselves, and in the process discover that other worlds are indeed possible (for better or worse). Our research, described above, took place in pre-pandemic times. Arguably the approach to archiving that we've described has since 2020 become more widespread as researchers have (largely) been stuck at home, in a collective moment of crisis for social research methods, that has led many of us online to create projects for crowdsourcing experiences of the pandemic across the life course. In this chapter, we have shown how crowdsourcing relates to archiving and how it enables the assembly of a flatter and more democratic archive, one which is 'live' (Giannachi, 2016) and public, and in constant conversation with its crowds and audiences.

Acknowledgements

The 'ERC Connectors Study' was funded by the European Research Council Starting Grant, ERC-StG-335514, to Sevasti-Melissa Nolas. We thank Robyn Long, who managed the digitisation and daily blogging of the earliest political memories, and Alice Corble, who carried out some of the background literature review on archives used in this chapter. We thank the editors, especially Rebecca Coleman, for the feedback on an earlier draft of this chapter.

References

Andrews, M. (2014) *Lifetimes of Commitment: Ageing, Politics, Psychology.* Cambridge: Cambridge University Press.

Bruce-Jones, E. (2020) 'Themed book review of Saidiya Hartman's *Wayward Lives, Beautiful Experiments: Intimate Histories of Social Upheaval*', *Feminist Review*, 125, pp. 110–116.

Carsten, J. (ed.) (2005) *Ghosts of Memory: Essays on Remembrance and Relatedness.* Oxford: Blackwell Publishing.

Cook, T. (2013) 'Evidence, memory, identity, and community: Four shifting archival paradigms', *Archival Science*, 13(2–3), pp. 95–120.

Derrida, J. (1995) 'Archive fever: A Freudian impression', *Diacritics*, 25(2) (Summer), pp. 9–63.

Drake, J.M. (2016) 'RadTech meets RadArch: Towards a new principle for archives and archival description', *Medium*, 6 April. Available at: https://medium.com/on-archivy/radtech-meets-radarch-towards-a-new-principle-for-archives-and-archival-description-568f133e4325#.86ba9wqwf (Accessed: 18 March 2019).

Giannachi, G. (2016) *Archive Everything: Mapping the Everyday.* Cambridge, MA: The MIT Press.

Holloway, J. (2010) *Crack Capitalism*. London: Pluto Press.

Keating, M.D. and Furberg, R.D. (2013) 'A methodological framework for Crowdsourcing in research', in *Proceedings of the 2013 Federal Committee on Statistical Methodology Research Conference*, Washington, DC. Retrieved from: https://nces.ed.gov/FCSM/pdf/H1_Keating_2013FCSM_AC.pdf

Kraftl, P. (2015) 'Alter-childhoods: Biopolitics and childhoods in alternative education spaces', *Annals of the Association of American Geographers*, 105(1), pp. 219–237.

Moore, N., Salter, A., Stanley, L. and Tamboukou, M. (2017) *The Archive Project: Archival Research in the Social Sciences*. London: Routledge.

Nolas, S-M. and Varvantakis, C. (2019) 'Fieldnotes for amateurs', *Social Analysis*, 63(3), pp. 130–148.

Nolas, S-M., Varvantakis, C. and Aruldoss, V. (2017) 'Talking politics in everyday family lives', *Contemporary Social Science*, 12(1–2), pp. 68–83.

Puwar, N. (2021) 'Carrying as method: Listening to bodies as archives', *Body and Society*, 27(1), pp. 3–26.

Ranade, S. (2018) 'Access technologies for the disruptive digital archive', in Brown, C. (ed.) *Archival Futures*. London: Facet Publishing, pp. 79–98.

Sutton, D. (1998) *Memories Cast in Stone: The Relevance of the Past in Everyday Life*. London: Routledge.

Warner, M. (2002) *Publics and Counterpublics*. Brooklyn, NY: Zone Books.

Wexler, M.N. (2011) 'Reconfiguring the sociology of the crowd: Exploring crowdsourcing', *International Journal of Sociology and Social Policy*, 31(1–2), pp. 6–20.

3

How to do social research with... body mapping

Fay Dennis

Upstairs in a south London drug service, we are gathered around a collection of trestle tables covered in encrusted paint, splayed out magazines, and various collaging, painting, and drawing materials. I am talking to Jamil,[1] asking him how he plans to use the session, when I spot a piece of 'gauze' (enmeshed metal wire broken off from a scouring pad). What are you going to be using this for? Jamil, surprised by my question, starts scanning the table looking for something, then stretches out, and grasps a plastic 'Bigga' bottle another participant, Sam, had brought in. Holding it up, he explains how he would use the gauze and a piece of foil from a Kit Kat to assemble a crack pipe. With this, Alicia, sitting next to us, who had been listening silently until this moment, says: 'Last week, when he brought the gauze in, I started sweating'. An object that was once so familiar to her had affected her body in an unwelcome and troubling way.

The gauze then started to gain wider attention as other members wanted to know what we were talking about, triggering an exchange of stories, which led Jamil to conclude: 'See, there's a lot of stories around a little bit of metal.'

This fieldnote is based on an encounter that happened during a series of body-mapping workshops that took place in the summer of 2019. The participants were all clients at the hosting drug service and hoping to abstain or currently abstaining from drug and/or alcohol consumption. The workshops sought to explore participants' experiences of 'living with' and 'without' drugs/alcohol and, through this, alternative ways of thinking

---

[1]All names of participants have been changed for anonymity.

about substance use and recovery beyond addiction.[2] By zeroing in on the body and embodied practice, I hoped to bypass addiction narratives that focus on the 'diseased brain'. Defined by a loss of control and agency, an addiction diagnosis and the infrastructure that surrounds it, like its treatment systems, can shut down an imaginary on what else substances can do and be part of – for example, the many stories a little bit of metal can tell! – and the lives and identities people can have outside of addiction. As an individualised pathology, addiction also works to depoliticise dependency and the multiple forms of oppression it intersects with such as the war on drugs, poverty, racism and sexism.

Trying to open up this imaginary on what substances can do and be part of beyond addiction, in the two projects I describe in this chapter, I wanted to pay attention to the skilled embodied ways participants negotiate substances' effects. Rather than thinking of substances as having inherent properties and linear causal effects, body mapping traces where these effects materialise and continue to reside after the event as a complex interaction of substances, bodies and environments. This approach was initially inspired by Gilles Deleuze and Félix Guattari's (1987) imagining of the body as an assemblage in *A Thousand Plateaus* and as notably developed in relation to the drug-using body by Peta Malins (e.g., 2004). For Deleuze and Guattari, bodies are not independent of their environment but are made up of it and are defined and gain their capacity to act in relation to it. Body mapping was a way of mapping these assemblages, while also becoming part of the assemblage itself, in terms of body mapping's own power to prompt memories and stimulate embodied feelings. What becomes important, then, for body mapping, as I use it in my work, is not simply how accurately it can represent the substance-using or recovering body. This is a question of validity that I return to later. Instead, what is important is what it can enable us to think and do in this interaction. For example, what more ethical alternatives to addiction might body mapping generate? With this, I have been more recently helped by Donna Haraway's (2016) notion of storytelling as a more-than-human practice of

---

[2]The workshops formed part of a broader early-career fellowship research project that sought to observe and create its own methodological ways to 'make people who use drugs matter.'

return and relay. Using string figuring as her metaphor, Haraway describes the giving and receiving of patterns to not only tell stories but construct more liveable futures.

> Playing games of string figures is about giving and receiving patterns, dropping threads and failing but sometimes finding something that works, something consequential and maybe even beautiful, that wasn't there before, of relaying connections that matter, of telling stories in hand upon hand, digit upon digit, attachment site upon attachment site, to craft conditions for finite flourishing on terra, on earth.
>
> (Haraway, 2016, p. 10)

Body mapping, and its constituting parts, therefore, are very much part of the stories that can be told, and the realities made possible for how we can live with substances. In this chapter, I look at three ways this opening has emerged – through the materials, the act of drawing/image making and the images – before revisiting the aforementioned question of validity.

Two Studies

In this chapter, I focus on two research projects that used body mapping as a drawing method during in-depth interviews and as a collaging method in a series of workshops. Both took place in London drug services. The first study (Study 1: 2012–2016) used body mapping to explore experiences of injecting drug use (predominantly heroin and crack cocaine) with a particular interest in pleasure.[3] Using an A1 piece of paper and a selection of drawing equipment including felt-tip pens, crayons and highlighters, I invited participants to draw a picture of their body before, during and after injecting drugs, and mark on and around the body what would be going on at the time (who and what would be present, including people, objects, sounds, smells, etc.) and what they would be feeling (for more details, see Dennis, 2019). The second study (Study 2: 2018–2022) used body mapping to explore experiences of abstaining and living without substances. A group of seven participants were invited over a

---

[3] I will always be indebted to Ruth Lewis for suggesting body mapping to me for this project.

series of four three-hour workshops to produce images about 'living with' and 'without' substances. They drew outlines of their bodies formed by the shadow of an overhead projector and then populated these outlines with various collaging materials, including paint, magazine cuttings and objects brought in by themselves, myself and an artist working on the project (see Figure 3.1).

Rather than focusing too much on the mechanics or the 'about' question of the method (which can be found elsewhere; see Dennis, 2019), in this chapter I want to think more about what body mapping *does*. This is a different kind of question. Method, here, is seen as an active part of the research process, rather than a tool for accessing the world 'out there' where its purpose is to interfere as little as possible, in the pursuit of objectivity. In this, I want to think about some of the ways body mapping actively changed the research encounter, enabling new thinking and ways of being to emerge.

Figure 3.1 Photograph of workshop showing participants engaging with the collaging materials and making their body maps.

Materials

For my first example, I ask the reader to revisit the fieldnote at the top of the chapter. In this excerpt from Study 2, we witness an exchange of things, bodies and affects. Jamil is prompted by the fizzy-drink bottle belonging to Sam, while Alicia's body acutely responds to the gauze Jamil brought in, and a series of stories are exchanged. Although there is not the space to expand on these stories here (for full details, see Dennis, 2022), they explored the skill, pleasure, harm and friendship involved in smoking crack. As with Haraway's (2016) conceptualisation of storytelling as a mode of more-than-human 'string figuring', body mapping is operating as a practice of return and relay. While Jamil had brought the gauze to the workshop to tell a story of repetition, sticking it to his body map and writing 'lost my gorze 4 my pipe again', it takes on a life of its own, and we soon witness the many stories 'a little bit of metal' can tell in this collective setting.

The Act of Drawing/Image Making

Mid-way through an interview with a participant named Jim in Study 1, I nervously re-introduced the idea of body mapping. While people are familiar with the verbal interview, reminiscent of a key-working session or doctor consultation, asking them to draw changes this dynamic. There is a disruption to the order of things as the drawing equipment is brought out but also as the room layout is changed to facilitate the activity. There is also an intimacy as we move in closer so I can see what is being drawn. Body mapping opens out the interview, allowing for a different kind of knowing to be produced. In Jim's case, he audibly uses the mapping as a mode of embodied remembering. He draws an outline of his body and says:

There was me. I was sort of thinking, today, to give you an example, I was thinking about *the clinic* (he writes the word clinic on the piece of paper), and *the time* that it's going to take for me to *flush this beer through me* [metabolise it], and, should I even have the beer ... I'm hoping that I blow below [on the breathalyser]. I know I'll blow something. Normally, I go back to zero because I drink at like half nine, quarter to ten, but I'd have had a Special Brew. Today, I only had a Kronenburg, which is 5% [alcohol], which is nearly half the percentage ... So, I was hoping, *I'm balancing all of this up in my mind* (he draws a set of scales), and then I was thinking ... 'aha, I'll get some *money* if I go down there'. ... And this was another question as well (he draws a thought bubble), because, I was thinking, 'aha', here's the (he draws a £20 note), 'bubububum' (he makes noises to accompany the drawing). And, I mean, the question is, am I gonna go straight and 'bum', straight back into the *needle* [inject heroin] (he draws a needle)? In fact, I'll do that in a red one (he chooses a red pen), more of a dark red one, it's more dominant, it's sort of playing a big part on my brain at the moment, I don't know why, but it is...

(Dennis, 2016, p. 136)

In this physical act of drawing, we are introduced to an intricate network of entities and processes informing Jim's use (or not) of licit (diamorphine, alcohol) and illicit (injecting heroin and crack) substances on the day of the interview. We get a real sense that Jim is not acting alone in the research process or events he describes as he depicts a complicated negotiation of timings, objects (breathalyser, money, syringe), substances (beer, heroin) and bodily processes ('flush the beer through'). As Jim relaxes into the practice, there is a rhythm to this drawing-remembering as he makes accompanying noises. There is also a representational element in which he thinks about the colours to represent what he is trying to communicate. Unlike a verbal interview, there are prolonged points of silence as participants concentrate on the drawing and can become attuned to what they are describing. One man even broke into song as he remembered some of the joyful ways heroin had affected him. The act of drawing/image making, therefore, affects and opens up the body and what is possible to think and feel in these moments.

Images

The images in themselves should not be imagined as an end point of the body mapping process but part of the relay of bodies, things and affects. In Study 2, we exhibited the body maps to the general public alongside an art installation made by two artists, Isla Millar and Penny Maltby, in response to them (see https://sites.gold.ac.uk/sociology/i-am-a-work-in-progress/). By inviting the body maps to be perceived as art and inviting artists' and publics' bodies into the storytelling, there is an opening out of what the maps can mean and do.

In what Nirmal Puwar and Sanjay Sharma have called a 'call and response' between sociology and art, textiles, like the gauze, became particularly important as a material and metaphor for understanding and representing the fragility of people's lives without substances. This follows Puwar and Sharma's conceptualisation in which researchers and artists collaborate in a process of exchange that involves stages whereby materials are passed and returned, transformed, only to be carried over to the next practitioner involved in the relay of co-production (2012, p. 54).

In this relay of body maps, textiles, metaphors and bodies, we became attuned to the tensions, burdens and the unending 'work' of recovery, encapsulated in one participant's phrase: 'I am a work in progress', which became the title of the exhibition. In this, the exhibition challenges a narrowly-defined addiction disease and treatment system that is often time-limited and considered successful as soon as the person is 'drug free', highlighting the need for longer-term support and diversifying what success and recovery mean for those they concern.

Through this process of working *with* the body maps in curating the exhibition we had to think through the kinds of affects we wanted them to have: how they should be hung, arranged, under what lighting, with what information and in what space. But this is only ever a suggestion. The images and installation will affect people in different ways as visitors to the exhibition are invited to use their bodies in moving around and getting a *feel* for them. By becoming affected, publics too are weaved back into this relay and re-imagining of what substance-using and recovering bodies can be and do after addiction.

Returning to the Question of Validity

The question is not: is it true? But: *does it work?* What new *thoughts* does it make possible to think? What new *emotions* does it make possible to feel? What new *sensations* and *perceptions* does it *open up* in the body?

(Massumi, 2004 [1987], p. xv, emphases added)

As we have seen, body mapping is not an inanimate, window-like portal into the world, but rather works to bring about new constellations of bodies, things and affects. As with Brian Massumi's (2004 [1987]) often-cited reflection on validity inspired by Deleuze and Guattari's *A Thousand Plateaus*, the question is not whether method can access truth but what it can *do* in the process: how it affects and moves us. In this, we have witnessed how bodies are opened up by the materials, the act of drawing/image making and the images themselves. With the materials, we see how the gauze and bottle affect the group and provoke different stories. In the act of drawing, the traditional interview participant who is deemed to be in control of their decision and meaning making quickly gives way to a wider form of participation *with* the drawing and with the entities and processes they describe. Moreover, in working *with* the body map, images as art threads are added to the storytelling relay, meaning that drug-recovering bodies become knowable as 'works in progress' and publics are invited into this understanding through a carefully curated exhibition.

Having focused on studying drug practices with body mapping, I now want to briefly extend this focus to social research more broadly by looking at where this opening up of the body – to new thoughts, emotions, sensations, perceptions – could be useful for researching other kinds of *disembodied*, heavily *narrativised*, *hard-to-verbalise* and *sensitive* practices.

Body mapping may be particularly useful for topics where the mind has tended to dominate and yet the body holds memories, like trauma and grief. By extending the research subject through the body, we get to know these 'problems' differently. This is similarly the case for phenomena that are heavily researched or narrativised, especially where discourses of pathology prosper. Furthermore, due to our oral Western 'traditions' tied up with colonial and patriarchal power relations, word-based methods may find it hard to avoid discriminatory and stigmatising stories and tropes. By introducing drawing or a creative practice that focuses on the body, we can help to circumvent these dominant ways of knowing.

By asking participants to map out various entities and forces, we get to see how bodies are constituted and curtailed, and where to intervene. This may be useful for understanding how even small acts, of violence, for example, or things, can cause what Deleuze and Guattari (1987) might call a 'blockage', inhibiting what bodies can 'become' (see Dennis, 2019, p. 133 for examples). However, by the same token, in treating bodies as assemblages, the method is intrinsically hopeful about how bodies might become otherwise and where openings may appear (Gunaratnam and Hamilton, 2017). Therefore, researching with body mapping, as seen here through its materials, practice and images, is not only useful for studying subjugated bodies and what might be deemed ethically or politically sensitive topics but for imagining and enacting more liberated futures.

References

Deleuze, G. and Guattari, F. (1987) *A Thousand Plateaus: Capitalism and Schizophrenia.* Minneapolis, MN, London: University of Minnesota Press.

Dennis, F. (2016) 'Encountering "triggers": Drug–body–world entanglements of injecting drug use', *Contemporary Drug Problems*, 43(2), pp. 126–141.

Dennis, F. (2019) *Injecting Bodies in More-than-Human Worlds.* London: Routledge.

Dennis, F. (2022) 'Chemical species: The art and politics of living with(out) drugs after addiction', *BioSocieties*. Available at: https://doi.org/10.1057/s41292-022-00281-9

Gunaratnam, Y. and Hamilton, C. (2017) 'Introduction: The wherewithal of feminist methods', *Feminist Review*, 115(1), pp. 1–12.

Haraway, D.J. (2016) *Staying with the Trouble: Making Kin in the Chthulucene.* Durham, NC: Duke University Press.

Malins, P. (2004) 'Machinic assemblages: Deleuze, Guattari and an ethico-aesthetics of drug use', *Janus Head,* 7(1), pp. 84–104.

Massumi, B. (2004 [1987]) 'Translator's foreword: Pleasures of philosophy', in: Deleuze, G. and Guattari, F. (eds.) *A Thousand Plateaus: Capitalism and Schizophrenia.* London, New York: Continuum International Publishing Group, pp. ix–xvi.

Puwar, N. and Sharma, S. (2012) 'Curating sociology', *The Sociological Review*, 60, pp. 40–63.

4

How to do social research with... a bowling ball

Emma Jackson

Introduction

This chapter reflects on the experience of conducting participant observation between 2015 and 2017 in a London bowling alley that is used by a highly diverse group of people. At the time of the research, the area surrounding the bowling alley was undergoing redevelopment and the building, earmarked for demolition, had become central to arguments about the future of the area. As a threatened diverse and well-loved local leisure space that was out of step with the official future vision for the neighbourhood, the bowling alley provided a lens on how ideas of urban diversity are deployed to make competing value claims in moments of urban change (Jackson, 2018). In order to understand how the bowling alley was used and valued (or not) by those who frequent it, I took to the lanes.

This chapter focuses on the ethnographic research process, exploring how the object of bowling ball acts as a tool for participation for the researcher, while also being imbued with layers of social, aesthetic and performance-focused meaning by those who use it. I ask: how does taking part in an activity like bowling with research participants offer insights into the social world of bowlers? How does this help us to access the meanings attributed to objects, like bowling balls and bowling shoes, by those who use them and how do they 'act back' on the bowler?

I am not the first sociologist to lace up my bowling shoes. Back in the 1930s, William Foote Whyte (1943) explored how social status and hierarchy were reflected and confirmed through bowling performance as part of his highly influential Boston-based study *Street Corner Society*. I decided to read his account of bowling one night before leaving my office as some sociological bowling inspiration, but instead it brought on profound jealousy. According to the book, Whyte was instrumental in winning a key game and was henceforth known by the men in his study as 'The Champ'. This reminded me of Loïc Wacquant's Chicago-based boxing ethnography *Body and Soul* (2004) where he becomes a boxer, nicknamed 'Busy Louie'. I noted in my field diary (29 May 2015), 'Do all male sport-related studies involve the researcher becoming amazing at said sport? I'm determined to be both a better ethnographer and a better bowler tonight.' Somewhere, deep down, I imagined a personal 'journey' involving high scores and an earned nickname. These aspirations do not reflect favourably on me, but also provide a window onto issues in doing research that involves taking part in an activity where the researcher might lack technical skill, and also are revealing of the prevalence and attraction of masculine heroic tropes within ethnography.

My (lack of) bowling skills aren't the only difference between my own and Whyte's approaches to research and writing about bowling. Whyte provides an account of what the bowling competition between two rival gangs means in terms of establishing the reinforcement and hierarchy in the social world he seeks to understand. Like me, he was interested in the social uses of bowling. But there is no description of what it *feels* like to pick up a bowling ball as part of his research – was he nervous? Did he manage to concentrate? – which is in step with sociological ethnographic writing of that period. Whyte does, however, provide a more reflexive account of his fieldwork in the later (1955) methodological appendix to the book, which gives a much more visceral account of the challenges and small humiliations involved with ethnographic research.

A more contemporary sociological bowler can be found in Douglas Harper (2004), who writes about a rural league in New York state. Harper reflects on what his all-male league participants discuss at bowling and the relationship to their working lives while also discussing the embodied rituals of bowling. However, Harper was already a member of the league and so didn't have to *become* a bowler as part of the research process. But what happens to 'doing research with...' when the researcher does not possess the technical skills of those she is researching? How does she balance keeping an eye on the ball and on the wider field that she hopes to observe?

Embodiment and Picking Up the Bowling Ball

The contradiction at the heart of participant observation has long been discussed by ethnographers. Ruth Behar (1996, p. 5) writes that the practice is 'split at the root' while Pierre Bourdieu (1993) describes it as an oxymoron. This paradox – of being 'with' while also attempting to document and analyse – resonated strongly in this research project, from the practicalities of combining observation with forging relationships while also trying to gain the skills to knock down ten stubborn pins, to the classic methodological and ethical questions of the extent to which I was in the league or a researcher, and the blurring of the boundaries between these positions. These practical and methodological issues have also been a feature of my previous projects, but the bowling study brought the embodied aspect of this process into particularly sharp focus.

While Wacquant advocates for a 'carnal sociology' (2015, p. 5) where the ethnographer puts their body into the situations of research participants in search of a sociology 'from the body', his theorising of what this means can slip into an account of ethnographic heroism. Can someone researching homelessness really get closer to the homeless experience by

Figure 4.1 A league member skilfully goes for a 'spare' (photo by Andy Lee).

putting their body through staying out overnight on the street as he suggests (2015, p. 6)? Researchers have to be very careful about the claims they make and what can become a performance of authenticity. Wacquant also overlooks other traditions in feminist research, where an embodied approach (for discussion, see Pitts-Taylor, 2004) has long been advocated. However, while we may want to steer clear of heroic ethnographic tropes, the body is nonetheless a resource and can offer clues and avenues of inquiry for the researcher. The rush of getting a strike, the increase in size of my right bicep and the onset of a foot problem exacerbated by the frequent wearing of ill-fitting bowling shoes – all of these experiences show how the body is a tool for the researcher, but also how this is not a one-way process; research acts back on the body of the researcher.

Bowling alongside my participants gave me insights into the embodied rituals and etiquette of bowling as they are experienced and interpreted by the bowlers. As a pure observer I might have noted the high-fives and fist bumps or the flashpoints of excitement when bowlers stop their games to gather around a particular lane. But I would not have the same sense of what it *feels* like. My own struggles with becoming a bowler also provided insights into the experiences league members described to me. For example, Tom[1] explained the issues of trying to improve while also maintaining a conducive headspace.

I had this period of time I was so frustrated, nothing was going my way and one time John [league organiser] came to me and he was like 'the thing is about bowling you need to get around ten different things right to have a perfect shot. And if you have something on your mind, something stressing you out outside of this, you are not relaxed' and it's absolutely right. And some of the best nights you are relaxed and you haven't planned anything in your head. Don't think about your shot … and you just clear your mind basically, and that's where it happens.

This proved difficult advice to follow when bowling as part of ethnographic research where the mind inevitably wanders over to the next lane.

Bowling alongside participants also enabled discussions about what participating meant to bowlers in the context of their lives. One bowler, Robert, explained the importance of progressing as a bowler:

[1]All names have been changed for anonymity.

For me, the competition is ... is how much better can I be than I was last year? That for me is what's important. Can I do what I couldn't do last year. And *I don't have any improvements in my work or social life so it's nice to have that one thing.* (emphasis added)

Going into the project with a set of research questions about space sharing, urban multiculture and city space, I had not thought about this motivation of improvement as a reason for people going to the bowling alley. Through conducting participant observation, I was challenged to think about how these individual aspirations and practices of belonging that embedded people in a group were linked (Jackson, 2020).

As well as taking part while observing, the other aspect of research that the ethnographer must juggle is how to document her thoughts and observations. Taking extensive notes while participating in the league was not practical or appropriate. I would note down the odd prompt for later and then would sit on the East London line train on the way home, furiously typing on my phone and then filling the notes out the morning after. This strategy worked for the most part, but on one particularly eventful night, I noted in my field diary (20 April 2016), 'I have that "ethnography feeling" where you feel brimming with stories and like if you don't write it down you will burst.' Others have got around this problem by periodically diving into toilet cubicles, giving rise to the expression 'ethnographer's bladder' (Dingwall, 1980).

I never did become The Champ. There was no cool nickname waiting for me and the doors that becoming a better bowler might have opened for me - invitations to bowl elsewhere and the respect of my bowling peers - never materialised. The challenge, then, was to find and accept my place in the league. That of enthusiast and that of the researcher. At one stage of the research, I also found a role in doing some of the admin of bowling night. A tradition peculiar to this particular league is that when someone gets a 'Turkey' (three strikes in a row), they are given a novelty hat in the shape of a turkey to wear. This gets documented with a photograph that is posted on the league's Facebook page. The tradition was initiated by an American bowler, Amy, who moved back to the USA during the fieldwork period. Amy bequeathed the role to Lisa, an enthusiastic, relatively new member of the league but the hat duties kept interrupting her game. I started helping out, fetching the hat from the store cupboard, taking a photo and then sending that to the league organiser, John. This is one of the many examples of how objects play a vital role within the league – and how researchers sometimes find their place in a group by making themselves useful.

Cursed Balls and Other Objects

> I unfasten the velcro and slide my feet into the shoes and feel the familiar sensation of shoes moulded by other people's feet ... I enter my name on the console then try to find a decent 10-pound ball on the racks – and fail. They all look a bit bashed up. Some are heavily chipped and resemble the boulders that *The Flintstones* use for bowling. I try a couple of goes with a rubbish ball. Clunk, clunk, clunk it goes down the lane.
>
> (Fieldnotes: 15 April 2016)

Balls and shoes – alongside trophies, bowling shirts and other pieces of equipment and ephemera – are part of the rich material culture of bowling. Often reflecting the aesthetic of 1950s Americana, in keeping with bowling alleys across the world, these objects can be read as expressing the bowler's sense of identity ('If lost return me to ... Lane 17' reads a t-shirt worn by three of the bowlers) but they also circulate in place, reaffirming group identity – and at times causing friction.

Putting on a pair of shoes from behind the counter of a bowling alley and selecting a ball from the racks is part of the ritual of bowling for many people. However, some league members came to the league with their own balls (and shoes), or else, once they became serious about bowling through regular league attendance, chose to buy their own. Going to get a first bowling ball drilled to fit the bowler's hand was an important part of becoming a bowler and honing a personal technique and style. It also means not having to rely on the variable quality of 'house balls' (see above). I noticed that at the end of a few of my interviews with league members they would ask me if I was going to get my own ball. I read this as a query about my own relationship to bowling. Was I sticking around or just passing through?

The bowling balls of others were read by other members of the league. To bring your own ball to the alley was a marker of seriousness and commitment as a bowler. League members described how they had come to the bowling alley on a regular night and having their own ball was a cause for comment from the league regulars who then suggested they come along to the league. Robert recalls,

I took some friends to [bowling alley] for a party. Pete [league stalwart] was like 'Oh you have your own ball but you're not very good!' Something like that. He said, 'you should come upstairs and get better'. So, I thought, 'OK yeah that sounds like fun.'

Interestingly, Robert, who liked the vintage Americana aesthetic of bowling, did not get his own shoes because he disliked the trainer style of modern bowling shoes, and because getting shoes would mean trading in his traditional 1950s bowling bag (which fits one bowling ball) for a contemporary wheel-along bag which did not fit his preferred aesthetic. Bowling balls are also passed on. Robert generously offered to give me one of his, but I could not get used to the fingertip style. And Lisa who took over the hat responsibility from Amy also inherited a glittery red bowling ball at the same time. It was as if Amy was passing on her league role through the ball.

While house balls were sometimes blamed for bad scores, others took on meaning as particularly lucky or unlucky. The most extreme example I came across was relayed by Tom who told me about a 'cursed ball'.

I had a friend back in the day who was really into it. I think he was the first one to buy his own ball and after he bought his own ball he went way, way, downhill. He could not get over 40 in 10 frames. Forty! And he was literally struggling with it. He even took lessons and it was terrible. Like, what happened? He's trying so hard. He got a ball. It doesn't make any sense and one day he'd just had enough. He said, 'I'm done' and he left the ball in there and nobody wanted to touch it because everybody thought it was the cursed ball ... There's no other explanation why the ball doesn't reach the end and knock something down.

Here the ball itself becomes imbued with agency by the frustrated bowler and his friends. Such abandoned balls would sit in the store cupboard until a clean out. The ball thus acts back on the bowler in terms of the feelings attached to it, but also physically. A change in ball can destabilise a bowler as they adjust to the new object. Making sense of this a little more pragmatically than in the tale of the cursed ball, Steve told me how retrieving his own ball that had been drilled for his hand from his parents' house and bringing it to bowling night had initially had an adverse effect on his scores, 'The ball I have is much more of a hook ball so it's trying to find the skill that I had before and trying to bring it back.' His reunion with his ball thus took some work.

At the other end of the spectrum, bowlers deploy strategies to hang on to 'good' house balls. One bowler used to stash a particularly unmarked and shiny 12lb house ball in the store cupboard. When he stopped coming to the league, I started to use that ball and rather guiltily carried on keeping it in the store cupboard. Eventually, the ball was put back out into general circulation. Through these strategies, bowlers attempt to make pieces of the communal furniture their own.

The circulation of objects both cements a sense of belonging to the league while also potentially generating other kinds of feelings – annoyance and possessiveness over shared equipment, frustration at a ball that must be cursed.

Conclusion

The example of the bowling ball shows how objects become imbued with meaning within this social scene. Bowling alongside others, with its combination of participating in a physical ritual, chatting between games and relating to the same kind of objects, allowed me to experience some of the shared emotions and physical experiences of others in the league. Albeit with a different kind of intensity and motive – I never did end up getting my own ball. Despite being a poor to average bowler, picking up a bowling ball was crucial to my research. By getting to know the bowling league, I became more at home in the space of the bowling alley. Bowling alongside others gave me insights into the kind of micro-interactions and processes I describe here, but also into the space of the bowling alley and its place in the neighbourhood. Through taking to the lanes, I was able to explore what places like the bowling alley mean to those who use them and contrast this with how the bowling alley figured in official accounts from local government, which framed the bowling alley as an impediment to progress (see Jackson, 2018; 2020). Doing research through joining in a physical and social activity like bowling poses challenges for the researcher, but can also provide an entry into understanding rich social worlds.

References

Behar, R. (1996) *The Vulnerable Observer*. Boston, MA: Beacon Press.

Bourdieu, P. (1993) *The Weight of the World*. Redwood City, CA: Stanford University Press.

Dingwall, R. (1980) 'Ethics and ethnography', *The Sociological Review*, 28(4), pp. 871.

Harper, D. (2004) 'Wednesday bowling night', in Knowles, C. and Sweetman, P. (eds) *Picturing the Social Landscape*. London, Routledge, pp. 93–114.

Jackson, E. (2018) 'Valuing the bowling alley: Contestations over the preservation of spaces of everyday multiculture in London', *The Sociological Review*, 67(1), pp. 79–94.

Jackson, E. (2020) 'Bowling together? Practices of belonging and becoming in a London ten-pin bowling league', *Sociology*, 54(3), pp. 518–533.

Pitts-Taylor, V. (2004) 'A feminist carnal sociology? Embodiment in sociology, feminism, and naturalized philosophy', *Qualitative Sociology*, 38(1), pp. 19–25.

Wacquant, L. (2004) *Body and Soul: Notebooks of an Apprentice Boxer*. New York: Oxford University Press.

Wacquant, L. (2015) 'For a sociology of flesh and blood', *Qualitative Sociology*, 38, pp. 1–11.

Whyte, W.F. (1943) *Street Corner Society: The Social Structure of an Italian Slum*. Chicago, IL, London: University of Chicago Press.

Whyte, W.F. (1955) *Street Corner Society: The Social Structure of an Italian Slum*. Second edition. Chicago, IL, London: University of Chicago Press.

Further Listening

Lessons from the Lanes 1 https://cucrblog.wordpress.com/2017/11/02/bowling-together-lessons-from-the-lanes-by-emma-jackson/

Lessons from the Lanes 2 https://cucrblog.wordpress.com/2017/11/06/bowling-together-lessons-from-the-lanes-part-2-by-emma-jackson/

5

How to do social research with... a chilli

Alex Rhys-Taylor

Figure 5.1 Chilli cultivars and their origins, The Festival of Heat, London (author's own photograph).

17.00, late November in East London. An elderly man with rose pink skin, an even rosier nose and a full head of bright white hair enters the neon lit Bengali canteen just off Whitechapel High Street. He rubs his hands to warm them as he stands in his long black woollen coat behind a young British Bangladeshi woman and her ten-year-old daughter. The mother and daughter are ordering their dinner on the way home from an afterschool club and are arguing over their order.

'I don't want that one.'

'You're sharing with us all.'

'The chicken is too spicy.'

'Ok. What about...'

'I want chips!'

'It's something from here, or you go hungry.'

The mother, looking around her, suddenly self-conscious, catches the eye of the older man behind her who offers a polite grimace. An acknowledgement of the universal truculence of children.

She pays before pulling her daughter aside to a nearby table where they wait for their order.

The elderly man approaches the counter.

The server smiles 'Good evening sir.'

'Good evening. Good evening.' The old man speaks with the enunciation typical of monied residents from a nearby cluster of Georgian terraces.

'What can I get for you?'

The old man jabs his finger towards one of the large dishes beneath the glass service counter 'Is this ... this one here ... is this the garlic chicken?'

'Yes, it is sir. You want one of those? With rice?'

'What? Um. Is it spicy today?'

'A little sir. Not very I think. No, not really. I think you'll be ok.'

'Oh. Oh. No. No.' The man shakes his head, apparently in disappointment.

'Oh. Haha. Ok. Sorry sir. You want it spicy? You can have this one here. But this one has bones in. Or I can serve you the garlic chicken with some chopped up green chilis if you like.'

'Oh. Yes! That would be much better. Yes.' The man rubs his hands together again. 'I'll have that to eat here if you don't mind.' The man gestures to a small table in the corner. 'Will you bring it over to me when it's ready.'

'Yes sir.'

As he hands over his money to the cashier, another man comes up some stairs behind the counter carrying two large ghee-spotted brown bags that he hands to the waiting mother.

As they leave the shop the mum smiles again at the elderly man as he moves towards his table.

After five minutes of banging microwave doors and mechanical buzzing noises the man is served at his small Formica table with a small porcelain bowl of steaming chicken curry, a plate of rice and saucer of chopped green finger chilies (*Jawla*). The server returns with some water and a cup. The old man appears to pour the chilies over the curry before hunkering down over the bowl. Even from behind it's possible to see the heat from the bowl spreads through his body, the pale rosy flesh of his ears turning ever closer to fuchsia with each mouthful.

Whatever the strain of materialism that they subscribe to, the realm of 'objects' plays a well-acknowledged part in mediating the social world. Over the years, the sociology of objects has revealed a number of key materials around which 21st-century human life is organised. Of the gaggle of objects accused of making social worlds, those that are digestible – foodstuffs, drinks and pharmaceuticals – seem particularly capable of influencing humanity's collective existence. Whether it is through sating the raging desperation of hunger or stirring sentiment, the act of eating and digesting can radically change the way in which an individual body, or a collective, acts. In this respect, foodstuffs might be *the* most important class of objects in human history. Look at any history of bread, for instance, and you will see how hunger for bread and revolution are common bed-fellows. Beyond stirring revolution, food also brings bodies together and connects them through production, markets, procurement or otherwise some sort of cultural ritual related to their consumption. This was certainly the case, for instance, for a range of spices and comestibles, upon which the brutal circuitry of colonial trade was founded (Mintz, 1986; Schivelbusch, 1993). In this sense we might think of foodstuffs as what the philosopher Michel Serres (2008) famously referred to as 'quasi-objects'; objects that become intertwined with multiple individuals and, in doing so, catalyse social relations between them.

However, to really understand how human history is nudged one way or another by materials around us, we not only have to take material objects seriously. We must also put the *bodily sensations*, the feelings afforded by and meanings ascribed to these objects at the centre of our focus. This is where a 'sociology of the senses' is of particular importance. Combining sensorially attuned scholarship with an aforementioned social science of objects, we stand to get a much better understanding of history, the present and the possible future of our life amongst these things.

Taking sensations seriously is crucial to understanding humans and their collective activity. That is not to say, however, that all sensations are as sociologically illuminating as one another. Not all sensoria – as distinct from 'sensations' (embodied experiences) – are equal in this respect (Rhys-Taylor, 2017, p. 12). Within the assortment of sensoria that make up 21st-century cultures, some sensations have more potential to set the world in motion at a given moment. In many instances, this 'potential' seems related to the affectivity of the objects in question; their ability to precipitate changes in the bodies around them. As such, to understand how we can do contemporary social research with these objects and the sensations they afford us, it serves to consider ingredients whose enhanced affectivity has moved, connected and altered cultures and communities across the world. Consider then, one of the most obviously affective ingredients on the shelf of the 21st-century grocers: the chilli pepper.

Worldly Berries

Purportedly originating somewhere around what is now central-eastern Mexico, the chilli pepper was cultivated into edible, sweet and spicy forms across the pre-Columbian Americas and is known as one of the first domesticated crops across those continents. Therein it served as both a regular ingredient and a ritual device within a range of different cultures and events (Anderson, 2016, pp. 34-44). The berry of the chilli plant spread around the world following the great 'Columbian exchange' of botanicals between Western and Eastern hemispheres in the 1500s, and subsequently – by way of gunboat diplomacy and colonial conquest (Schivelbusch, 1993; Czarra, 2009) – became an integral part of many 'heritage cuisines'. For the first 300 years of this process, the chilli moved from its European ports of arrival back into tropical latitudes into the local culture and cuisines across Africa, India, China and beyond. As it did so, it spawned new cultivars (scotch bonnets in the Caribbean, finger chillies in India, birdseye chillies in East Asia) and synchronised with the pre-existing use of peppers and other fiery spices. The descendants of the Americas' chilli now abound in cuisines the world over from Lagos to Lahore and London, to Bangkok, Budapest and Beijing. Importantly, in each location the chilli plays a unique role, appears in dishes with diverse meanings, and also gets involved in a diverse range of rituals and social processes, each one different from the next.

We get much of our understanding of the historical entanglement of cultures by way of foodstuffs over the last 400 years, and a sense of the post-colonial legacy, by looking for traces of ingredients like chillis in accountancy records, recipe books and cultural artefacts of the past. However, as advocates of stalking objects have intimated (Appadurai, 2006; Cook and Harrison, 2007; Bauer, 2019), we get a stronger sense of the current sociological significance of all this if we supplement the documented social history with real-time ethnographies of the thing in question. For instance, were we to trace the chilli pepper from the fields of the global south where it is grown, through the co-operatives where it is aggregated and exported, to the distributors of the global north, we would build up a particular gestalt of the contemporary world; a picture of the flows and bottlenecks within 21st-century global food systems. Tracking the object through its production, we would get broad answers to the 'where', the 'when' and the 'how much'. Tracing the object that far does not, however, tell us much about the 'how' or the 'why', nor does it give us much of an answer to 'so what?'. Tracing the sparks that the thing makes as it moves through from the retailers into the homes of consumers and across their tongues, however, yields a much higher-resolution picture of what a specific ingredient does and to whom it does it. Zooming in *even closer*, to the movement of sensations across taste buds and through the bodies in those scenes, we can add to 'where', 'when' and for 'whom', a fuller understanding of 'how' and 'why'. And in doing so, an attention to sensory experience opens into a much more complete understanding of the processes upon which the larger global food system rests.

Sensed Communities

Nosing around for the preparation of chillis, and watching out for where and how people use them, can be particularly revealing. Shadowing the chilli pepper through South East England, for instance, we discover a middle-aged Thai woman who, from her arrival in the 1980s, has carried little sachets of chilli powder in her purse. These are for sprinkling over the various beige dishes that her husband orders for her in the country pubs that they visit during their weekend walking trips. He doesn't mind a bit of heat now and again and will pinch things off her plate. But when she gets together with friends to play cards, they deliberately make food so hot that none of their husbands can eat it, nor interfere with their evening. Pursuing the chilli into East London, we discover a contrapuntal story: for the young girl featured in the opening vignette, the refusal to eat her parents' chilli-spiked lunches and family dinners, in her own eyes, marks her off as distinct from her parents' 'first-wave immigrant' generation, and less distinct from her peers. Her parents mourn the loss and repeatedly secrete occasional flakes of chilli into her meals. Tracking the fiery berry a few hundred metres up the road from this domestic setting, we arrive at a local Bangladeshi cookery class. One attendee, a bearded British farmer from Dorset repeatedly restates his knowledge of chilli cultivation to other white middle-class cooks in an unveiled effort to assert his mastery of the exotic. The elderly female instructor smiles politely as the man talks. And a mile up the road, in a student union bar we discover that for initiates into a rugby team, machismo and masochistic acceptance of pain are displayed by ritually swilling the initiation cocktail of vodka and inhumanly-hot pepper sauce.

In each of these scenes, the peculiar sensation of the pepper's consumption is important to senses of self, other and community. But as the diversity of scenes in which the pepper appears also suggests, it is not just the raw experience of eating the pepper that does this. None of the idiosyncratic meanings ascribed to the pepper here are innate to the object. In each of the instances, the associational work of the chilli pepper emerges from the process of ascribing biographically and culturally specific meaning to the sensations afforded by the pepper. Through combining the *sensoria* of the pepper's flavour and the meaning acquired through *sensibility*, the resultant *sensation* can stimulate a culturally specific sense of commensality. Not least, these sensations gives consumers the experience of a 'sensed community', and affinity between others who ascribe the *same* meaning to the sensation (Howes and Classen, 2013, p. 84). But, as the disparate examples above suggest, the chilli does this in different ways in each case.

Transcultural Sensations

The chilli appears as a bit part in any number of different cultural rituals and has specific emotional resonances for different individuals and groups. However, the spread of the berry is related to something that *all* chilli eaters, for all time, have experienced irrespective of cultural meanings: the pepper's iconic 'heat'. This heat is derived from a biological trick that the chilli plant evolved to trick ground-dwelling creatures into thinking they have encountered a threat when they bite into it (birds apparently do not feel this sensation, and thus serve as propagators of the shrub). This sensation is created by the chemical capsaicin and all mammals, apart from tree shrews and humans, are entirely perturbed by it (Chu *et al.*, 2020). Humans will eat the berries with no ill effect because they are able to realise that it is not literal burning that one feels when biting into a chilli, but rather a simulation, a gustatory illusion. Humans sense the 'heat'. But they also see through the evolutionary ruse. And on the other side of the illusion, the consumer swims in the dopamine secreted in response to the burning pain. As with the pain of tattoos, acupuncture and BDSM (bondage, domination/discipline, sadism/submission, masochism), we have a capacity to ascribe a 'positive' meaning to the pain. This might be the case with tree shrews too, but we've never asked them.

Importantly all this burning, sweating and euphoria happens at a very corporeal level, in the realms of affect, below the level of discursive consciousness and prior to culturally specific meaning. As such, it might be said that beneath the layers of culturally specific significance that the chilli acquires, the pepper might also be said to have less arbitrary, non-idiosyncratic meaning for all human bodies; that is, the pepper signifies the experience of a benign burning sensation and the pleasure derived from it. That this sensation is apart from the culturally specific connotations of the pepper does not, however, mean that it is *asocial*. Rather, the benign burning sensation might also play an important role in establishing commensality. This applies both within cultural groups but also, crucially, across difference. That's because the intensity of the affect the pepper produces, the burning sensation it elicits, has the potential to produce – between diners – an empathetic sensation. A sense, when consumed as part of a group, that 'you' are feeling what 'I' am feeling. At the most, this sensation facilitates a moment of mutual recognition. At the least, it creates an opportunity for translation. While the chilli is an important player in a kaleidoscope of different cultural rituals, the unequivocal nature of the sensation it precipitates might also be active in the development of recognition and translation across differences.

Intensely affective objects can do this. In his anthropology of the Cuban cultural formation, the work of anthropologist Ortiz suggests that objects such as tobacco and sugar played a particularly important point in the development of new 'transcultural' artefacts, practices and cuisines (Ortiz, 1995). Ortiz uses the term 'transculturation' to specify the emergence of new cultures in intensely transnational spaces of early modernity, in situations where multiple 'exogenous influences converge' (Ortiz, 1995, p. 177) on the same human group and mutate to produce something new. It is no coincidence that the materials Ortiz saw as entangling communities with one another, tobacco and sugar, are deeply affective materials. As the anthropologist details, each of these sensuous objects had its own culturally specific meanings and social functions for the residents and settlers of the Caribbean island. But the substances each also had 'physiochemical properties' (Ortiz, 1995, p. 184) that relate directly to the 'sensual pleasure' that *anybody* could derive from them. It is the experience of these sensations that led tobacco use to spread first from native Americans, to African slaves, and later to white European settlers. While it spread, the production and consumption brought disparate constituencies together into shared spaces, institutions and rituals. 'In the service of tobacco', Ortiz wrote, 'strangers are brought together' (Ortiz, 1995, p. 251). Ortiz's focus on objects in newly emergent cultures offers a conceptual framework that is also relevant to understanding contemporary forms of cosmopolitanism (Berg, 2022). But it does so best, only when we pay attention to the sensuous role of objects within those situations.

When it comes to nudging human history one way or another, comestibles are amongst the most potent materials. They tangle themselves up with our bodies, and catalyse sociality with other bodies. As they do so, the sensations stimulated by simple ingredients acquire deep and culturally specific meanings. And once these meanings are learned, they can help to forge a sense of community through enabling people to recognise other people who share the same 'sensibility'. But it is also the case that, beneath the idiosyncratic meanings attached to sensations, the very physical experience of eating particular ingredients can, at least potentially, foster a sense of a shared experience between, and translation across, different cultural milieus. This is especially so when such intensely affective ingredients are involved. We can glean aspects of this through crude empiricism, through counting and accounting for where ingredients go, who buys and who sells them, and who consumes them. But if we are to really understand how and why each ingredient or foodstuff does this, we cannot ignore the social import of the sensuous side of consumption. In fact, we must take the sensuous side of consumption seriously, because the sensations themselves are what set the human world in motion.

References

Anderson, Heather Arndt (2016) *Chillies: A Global History*. London: Reaktion Books.

Appadurai, Arjun (2006) 'The thing itself', *Public Culture*, 18(1), pp. 15–22.

Bauer, Alexander A. (2019) 'Itinerant objects', *Annual Review of Anthropology*, 48, pp. 335–352.

Berg, Mette Louise (2022) 'Anthropological perspectives on super-diversity: Complexity, difference, sameness, and mixing', pp. 1–10. https://discovery.ucl.ac.uk/id/eprint/10138189/1/Berg_ML%20--%20Anthropological%20perspectives%20on%20superdiversity%2022%2009%202021.pdf

Chu, Ying, Cohen, Bruce E. and Chuang, Huai-hu (2020) 'A single TRPV1 amino acid controls species sensitivity to capsaicin', *Scientific Reports*, 10(1), p. 8038. doi: 10.1038/s41598-020-64584-2.

Cook, Ian and Harrison, Michelle (2007) 'Follow the thing: "West Indian Hot Pepper Sauce"', *Space and Culture*, 10(1), pp. 40–63.

Czarra, Fred (2009) *Spices: A Global History*. London: Reaktion Books.

Howes, David and Classen, Constance (2013) *Ways of Sensing: Understanding the Senses in Society*. London, New York: Routledge.

Mintz, Sidney Wilfred (1986) *Sweetness and Power: The Place of Sugar in Modern History*. London: Penguin Books.

Ortiz, Fernando (1995) *Cuban Counterpoint: Tobacco and Sugar*. Durham, NC: Duke University Press Books.

Rhys-Taylor, Alex (ed.) (2017) *Food and Multiculture: A Sensory Ethnography of East London*. London: Routledge.

Serres, Michel (2008) *The Five Senses: A Philosophy of Mingled Bodies*. London, New York: Continuum International Publishing Group.

Schivelbusch, Wolfgang (1993) *Tastes of Paradise*. London: Vintage Books.

6

How to do social research with... collaging

Rebecca Coleman

In a classroom in a secondary school in Oxfordshire in 2003, a group of young women and I eat chocolate and paste the empty wrappers onto paper torn from a roll of lining wallpaper. Two young women put on make-up and take polaroid photographs of themselves to glue on to their paper.

(Fieldnotes, 2003)

Figure 6.1 Collaging materials, 2016.

As this scene from a research project in the early 2000s indicates, I have worked with collaging as a social research methodology for a number of years. In this particular project, I was exploring how young women experience their bodies through relations with different kinds of images. Most research on this topic seemed to rely on verbal methods such as interviews and focus groups. Building on creative, often arts-based methods that were emerging at the time, I was considering how I might study images through image-making methods. The sessions were a hit; the girls seemed to really enjoy making images of their experiences, and some girls stayed on through their lunch break to continue their making. I enjoyed the sessions too, as I felt us all relaxing into the project and articulating experiences not only through words but also the materials I'd brought with me in a large suitcase, including young women's magazines, stamps, stickers, pipe cleaners, make-up, paper, glue and scissors, a box of chocolates and a Polaroid camera.

I didn't call their making 'collaging' at the time, as I was uncertain whether it was possible to bring such an activity into what I hoped was my serious piece of social research. Collaging seemed to me, at once, artistic, and therefore demanding years of study and practice, which I did not have; idiosyncratic in that I didn't really know how participants would respond to the prompt to make a collage or the materials I'd provided, or the collage that they'd make; and a bit too playful – was collaging really a rigorous method when it seemed so fun? Over the years, however, I have tried to reframe these uncertainties into potential strengths. In this chapter, I consider these three points – collaging as artistic, idiosyncratic and playful – reflecting on some instances across my research and teaching that have sharpened my understanding of how it is possible to do social research with collaging.

Art, Interest and Accessibility

I am in a room at the far end of the Turbine Hall at Tate Modern with my friends and colleagues Tara Page and Helen Palmer and a group of early career researchers who are participating in a practice workshop. They arrange the found materials they had brought with them on a large table. Twigs are piled on top of each other, leaves are laid next to signs for cyclists next to bars of liquorice next to written words...

(Fieldnotes, 2016)

Brandon Taylor begins his book, *Collage: The Making of Modern Art* (2014 [2004]) by describing a piece of art work Picasso made in 1908 called *The Dream*. On 'a brown cardboard sheet, perhaps the side of a packing box, bearing a label from the luxurious Magasins du Louvre department store in Paris', Picasso paints over the label and sketches the curves of two figures (probably women) and some swooping trees and branches (2014 [2004], p. 7). Taylor argues that '[w]hile not strictly a collage (Picasso did not, after all paste the label on)', this artwork can be understood as a precursor to the artistic movement of Cubism, which emerged shortly afterwards, and established collage as a particular kind of artistic form.

Taylor defines collage, 'in its first and usual meaning' as 'the pasting-on of scraps that originated beyond the studio, in the department store or on the street' (2014 [2004], p. 8). In this short definition, we are alerted to two points about collage. The first is that collage refers to 'the pasting on' of one thing onto another thing ('collage' is derived from the French '*coller*', which means 'to glue' or 'to stick'); the second is that what is pasted is a found object that typically comes from everyday life and popular, or 'low', culture; 'scraps' that come from 'beyond the studio' of the artist. Taken together, these points draw our attention to how collaging involves the transformation of a thing (a found object, a scrap) from one context to another – the 'imported object ... has to join another surface where it does not strictly belong' as Taylor puts it (2014 [2004], p. 8) – and that this transformation might be 'inappropriate, jarring or wrong – but interestingly so' (2014 [2004], p. 8). Just as with my hunch that collaging might disturb some of the professionalism of research methods (in its playfulness and idiosyncrasy), collaging is also often seen as disturbing an understanding of art as 'high culture'. Artistic practice is democratised through the focus on and use of readily accessible materials and collaging's ability to be done in different locations.

Today, there is a wide range of collage artists, including increasingly those who work digitally (indeed, the cut and paste function so ubiquitous to writing, editing and searching online might be understood in terms of the key definition of collaging). Gwen Raaberg (1998) argues that the routes of collaging in making use of accessible, everyday materials and in critiquing dominant culture (including that of 'high art') have, on the one hand, resulted in it being a subordinated art form. On the other hand, this alternative history of collaging makes it especially appropriate to those interested in challenging and re-working norms and values, including gender, sexuality, race, class and dis/ability. For example, collage artist Barbara Kruger has juxtaposed classical and popular images of women's bodies with cultural slogans, such as *Untitled (Your Body Is a Battleground)* (1989); Martha Rosler juxtaposes images of war, white femininity and domesticity (e.g., *House Beautiful: Bringing the War Home*, 2004), and Wangechi Mutu combines images of black African women's bodies and medical images (e.g., *Complete Prolapse of the Uterus*, 2004).

A number of points from these discussions of collaging and art are helpful to understand collaging as a social research method. First, its interest in 'low culture', everyday life and challenging dominant norms and values means that collaging has many intersections with the critical dimensions of social research. This involves the kinds of issues that collaging might be deployed to address (as I discuss below), and where it might be done – in London's Tate Modern gallery as the scene that begins this section indicates, but also in the classroom and the home. Second, the accessibility of collaging means that it is a relatively straightforward activity to organise and one that participants are usually already familiar with. In the scenes above, note how I brought a range of everyday materials to the image-making sessions, most of which I purchased from a local pound store, and how participants bring their own found materials to the session, including twigs, leaves and signs. In other sessions, I've asked participants to gather free flyers, cardboard packages, newspapers and magazines, sticky notes and used paper. In some sessions, we've deliberately worked without scissors or glue, exploring how different materials afford techniques of folding, tearing, crumpling, as well as the ephemerality that results from being unable to permanently fix things in a place.

Third, the movement of materials from one context to another and the juxtaposing of materials is productive; participants may explore and express their opinions or experiences about a particular topic, putting together potentially disparate materials to make new relationships and connections. The practice can also 'evoke ... embodied responses, and use ... the juxtaposition of fragments and the presence of ambiguity to engage the viewer in multiple avenues of interpretation' (Butler-Kisber, 2018,

p. 103). Discussing her research with black and Latinx youth on health and fitness, Carrie Safron (2019) notes how collaging introduced slowness and hesitation into the research process as both participants and she herself reflected on their multiple intentions in making and analysing the collages. Fourth, while the technique certainly matters, and most artists and some social research participants make beautiful collages, the movement and transformation of materials from one situation to another is itself interesting and rendered visible; the finished product is significant, but the process of making is both highlighted and important too.

Idiosyncrasy, Materials and Vibrancy

In a classroom in a girls' secondary school in South East London, a small group of young women chat to each other as they pass around crafting materials, paper, magazines, scissors and glue. The tubs of glitter prove to be particularly popular.

(Fieldnotes, 2016)

This scene from a collaging workshop in 2016 highlights not only the importance of accessible materials in collaging, but also the ways in which certain materials can stand out as especially vibrant or engaging to participants. Among a range of crafting materials, glitter emerged as the one that most of these participants wanted to work with; tubs were passed around the table and the glitter made its way on to the collages, as well as on to clothes, bodies, the table and floor. I've learnt through organising and participating in collaging workshops to be open to the materials that might become popular; indeed, this workshop inspired me to trace the popularity of glitter within this specific group of young women to how glitter often makes things luminous, exciting and aspirational in mainstream girls' culture (Coleman, 2020). I also began considering how working, hands on, with tactile objects focused my attention on the materials. The collaging method, then, brought into focus the materials via which research was composed, and demanded I think carefully about the materials that both I and the participants selected.

In a classroom at Goldsmiths, a group of MA students studying feminist methods sit in a large circle on the black carpet. In the middle of them are collections of pages torn from magazines, sticky notes, ink stamps, stickers, glitter (again). They talk to each other about what they are making as they select the materials that are somehow vibrant to them.

(Fieldnotes, 2015)

This scene ends with me noting how participants discuss their selection of specific materials. One way I responded to the demand that materials seemed to place on me was through building opportunities into the workshops for participants to consider which ones stood out to them. Rather than trying to temper the quirks of collaging, or to produce social research data that are representative, generalisable or replicable, it seemed important to stay with its idiosyncrasies. All materials, whether they be words or twigs, generate certain affects and possibilities, and limit others. In some sessions, we reflected on this by engaging with feminist theories of the agency of materials (e.g., Bennett, 2010) and archives and subjectivity (e.g., Campt, 2017; Tamboukou, 2019) in order to explore how certain materials become vibrant to us and how this connects with personal and/or socio-cultural histories. In other sessions, we have critiqued the materials that we work with. This has been especially the case with mainstream women's magazines; their representations of white, able-bodied, young, normative femininity have led to reflections on why I brought them in, to broader discussions of the limits and problems of mainstream media. Sometimes this has been the focus of the collages themselves. One memorable collage involved cut-out pictures of scissors pasted onto ripped-up parts of women's bodies, reflecting the maker's rage.

Playfulness, Making and Contemplating

In a classroom at the Polish Academy of Sciences in Warsaw, an international group of women academics scribble words describing their journey to the room onto small pieces of paper. They throw the paper into the air, and assemble and re-assemble words on the wooden parquet floor. On four hard plastic chairs she had pushed together at the start of the session, one of us sleeps.

(Fieldnotes, 2016)

This scene is from a workshop I organised with Tara Page and Helen Palmer, as part of a large international academic conference. The call for the conference explicitly encouraged proposals for creative sessions such as this one, although the majority of sessions were, understandably, the more typical verbal presentations. The conference had an overwhelming number of proposals, sessions were scheduled between 8am and 8pm, and evenings were often spent catching up with new and old international friends and colleagues. Although we, the conference organisers, and participants saw this practical making as a continuation of, rather than an opposition to, the more cerebral sessions, we had set up a different kind of space, and one of the participants used it as a chance to rest. We began the workshop by asking participants to write down a few words about their journey to the conference room. We stood in a circle and, as described above, threw the words into the air. Once they'd settled, we each selected from the spread of our collective words a handful of words that meant something to us, and arranged them into a short poem. We then invited participants to go for a walk around the local area, and to collect found materials to bring back and collage with their words. The final part of the session was spent reflecting on what we had made, as well as on what we thought of the workshop and its relationship to the wider conference and conference topic.

Part of what had made the session different from other parts of the conference was its playfulness, at least in the context of an academic conference: the chance to go for a walk around a city that many conference attendees had not visited before; to notice and collect 'the scraps' of everyday life on the streets surrounding the university; to think about the often overlooked aspects of attending an academic conference, including its impacts on our bodies; to work collectively with other people's words and reflections; to collage different media (words, flyers, leaves, receipts, bodies, the wooden floor) and transform their meanings and affects. This made me question how far and how often social research methods are enjoyable for our participants, and what might happen if we augment our usual suite of social research methods with techniques often employed in museums and galleries where visitors are encouraged to make and display things, and in social and market research, where methods can be quite agile and participatory (Taylor *et al.*, 2014).

Part of the playfulness came from letting go of what a finished product of the workshop might be and instead focusing on the process itself. I've found that it is often difficult for participants to articulate verbally on what their collage 'is of', and so shifting to focus on the process of making has enabled us to explore its opportunities and limitations as a method and a practice. This has sometimes involved a contemplation of what materials we had collected, why and how, what the materials afford (could we fold, rip, stack, slide, crumple them?) and what kinds of interesting relations we could establish between them. On occasion, these contemplations are individual and personal; on others, they have been collective, grappling with and sharing thoughts and questions about ways of making. Discussing how she deployed collaging with migrant, refugee and asylum-seeking women, Elena Vacchelli (2018) notes how the method directed her attention to what her own and the participants' bodies were doing – laughing, asking questions, speaking quietly, sharing materials, moving closer to each other – which brings critical attention to the processes and practices through which research data are made. All of these occasions can be understood in terms of what Brian Massumi and Erin Manning call 'thought in the act' (2013), or – to twist Kat Jungnickel's (2018) enticing term – a making sense of things through the making of things.

Reflecting

Working with collaging as a social research method is not a standard or standardised practice; as these scenes show, there is not one way of organising a collaging session, nor is there one particular topic that collaging lends itself towards exploring. This capaciousness of collaging is both an opportunity and a challenge. Collaging provides playful and accessible ways for our participants and us to explore and express our understandings and experiences of specific questions and issues through a range of materials that might be both unusual to social research and familiar, if sometimes overlooked, in our everyday lives. It enables an expansive and inclusive approach to the materials that might be used and become important in social research. Its idiosyncrasy requires us to pause in our assumptions about what might count as social research data and what a finished output might be, and to place our attention on what happens during the process of making, including critical questions as to what the archive of materials includes and doesn't. It also requires us to consider what we do with the collages that are made, leaning us towards a series of other questions concerning what happens with the data that are generated through our methods.

In a (different) classroom at Goldsmiths, a group of people collage with glitter. Prior to the workshop, some of the participants had contacted my co-organiser Jayne Osgood and I, asking about the environmental damage that the glitter would create. During the workshop, we discussed this issue, including our use of standard glitter, sustainable glitter and recycled glitter. We also debated various things that we might do with the collages after the workshop had ended, including organising an impromptu or more carefully planned exhibition, participants taking their collages home with them to display, and the collages being thrown away. In the end, most of the collages went in the bin.

(Fieldnotes, 2018)

References

Bennett, J. (2010) *Vibrant Matter: A Political Ecology of Things*. Durham, NC, New York: Duke University Press.

Butler-Kisber, L. (2018) *Qualitative Inquiry: Thematic, Narrative and Arts-Based Perspectives*. London: Sage.

Campt, T. (2017) *Listening to Images*. Durham, NC, New York: Duke University Press.

Coleman, R. (2020) *Glitterworlds: The Future Politics of a Ubiquitous Thing*. London: Goldsmiths Press.

Jungnickel, K. (2018) 'Making things to make sense of things', in Sayers, J. (ed.) *The Routledge Companion to Media Studies and Digital Humanities*. London: Routledge, pp. 492–502.

Massumi, B. and Manning, E. (2013) *Thought in the Act: Passages in the Ecology of Experience*. Minneapolis: University of Minnesota Press.

Raaberg, G. (1998) 'Beyond fragmentation: Collage as feminist strategy in the arts', *Mosaic: A Journal for the Interdisciplinary Study of Literature*, 31(3), pp. 153–171.

Safron, C. (2019) 'Reimagining health and fitness materials: An affective inquiry into collaging', *Reconceptualizing Educational Research Methodology*, 10(2–3), pp. 40–60.

Tamboukou, M. (2019) 'New materialisms in the archive: In the mode of an œuvre à faire', *MAI: Feminism and Visual Culture*, 16 May. https://maifeminism.com/new-materialisms-in-the-archive-in-the-mode-of-an-oeuvre-a-faire/

Taylor, A.S., Lindley, S., Regan, T. and Sweeney, D. (2014) 'Data and life on the street', *Big Data and Society*, 1(2), pp. 1–7.

Taylor, B. (2014 [2004]) *Collage: The Making of Modern Art*. London: Thames & Hudson.

Vacchelli, E. (2018) 'Embodiment in qualitative research: Collage making with migrant, refugee and asylum seeking women', *Qualitative Research*, 18(2), pp. 171–190.

7

How to do social research with... comics

Monica Sassatelli

Social research themes come from many sources with diverse purposes, but they all need to find a form, usually the verbal form of research questions expressed in the language and concepts of a given discipline and approach. Expanding the range of possible ways to formulate questions as well as answers expands our horizon beyond unexamined, implicit assumptions. At this fundamental level, drawing can be integrated into social research as an ongoing practice of *thinking through drawing*. The first example is the illustrated fieldwork diary, although the approach can equally be applied to theoretical research (Sousanis, 2015). As for writing – where digital advances provide many alternatives, but the basic activity can still be done with just pen and paper – similarly for drawing, what is needed is just paper and, rather than pen, pencil and eraser (a good reminder of how research is trial and error and seldom linear).[1] The simplicity of it is what makes it difficult: all the labour falls on you and your perseverance. All you need is a composition notebook, with plain, or ruled or graph-ruled sheets as you prefer – I like the versatility of graph ruled that allows me to write both words and numbers and disappears into a kind of supporting grid where I can create frames easily when drawing; it is freer than a ruled sheet and less messy than a plain one. It is good to have both pen and pencil, colours even if you like, but the most important thing is to *always* be ready to make the note or the sketch as the idea or

---

[1] The 'ratio' between the hand-made and the digital medium is contentious and shifting in a rapidly developing scenario. Software to create and manipulate images can be used from the beginning or variously combined with hand-drawing; for instance, by scanning hand-drawn images for editing. The two drawings in this chapter have simply been hand drawn and then scanned.

the observation comes to you. As a habit of regular journaling, precisely in the tradition of ethnographic notebooks, but also to rekindle us with this primary form of expression, drawing.

Michael Taussig (2011) reflecting on the role of drawings in his journals, remarks that drawing is an opening between the inner and outer world, a seeing that materialises in the act of drawing. Drawing, Taussig continues, enlisting John Berger as a source, is a *making* and encompasses time:

[D]rawing is an activity much older than writing or architecture. It is as old as song, that inflection of language. Indeed 'drawing is as fundamental to the energy that makes us human as singing and dancing.' Drawing ... has something that painting, sculpture, videos, and installations lack – corporeality.

(Taussig, 2011, pp. 22–23; citing Berger, 2007, p. 106).

The act of drawing is what counts, more than drawings. Drawing is indeed a way of seeing and even a way of *sensing*: in the struggle to depict what we see, remember or feel, no matter how successful the actual resulting depiction, we see and experience in a new way.

What I have in mind here are ways to insert drawing and comics organically in social analysis, ways in which a research project can be informed from the beginning by the specific affordances of drawing and comics as *narrative drawings*, an operational definition both more inclusive and theoretically precise (Grennan, 2017). That is, how the specificity of narrative drawing – sequential drawings in combination with words, including a narrative dimension and a spatial unfolding highlighting a relational dimension – can inform a whole project. In particular, how its display of the tension between verbal and visual narration, between object-based and relation- or practice-based logic can be used not only in gathering research material and developing rapport with research participants, or in engaging the audience, but also from the very beginning when formulating a problem or question, as well as in analysis and giving shape to interpretation.

Once drawing stops being an unusual practice within research, it will start making its way out of preparatory notebooks into actual research projects, in the more canonical phases of collection, analysis and dissemination. Here one of the advantages of narrative drawing becomes prominent: its contribution to collaborative practice-based research. You can ask participants to draw, trace, make comics and you can collaborate with them, engaging in conversation: 'as a "draw and talk" methodology, drawing [is a process] that constructs a specific dynamic between researcher, participant and the subject/object of enquiry that has the potential to produce *different kinds of insights and understandings*' (Reason, 2018, pp. 48–49, emphasis added).

So far, comics have mostly been added towards the end of a project to promote communication and dissemination of research results – precisely for the attractive quality of being considered a popular, easy medium. In this scenario, there is often the involvement of a comic artist who is not the researcher. Alternatively, simple comics may be elicited from research participants, often children, as part of interviews and included as data to be interpreted by the researcher. These are, however, only two of the possible uses and arguably ones that, in leaving almost untouched the main development of a research trajectory, miss many of the potentialities of the combination of words and drawings more generally.

As a conscious attempt to develop that greater integration, comics-based research (CBR) (Kuttner *et al.*, 2017) is on the rise. Topics vary considerably; however, medical comics, auto-ethnographic and ethnographic comics are the most developed so far, with new book series, conferences and networks. This is a rather lively and diverse emerging sub-field; it can be an articulated methodology that may require the involvement of artists, but it can also be applied in more low-key ways in small projects with a single researcher. Comics can be involved in research in a number of ways, ranging from participants being asked to draw and comment; to researcher-made comics as part of data gathering and analysis; to professionally drawn comics to disseminate research results. Even if there are clearly cases in which comics are added at the end of a project as a means of dissemination, as well as a long tradition of research *on* comics, CBR's innovative strength lies in comics being used to do research work (a useful review and selection of some of the most interesting current experiments and established programmes can be found in the overview by Barberis and Grüning, 2021).

Using comics or narrative drawing does not mean you have to produce a graphic *novel*. The logic of the sequential combination of words and images need not be narrative in its basic sense; it can also be descriptive, interpretative, analytical and so on. It can be a way to expose contradictions and paradoxes, often precisely those of different forms of representation (Sassatelli, 2021; for an example of a non-narrative structure based on thematic analysis, see Figure 7.1B discussed below). You can draw comics to visually chronicle the social world or phenomenon (or theory) you are studying, and in so doing discover connections and points of view, revealed by the visual proximity of things that may stay verbally distant. A model of how the typical conventions of comics based on a narrative framework are used within qualitative research, in particular, is shown in Figure 7.1A. Here I have re-drawn, with permission by the author, Rachel Marie-Crane Williams's (2012) comic diagram, as reproduced in Kuttner *et al.* (2017). Instead of 'copy and paste' as one does for a normal citation, I opted to copy it as I would if I was, say, studying an old manuscript with text and pictures, found in an archive. This procedure applies the idea of drawing as research: staying with the diagram as I considered how to re-draw it (and after a few drafts) I inevitably appropriated it, adapted it, adding or changing details – although I tried not to omit any. I did not trace,

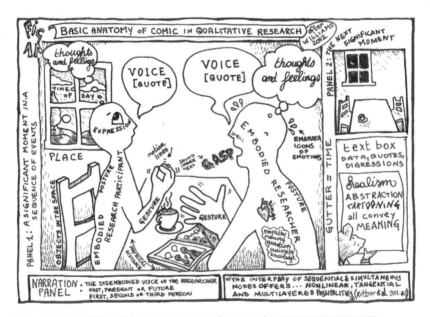

Figure 7.1A Williams's 'Basic Anatomy of a Comic' in qualitative research, redrawn.

nor did I try to copy closely, so the drawing is significantly different, and one can see a different 'hand'; it is a kind of visual paraphrasis. This raises issues regarding authorship, attribution, citation, all shifting in interesting ways from verbal to visual. The conceptual architecture of a research comic can be narrative but it can also be otherwise.

A pivotal feature in CBR is the issue of *visualisation* of concepts and arguments – or if you like, the issue of *translation* from a verbal to a visual language in ways that can both enrich analysis and help other types of translation, introducing different logics to make research more multimodal. In a way both expressions still reveal the predominance of the verbal – considered the default 'native' language of research and the one that may need translation either for dissemination purposes or in general to simplify or summarise complex matters. However, an idea also gaining ground is to confer independent dignity on the visual or graphic language itself. Looking for a term for this, we could adopt, following Clifford Marcus (2017) in his preface to *Lissa*, the graphic novel launching the series *EthnoGraphic*, the term *transduction*. The transduction of ethnography refers to a transition not just between languages, but of form, and not just as an addendum or illustration, but 'instructing anthropologists and academics more broadly in remaking their work into new forms' (Marcus, 2017, p. 11). On this subject, it is also important to acknowledge that in the broader field of comics (graphic novels, essay comics, documentary comics, etc.) this approach counts many insightful examples, well before its 'discovery' by sociology and other social sciences. Comics have long been, along with at least drama and novels, a medium for 'telling about society' (Becker, 2007). Even very simple line drawings can achieve that and it may be easier to ask for these from research participants. However, if your research topic or approach recommends a certain pictorial realism, one way to achieve this is combining photographs and drawings, especially through photo tracing – which I am going to briefly describe here through an example.

I recently explored the potentialities of line drawing by tracing over photographs, as I had seen it in Maureen K. Michael's (2020) research on education and artists' practice. The idea is to take or elicit photographs (and this can be done in various ways depending on the project's focus) and then, as part of the analytical phase, trace them to peel back layers and boundaries to get to the core of what – so one discovers – matters, focusing on objects/subjects but also on their relationships and on narratives. Michael argues that researcher-created drawings carry analytical content that is particularly useful to understanding relational dimensions otherwise obscured by categorising verbal analysis. The practicalities of the method involve the researcher taking photographs during fieldwork observation, then line tracing selected images (using translucent paper or other devices, including dedicated software on digital photos). The tracing can be done several times, each one focusing on different aspects of the selection, thus with interpretation involved in the act. This process can also be done collaboratively with research participants. I experimented with this method with the graduate students of a module on 'Art, Fashion and Society', where we wanted to explore how identity is expressed and performed via the material and social world that surrounds us, starting from what's closest – clothes and other objects that surround our body. Taking inspiration also from Doug Harper's activity 'portrait without self' (2012, pp. 225–229) as a way to render the personal into the sociological, students selected photos of themselves that they thought defined them; then they traced them concentrating on the clothes and details they felt were important, thinking, and in so doing often discovering, what they wanted to communicate. They could intervene as they wanted, selecting, pasting other images, using old photos or creating new ones, as long as they reflected as they went along and organised those reflections, putting the images in a sequence meaningful for them. I have then also collaged and re-traced some of them as part of my own reflections, and then shared them as inspiration for our class discussion – an example is reproduced below in Figure 7.1B. This image is my re-tracing and assembling of students' work, in which they had traced and put in a sequence, not necessarily temporal, a selection of images of themselves. As it emerged, both for me as I assembled their work, and for each of the students, it was a matter of finding a thread connecting layer after layer (selecting, tracing, assembling, re-tracing, possibly re-selecting and finding a logic that would work for themselves and for an audience), mainly through the slow and iterative process of tracing itself: 'Is this detail really worth the time it takes to draw it? Why?'. Recurrent themes, relevant distinctions and in general meaningful analysis emerged with the tracing and the juxtaposition and

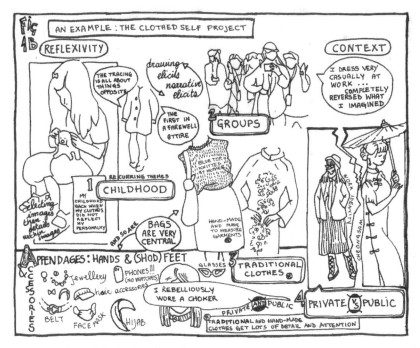

Figure 7.1B The 'Clothed Self' student project.

sequence of images, often a surprise for the drawer herself: the loving detail reserved for a top made by the mother of a student, or for clothes explicitly defined as 'traditional' and given a proper name; the omnipresence of smart phones among few accessories (and the disappearance of watches), the intentional use of an out-of-place accessory to make a statement of rebellion, again carefully drawn; perhaps above all the tension of private and public personae as expressed through clothing.

Tracing photographs or using digital filters and programs to turn photographs into comic art is a layered process that can involve participation at various levels. Drawing in the field attracts attention. Many practitioners have observed that a sketchbook and pencil create a more welcoming space for interaction, certainly more than a notepad, recorder or computer, and are therefore precious ways to build rapport, becoming a source of spontaneous conversation with informants. Graphic fieldwork can therefore help 'forge new knowledge and interact with informants in the field, creating possibilities for intimate and public-engaged inquiry' (Bayre *et al.*, 2016, p. 7). This is not meant instrumentally, to get quickly what would have taken longer; drawing is not a better 'extractive' model, as indeed it can be very time-consuming. It is instead, as mentioned before, a gateway to what we cannot get otherwise. Building on the specificity of drawing and the bridge that narrative drawing provides with more familiar forms of knowledge and narrativisation creates a space, in participatory or collaborative ways, for the production and translation of insights of researchers and participants, words and images. In fact, because of this exchange and porosity of authorship, comicization often creates the problem of how to portray the researcher: or, rather, it offers new ways to come to terms reflexively with the role of researcher and author by their personification in the drawings. The 'talking head' model – where the researcher becomes the omniscient and omnipresent narrator, often in the actual form of a talking head filling panel after panel – is the usual, but problematic solution of many essay comics. Yet, having a new canvas for raising the issue, particularly for reflexive social science, is more than a marginal advantage (Bonanno, 2018; Theodossopoulos, 2020).

With drawing – much as with research – it is never straightforward to say when one is really finished. Drawings bring to research an interpretative open-endedness which is precious in more exploratory projects, as a way to open the door to different forms of understanding. Given all the above, drawing may be better at generating new questions and nuancing analyses than at answering set questions or 'solving problems' of more mainstream research projects. Narrative drawing is useful to stimulate conversation with research participants as well as an inner dialogue of the researcher. It can 'mix raw material of observation with reverie' to activate the 'imaginative logic of discovery' (Taussig, 2011, p. xi). But once it is accepted beyond the initial phases and the private notebooks of researchers, readers and participants are trusted with that imaginative function too.

Taken as a primary and primal medium, drawing is as flexible as language and there are good arguments to make use of it, in a vast variety of ways and projects, especially in an era, like ours, which is predominantly visual but still lacking in visual literacy. If Geertz (1973, p. 19) was right in claiming that we are in no danger of running out of reality, but we always run the risk of running out of meaningful signs to navigate it – and our hyper-trophic culture does increasingly appear as an unwieldy second nature rather than a manageable tool of interpretation – the fact that we have drawing at our disposal as a whole realm of meaningful sign making is a strong argument to more fully draw comics into research.

References

Barberis, E. and Grüning, B. (2021) 'Doing social sciences via comics and graphic novels: An introduction', *Sociologica*, 15(1), pp. 125–142.

Bayre, F., Harper, K. and Afonso, A.I. (2016) 'Participatory approaches to visual ethnography from the digital to the handmade: An introduction', *Visual Ethnography*, 5(1), pp. 7–13.

Becker, H.S. (2007) *Telling about Society*. Chicago, IL: University of Chicago Press.

Berger, J. (2007) *On Drawing*. Cork: Occasional Press.

Bonanno, L. (2018) 'Drawing as a mode of translation', *American Anthropologist*. Available at: www.americananthropologist.org/ethno-graphic-bonanno/

Geertz, C. (1973) *The Interpretation of Cultures*. New York: Basic Books.

Grennan, S. (2017) *A Theory of Narrative Drawing*. New York: Palgrave.

Harper, D. (2012) *Visual Sociology*. London: Routledge.

Kuttner, P.J., Sousanis, N. and Weaver-Hightower, M.B. (2017) 'How to draw comics the scholarly way', in Leavy, P. (ed.) *Handbook of Arts-Based Research*. New York: Guilford Press, pp. 396–422.

Marcus, C. (2017) '*Lissa* and the transduction of ethnography', in *Lissa*, written by Hamdy, S. and Nye, C.; illustrated by Bao, S. and Brewer, C., lettering by Parenteau, M. Toronto, ON: University of Toronto Press.

Michael, M.K. (2020) 'Drawing relationally for an ethnography of practice', *Ethnography and Education*, 15(3), pp. 270–285.

Reason, M. (2018) 'Drawing', in Lury, C. *et al.* (eds) *Routledge Handbook of Interdisciplinary Research Methods*. London: Routledge, pp. 47–52.

Sassatelli, M. (2021) 'Show and tell', *Sociologica*, 15(1), pp. 311–319.

Sousanis, N. (2015) *Unflattening*. Cambridge, MA: Harvard University Press.

Taussig, M. (2011) *I Swear I Saw This: Drawings in Fieldwork Notebooks, Namely My Own*. Chicago, IL: University of Chicago Press.

Theodossopoulos, D. (2020) 'Solidarity dilemmas in times of austerity: Auto-ethnographic interventions', *Cultural Anthropology*, 35(1), pp. 134–166.

Williams, R.M-C. (2012) 'Can you picture this? Activism, art, and public scholarship', *Visual Arts Research*, 38(2), pp. 87–98.

8

How to do social research with... documents

Aoife Campbell-Franks and Margarita Aragon

Think of how often in your daily life you send or receive messages and emails; fill out forms; read blog posts, scroll through social media. As we move through the physical landscape, we encounter advertisements on the sides of buses, flyers on noticeboards, stickers on lampposts and so on. Documents permeate the fabric of our social world and thus form an important field of sociological inquiry. As Lindsay Prior has emphasised, documents are not just 'containers of content' but 'active agents in episodes of interaction and schemes of social organisation' (Prior 2008, p. 824). By this he means that documents make things happen in the social world. People generate them, read them, distribute them, deface and destroy them and so on.

A vast amount of our social interactions, whether with people close to us or with institutions, are mediated through documents. In particular, they are an important conduit through which state power is transmitted. Many people (and some more than others) may have face-to-face interactions with agents of the state – police officers, social workers, benefits assessors and so on – but our relations with state institutions are always heavily mediated through documents. As such, documents are a vital resource for social researchers. In this chapter, we think about documents not as inert objects but as an essential material through which processes – processes that have profound and violent implications – are given form and force in the social world. Specifically, we discuss Aoife Campbell-Franks' exploration of the Department of Work and Pensions (DWP) documents through which the UK Government's devastating cuts to disability benefit were set in motion.

Working with the Austerity Paper Trail

In my (Campbell-Franks') project, I was interested in *working with* DWP policy documents as a way of *working out* the ways in which disabled people have been constructed and managed by the state. My interest in this largely comes from my personal experience of my mother being physically impaired and seeing first-hand the ableism she has experienced, particularly in relation to work. Whilst I was undertaking my master's degree my mother was off work due to her disability. We were acutely aware of the Conservative government's austerity-inspired vandalism of the benefits system. As my mother navigated the re-configured sickness absence system, we felt how such changes made the lives of disabled people more precarious. Because of these experiences, I wanted to investigate the ableist impact of austerity more closely.

One morning as I was having a conversation with my mother about her current time off work and the documents she was filling out, we came across her 'fit note'. As I will explain further below, the government had replaced the traditional 'sick note' with a 'fit note'. Whereas a sick note was a document with which a doctor verified the patient's illness or disability in order to legitimate their absence from work, the new fit note asks them to provide their medical opinion on a person's 'fitness' for work. I became fascinated with the discursive shift from 'sick' to 'fit'. As the state manages disabled people in part through a flurry of paper, I chose to work with documents produced by the DWP for my dissertation project.

To begin with, I looked on the DWP website and found two policy reports: the 2008 *Working for a Healthier Tomorrow: Work and Health in Britain* (Black, 2008) and the 2011 *Health at Work – An Independent Review of Sickness Absence in Great Britain* (Black and Frost, 2011). Both documents set out the problems of the 'sickness absence system' and put forward revisions for its improvement. *Working for a Healthier Tomorrow* was published before the introduction of austerity. However, this was a significant moment in that it featured discourses of work and worklessness that would soon be mobilised by the government. *Health at Work* was co-written by the same author as *Working for a Healthier Tomorrow*, Dame Caroline Black, and can be said to function as its sequel in a time of austerity. Consequently, I found that working with both documents was equally important in understanding the discourses that the austerity regime has used to re-imagine and institutionally manage the disabled subject.

When I came across my mother's fit note, I went onto the UK Parliament website and searched 'fit note'. I found the transcripts of multiple debates in which Labour MPs challenged the government about a document called the ESA65B letter. This is a letter the DWP issued to general practitioners

(GPs) regarding the Employment and Support Allowance (ESA), a benefit that supports disabled and sick people not in work. Examining this letter gave me insight into how the DWP directly instructs other actors and reaches into the lives of disabled people. It shows us the specific tactics the state uses to implement punitive austerity reforms. To make sense of the letter, I held a physical copy of it in my hands and read it aloud. I tried to imagine the emotional weight of the letter and the impact of receiving it. I also cut out each paragraph of the letter and examined these isolated sections. This helped me to think about the importance of form and to examine why certain phrases had been situated in certain places.

As I examined the DWP documents, I was not looking for 'facts' about disability or work. I wanted to know how the people who created the documents have constructed particular versions of 'fitness', work and citizenship for particular purposes, as well as how these constructions are enforced and policed in practice. I examined the intended appeal of the documents and the 'objective evidence' they claimed to present, as well as what they obscured or left unsaid. I created a table of keywords and began highlighting them in the documents; from this process, common themes and imagery emerged. To understand how these documents create meaning about disability and create material impacts on people's lives, I tried to think about how they circulated within the social world, what they were responding to and what responses they might inspire. Examining the political debates on the Hansard website about the problems of the revised sickness absence system, and the ESA65B letter in particular, helped me to understand what the documents were working to actively obscure. I also sought to make connections between the DWP documents and the broader cultural discourses they draw from and feed back into – namely, the popular media stories in which those who fail to uphold the values of independence and self-sufficiency are demonised as 'scroungers' and 'benefit cheats' (Briant *et al.*, 2013).

Enforcing 'A Healthier Tomorrow'

As Amanda Coffey observes, 'Documents are usually part of wider systems of distribution and exchange' and make meaning in relation to other documents (Coffey, 2013, p. 377). The documents of the DWP, its reports, press releases, letters issued to GPs, benefit recipients and so on, work together as part of a larger institutional project. These documents serve different purposes and are created for different audiences, but they are all informed by a common logic.

Disability scholars (among others) have argued that austerity is made possible through neoliberal values that frame 'welfare reform' as a moral good, whereby the removal of welfare support is beneficial to those who are 'dependent' on it (Runswick-Cole and Goodley, 2015). The political discourses surrounding welfare reform policies put forward an image of the ideal citizen whose value is demonstrated by their capability to provide for themselves. In this context, disability benefit is treated as a crisis that can only be resolved through work (Brown, 2003; Gedalof, 2018). Though ostensibly 'positive' about disability, these narratives work to deny disabled people's needs and vulnerabilities. The message they convey is that disabled people should 'transcend their embodied impairments' by embracing the labour market (Gedalof, 2018, p. 106).

In contrast to the degrading tone taken in much of the media around disability benefit, the DWP documents I worked with were imbued with a tone of fairness and supportive concern that presented the revisions to benefit policy as 'helping' disabled people into work. This gives the DWP an air of positivity, while still reinforcing the logic that economic self-sufficiency is the moral foundation of citizenship. Work is described as inherently good for people's health, though ableist barriers in the workplace are not considered, nor the type of jobs available to disabled people. The documents present a narrative in which the removal of benefits is essentially a means of increasing health, an argument signalled in the title of its 2008 report on revising systems of sickness absence: *Working for a Healthier Tomorrow*. As part of its vision for a 'healthier' future, the report lamented that 7% of the population was workless and receiving incapacity benefit, reflecting 'patterns of poverty and social exclusion which blight entire communities' (Black, 2008, p. 21). Work is presented as a panacea to personal and social ills.

[In a recent study] the beneficial effects of work were shown to outweigh the risks and to be much greater than the harmful effects of long term worklessness or prolonged sickness absence. The fallacy persists, nevertheless, that illness is incompatible with being at work and that an individual should be at work only if 100% fit.

(Black, 2008, p. 21)

As it is a means of improving 'mental and physical health', disabled people should work not only for the good of the rest of society, but for their own well-being. The cutting of benefits is justified as championing disabled people by focusing on 'what people can do rather than what they cannot' (Black, 2008, p. 86).

Documents in Action: The ESA65B Letter

Such insights gave me essential context for working with the ESA65B letter, the letter sent to GPs about how to interact with patients seeking to claim Employment and Support Allowance (ESA). GPs were identified by the government as being central to implementing the 'fit for work' agenda. Before austerity measures, GPs would issue their disabled patients with documents referred to as 'sick notes' to authorise their absence from work. In 2010, however, the government replaced the 'sick note' with the so-called 'fit note', to encourage GPs to focus on identifying 'fitness' rather than on impairments; i.e., being 'unfit'. Fundamentally, the government wanted to discourage doctors from legitimating the subject position of 'unfit', since this designation entitles people to ESA. As discussed above, the DWP presented its policy as one of empowering disabled people to lead healthier lives. The 'fit note', it claimed, would 'provide a means for doctors to sharpen their focus on the relationship between health and work, which is particularly important given the strong evidence about the importance of work for health' (Black and Frost, 2011, p. 20).

As it was produced and circulated to instruct GPs how to implement this new regime, the ESA65B letter was a conduit through which DWP constructions of 'health' were materially imposed upon disabled people's lives. As discussed above, the DWP had already laid out their position in various policy reports that work is inherently good for health. We can see how the letter moves to operationalise this policy on the ground, as GPs are 'invited' to help their workless patients by also 'encouraging' them into work. The DWP has rejected the disabled subject's 'unfit' status, and so they are forced into an able-bodied position as, in the eyes of the state, they must be 'capable of doing some work' (DWP, 2017; see Figure 8.1).

The letter serves as a direct intervention from the state to ensure that GPs are relaying the message that work is good for health. This narrative of 'support' gives the impression that the letter is an invitation to the GP to help encourage their patients' 'healthy' efforts to pursue work, but a closer inspection reveals its true function: to instruct doctors to stop medically legitimising their disabled patients' absence from work and to enforce workability. This becomes more apparent in the next passage:

What this means for you

As a result of this decision, [Title] [Surname] is not entitled to ESA from   and **you do not need to provide any more fit notes to [select] relating to [select] disability/health condition for ESA purposes.**

Guidance for GPs on completing fit notes is available at: **www.gov.uk/government/publications/fit-note-guidance-for-gps**

Thanks for your help.

Yours sincerely,

Office manager

Figure 8.1 End paragraph of ESA65B letter.

When examining the letter, I paid particular attention to this passage as it misleads GPs about the workings of the policy.

The Work Capability Assessment (WCA), the test used by the DWP to determine whether a disabled person is 'fit for work,' has directly contradicted the diagnoses of medical professionals and therefore lacks any medical credibility (Gentleman, 2011). As a result, many individuals deemed 'fit for work' will appeal this decision. But whilst they wait for an appeal hearing (which can take up to 8–10 months) they will still need to receive fit notes from their doctor confirming their condition in order to obtain ESA (Bloom, 2019a). As you can see above, the DWP's letter to GPs makes this entirely unclear. The letter doesn't give any indication to the GP of the precarity that withholding the 'fit note' will inflict on patients deemed 'fit to work' by the DWP, but who are unable to do so. Indeed, the positive tone of the letter ('most people are better off in work') directly obscures the impact of removing vulnerable people's means of survival.

In 2017 an estimated 150,000 ESA65B letters were sent to GPs regarding their disabled patients. This had devasting consequences (Bloom, 2019b). Charities investigating the impact of this misinformation have found that it has left many disabled people without any income to support themselves (www.z2k.org, n.d.). Consequently, many have been forced into using foodbanks, increasing the risk of homelessness due to amplified poverty (www.z2k.org, n.d.).

Points of Reflection

Investigating even this small branch of the sprawling austerity paper trail illuminated the structural violence of austerity. I gained insight into how carefully the DWP cultivates long-standing classist and ableist notions of work, independence and self-sufficiency as the basis of good citizenship, and indeed personhood, through an insidious discourse of empowerment. As Prior notes, how a document circulates in the world might be different from what the author originally intended (Prior, 2008, p. 824). For example, I can't know from examining the ESA65B letter how individual GPs may have felt about or responded to the letter's 'invitation'. Nevertheless, it helped me to understand how the state encourages employers and medical professionals to have distorted views about sickness. The documents also shifted my understanding of my own lived experience. As I tried to pick apart the manipulative tactics that the DWP uses to force disabled people into work, I became aware of the extent to which I had also taken on the ableist common sense that work is inherently 'good' and being 'hardworking' and 'productive' should be a goal for everyone.

I realised that for most of my life I had not known the full extent of my mother's disability because she had 'pushed through the pain' and worked. Ironically, because she worked, I saw her as 'less' disabled when, in fact, working was making her increasingly sick, to the point where she had to apply for medical retirement at the age of 54. Contrary to the DWP's claims about the healthful benefits of work, as soon as she stopped working, she became more able-bodied; she is in less pain, takes less medication and can do more physically. Working with DWP documents, then, has helped me to understand how neoliberalism constructs norms of ability and work that deny disability and enforce able-bodiedness.

References

Black, C. (2008) *Working for a Healthier Tomorrow*. Available at: https://assets.publishing. service.gov.uk/government/uploads/system/uploads/attachment_data/file/209782/hwwb-working-for-a-healthier-tomorrow.pdf

Black, C. and Frost, D. (2011) *Health at Work – An Independent Review of Sickness Absence*. Available at: https://assets.publishing.service.gov.uk/government/uploads/system/uploads/attachment_data/file/181060/health-at-work.pdf

Bloom, D. (2019a) 'Disabled benefit appeals that defeat the DWP cost £26m to run in a single year', *The Mirror*, 12 June. Available at: www.mirror.co.uk/news/politics/disabled-benefit-appeals-defeat-dwp-16501426

Bloom, D. (2019b) 'DWP has sent 150,000 of the "fit for work" letters that "risk patients' health"', *The Mirror*, 30 April. Available at: www.mirror.co.uk/news/politics/dwp-sent-150000-fit-work-14968771

Briant, E., Watson, N. and Philo, G. (2013) 'Reporting disability in the age of austerity: The changing face of media representation of disability and disabled people in the United Kingdom and the creation of new "folk devils"', *Disability and Society*, 28(6), pp. 874–889.

Brown, W. (2003) 'Neo-liberalism and the end of liberal democracy', *Theory and Event*, 7(1), n.p.

Coffey, A. (2013) 'Analysing documents', in Flick, U. (ed.) *The SAGE Handbook of Qualitative Data Analysis*. London: SAGE Publications Ltd., pp. 367–379.

DWP (2017) ESA65B letter. Available at: https://data.parliament.uk/DepositedPapers/Files/DEP2018-0290/ESA65B_Letter.pdf

Gedalof, I. (2018) *Narratives of Difference in an Age of Austerity*. London: Palgrave Macmillan UK.

Gentleman, A. (2011) 'The medical was an absolute joke', *The Guardian*, 23 February. Available at: www.theguardian.com/politics/2011/feb/23/government-reform-disability-benefits

Prior, L. (2008) 'Repositioning documents in social research', *Sociology*, 42(5), pp. 821–836.

Prior, L. (2011) *Using Documents in Social Research*. London: SAGE Publications Ltd.

Runswick-Cole, K. and Goodley, D. (2015) 'Disability, austerity and cruel optimism in Big Society: Resistance and "The Disability Commons"', *Canadian Journal of Disability Studies*, 4(2), p. 162.

www.z2k.org (n.d.) #scraptheletterscampaign. Available at: https://z2k.org/scrap-the-letters/

9

How to do social research with... a dog

Mariam Motamedi-Fraser

I am giving a lecture on domestication, in a module I teach called 'Thinking Animals'. After I have been speaking for about 50 to 60 minutes, Monk, the black Labrador with whom I live, and who is at this moment lying to the left of the technology station where I am standing, will stretch out his four legs stiffly, turn his head to look briefly at me from the stretch position, before getting up and walking calmly to a spot directly in front of me. There he will sit, staring at me, shifting a little on each front leg. What Monk does in that moment affects us all. His actions, in that context, bring the lecture to a close.

Over the last two or three decades, a radical transformation has been unfolding in the animal sciences, and especially in cognitive science and ethology. Animal intentionality, agency and emotions are the focus of new approaches and new methods, which are generating striking and unantici-pated results. Topics once considered the property of the social sciences and humanities – interpretation, meaning, aesthetics, sociality, creativity, memory, psychic trauma, morality, humour – are now central to under-standing animals. Partly as a consequence, artists, philosophers and social science and humanities scholars across a range of disciplines and inter-disciplinary domains are actively inviting animals into human research projects not only as subjects of research, but also as research partners and knowledge producers (Bastion, 2017, p. 20). This flourishing body of work powerfully illustrates that humans and animals do not simply jostle along-side each other, but rather affect each other's individual and social worlds in substantive ways. While animal lives are shaped by political, economic and cultural forces – essential research topics in themselves – animals also contribute to social life as social and political subjects. Not only are the lives of animals meaningful to themselves, animals are also meaning mak-ers for others.

The concentration of the major part of Western scientific behavioural research on dogs is conducted with or on what are usually called 'family dogs' (or potential family dogs; e.g., dogs in shelters). This is problematic with regard to understanding 'what is a dog' (the title of Coppinger and Coppinger's [2016] critical analysis of this issue), because family dogs represent only a small proportion of the total number of dogs worldwide. Although there is some research on dogs who partner homeless people, and on free-ranging and feral dogs, 'cultures where dogs function mainly as food or pelt', for example, are underrepresented (Kubinyi *et al.*, 2011, p. 260). Family dogs are, by definition, part of families, and this too has implications for social research. As in the case of veterinary medicine, the 'complex triad' (Hobson-West and Jutel, 2020, p. 397) of the animal, their guardian and the 'expert' may raise questions of authority. Who is best positioned to interpret a dog's behaviour?

Going to work with a dog is not the same as researching with or on dogs. Some of the issues it generates, however, particularly the more contentious issues, parallel those of research and can perhaps further illuminate them. The brief discussion that follows is organised around four topics: anonymity and visibility, environment, consent and transformation. Each one is riven with contradictions and tensions.

Anonymity and Visibility

Why does it feel weird to ask whether an animal research subject should be anonymised? Perhaps it is because anonymity is the default position for most animals. Unlike humans, animals are usually conceived of as examples of a species, rather than as unique individuals who live and die once, and whose experiences between these two existential poles (whatever form those 'experiences' take) matter greatly to them. This is why animal biographies, whether they are constructed from historical or contemporary documents,[1] or traced through empirical case studies, have recently become the focus of increased research attention. Biography can serve as an analytic and methodological tool through which to make visible the individuality of animals and to take

---

[1]As historians such as Erica Fudge (2017) illustrate, the methodological issues raised by the use of textual sources are not uniquely different from any other kind of research that seeks to cross the boundaries between animals' and human perception.

seriously an individual animal's experiences. While it certainly has its pit-falls – among them the risk, for instance, of 'misrepresenting the realities of animal lives, given that animals are rarely treated as individuals but as flocks of chickens, herds of pigs or tanks of exotic pet fish' (Greenhough and Roe, 2019, p. 376) – biography nonetheless serves as an important reminder, in the context of research no less than in the meat industry, that no individual animal is substitutable with another species member (especially from the individual's perspective). This point has made its way into the animal sciences. '[W]hen I talk about *the dog*,' writes canine ethologist Alexandra Horowitz, 'I am implicitly talking about *those dogs studied to date*. The results of many well-performed experiments may eventually allow us to reasonably gener-alise about *all dogs*, period. But even then, the variations among individual dogs will be great' (Horowitz, 2012, p. 9, emphasis in the original). After all, '[i]f one man fails to solve a Rubik's cube in an hour, we do not extrapolate from that that all men will so fail' (Horowitz, 2012, p. 8).

Going to work with Monk has given him forms of individual visibility he would not otherwise have had. He has a staff card. He has a page on the department website.[2] He has a measure of local celebrity. Does Monk – sin-gular, irreplaceable, Monk – appreciate the *particular* forms of individuali-sation to which he is subject, and for which he must bear the consequences? 'Is that Monk?!' 'OMG, is that the Sociology Dog?' 'Hey Monk!' Monk is not in a position to object to any of this, or to what I am writing about him here in this chapter. I write with the fear of betraying Monk, and most certainly I do. Going to work with a dog, or conducting research with a dog/dogs, is poten-tially a way of making them visible as individuals. It is also a way of shaping their lives and, problematically, of speaking for and over them.

Environment

In order to work with Monk, policy at Goldsmiths had to be changed. Dogs are allowed on campus if they are guide or service dogs, and, now, if they aid in teaching. The college also required me to write an ethics policy for

---

[2]Regrettably, since writing this chapter, Monk's webpage has, after eight years, been taken down by Goldsmiths. All staff pages are now linked to contracts, and apparently no technical solution could be found. An alternative location was offered to Monk – among the Visiting Professors and Professors Emeritus – but I rejected this, on the grounds that it would margin-alise Monk's active contribution to departmental life, and his labour.

Monk, which I based on the Animal Welfare Act (2006). The Animal Welfare Act is limited to the most basic of needs. It is an echo of the 'five freedoms' (1979),[3] four of which are freedoms *from* (from thirst, for example, or from discomfort). How to ensure freedom from discomfort in a working and/or research environment?

At a most basic level, a dog's *Umwelt*, their perceptual and subjective experiences of their environment (von Uexküll, 2010 [1934]), differs from that of neurotypical humans. The very sensory architecture of a human environment – its lighting, sounds, smells, spatial organisation – can be an assault on a dog's senses. How aggravating is that flickering fluorescent light to a dog who sees more 'snapshots' per second than a human? How disturbing is its ongoing hum, which a dog can hear, but most humans cannot? A human nose has approximately six million sensory receptor sites; a beagle nose has over 300 million (Horowitz, 2012, p. 71). The classroom, the research space, is a working environment for dogs. Students and researchers can make a dog's job more easy or less so, by not wearing overpowering perfumes, for example, or by not eating.

Many scientific accounts of dog speciation/domestication come perilously close to suggesting that the near totality of the genetic, neurological, physiological, cognitive and affective processes that give rise to dogs' *Umwelt* have evolved in relation to/are organised around humans, and that a dog's 'natural' environment is 'the human social setting' (Kubinyi *et al.*, 2011, p. 259). In a rare example of a counter-narrative, Marc Bekoff and Jessica Pierce suggest that the 'high demand' for 'dog trainers and veterinary behaviorists' offers evidence of dogs' resistance to living – never mind working – with humans on human terms (Bekoff and Pierce, 2019, pp. 7–8). Dogs are not necessarily tolerant of human environments. Rather, dogs can 'tolerate high levels of abuse and handling' (Coppinger and Coppinger, 2016, p. 168). This makes dogs relatively easy to adopt, and relatively easy to live, work and research with. But therein lies the danger for dogs. To prefer not to be left alone at home does not mean that a dog *likes* to be in any or all other environments.

It would be polite (Despret, 2015), therefore, to ask the dog.

---

[3] The Five Freedoms paradigm was devised by John Webster in 1993 (FAWC, 1993). It is an extension of 'Brambell's Five Freedoms' which were outlined in the Brambell Report of 1965 (Brambell, 1965). The Five Freedoms model was originally intended to be a means of assessing husbandry systems with regard to animal welfare.

Consent

Although fraught with difficulties, animal consent is one of the ways in which the ethics of research with animals is currently being addressed. Claire Mancini describes two kinds of consent. First, consent which is mediated by guardians/carers of animals and/or by animal welfare scientists, who have a vested interest in the well-being of the animals, and 'the legal authority to consent on [animals'] behalf' (Mancini, 2017, p. 62) to research which is intended to be relevant to them, and to benefit their interests. Second, consent from the animals themselves, to the 'specific contingencies' (Mancini, 2017, p. 62) that arise during research. I will focus on the latter.

When I first started going to work with Monk seven years ago, I said that no student could touch Monk without *my* consent. Now that I have found a video on 'petting consent tests', which is mandatory viewing for all students who attend courses with Monk, I feel confident saying that no one can touch Monk without *his* consent. But how freely is consent ever given? Researchers on both sides of the science/social science divide recognise that dogs' so-called 'bond' with humans may mean that their ability to object is compromised. The neuroscientist Gregory Berns, for instance, suggests that dogs' orientation towards humans renders them 'particularly vulnerable to exploitation' (Berns *et al.*, 2012, p. 3). Scientists, he argues, must place 'the dogs' welfare above all else,' because '[d]ogs will do almost anything humans ask of them' (Berns *et al.*, 2012, pp. 3–4). Or as social scientists Eva Giraud and Gregory Hollin put it in their analysis of beagles who are bred to be 'amenable' experimental dogs: 'lack of substantive "objection"' does not always equate to 'lack of coercion' (Giraud and Hollin, 2017, p. 172).

One method of identifying resistance, Dinesh Wadiwel argues, is in the technologies and designs of instruments that are used to capture, control and kill animals. '[E]ven if we would prefer to imagine otherwise,' he writes, this point also extends to 'companion' animals (Wadiwel, 2018, p. 541). At work, Monk wears a harness, which signals to him that a different set of rules apply. On a harness, unlike a collar, at work, unlike at home, there will be little or no bartering, and for the most part Monk adopts quiet, even docile, attitudes. Students are surprised when they meet him outside of work. Who is this bustling, boisterous dog? The becomings of subjectivity, the opportunities to be rendered capable (or not), are in part given,

Vinciane Despret (2008) argues, by the research apparatus. The harness Monk wears is one part of his 'work apparatus'. So too are the treats in my pocket, for Monk, who is food-oriented, cannot resist a treat.[4] But where should one draw the line? Is *any* form of 'connection' a form of coercion? Dog behaviourist Suzanne Clothier writes:

One clue that the connection between you and your dog may need work is the dependence on equipment. If you need equipment to maintain control of your dog, understand that you have to control his body because you do not have his mind.

(Clothier, 2017, p. 48, emphasis in the original)

Is there an ethical difference between control of the body, and control of the mind? Intimacy in research is always an issue. The intimacy between a dog and their guardian can potentially blind both guardians and researchers to the limits on a dog's ability to refuse consent.

In a stroke of methodological genius, Jocelyn Porcher and Tiphaine Schmitt (2012) were able to illustrate that cows actively co-operate at work, that they actively invest in their work, by showing how, on occasion, they resisted their work, and made it difficult for the farmers to do their jobs. While Monk often expresses his opinion (by calling a lecture or a meeting to an end, for example, as I described at the start of this chapter), he rarely expresses an objection. On the one occasion that he did, the labour that Monk invests in 'being at work' was immediately made visible. At work, except at designated times and in designated places, Monk is *actively*: not playing, not seeking out things to eat, not nosing, not sniffing, not touching, not licking, not whining, not running, not chasing, not rolling, not mounting, not evacuating, not barking... In research, what a dog is *not* doing may be as significant as what they *are*.

Transformation

'Polite research', Despret (2015) argues, puts the burden on the researcher not to control, bore, patronise or diminish the animals with

---

[4] I say that *Monk* is food-oriented, rather than 'Monk is a Labrador, and Labradors are food-oriented', because breedism is often a projection that places burdens and expectations on individual dogs.

whom they are working, but rather to learn, with and from them, how to ask the right questions about what matters to them. This suggests that freedoms *from* are not enough, and that the ethical parameters of research with animals would be better defined by freedom *to*. Freedom to enjoy the research, to be invigorated by it, to benefit from it, to object to it. Students report that the sheer presence of Monk in the classroom transforms their understanding of that space, of the materials with which they are engaging and, sometimes, of their relationships with other animals in their lives. Is Monk transformed? In what ways? Is the university transformed?

Given the welcome but admittedly high bar set by polite research, most multi/interspecies researchers agree that research with animals requires being willing to relinquish established ways of thinking and acting, to be open to new ways of formulating questions, and to be flexible with regard to what counts as success or failure (Buchanan *et al.*, 2018, p. 387). The issues raised by interspecies research, Mancini writes, need to be explored 'with genuine curiosity, no matter how challenging or ironic they may appear' (Mancini, quoted in Bastion, 2017, p. 20). The difficulty of surrendering established ways of thinking and acting, however, should not be underestimated. There are considerable social pressures on humans in an academic setting, such as the pressure to 'do well' at research, or the pressure for teaching to 'go well'. In their study of dogs on campus, Nickie Charles and Carol Wolkowitz (2019) record that guardians of pet-assisted-therapy dogs are sensitive to their dogs' discomfort. It is not clear, however, to what extent they are willing or able to act on that distress, in that context (Charles and Wolkowitz, 2019, pp. 308–312).

The university – in all its material and immaterial dimensions – is designed by humans, for humans. It shapes and constrains human behaviours, and human expectations with regard to what is and is not permissible, and what counts or not as an achievement. On the one occasion of Monk's objection, his bark – his deep, intentional, meaningful bark; his unremitting, unrelenting bark; his bark so clear and loud and piercing – seemed to me to ring out across the university, shattering the defensive circle it has raised around all things human. There is an animal in the temple! He is barking down the walls!

References

Bastion, M. (2017) 'Towards a more-than-human participatory research', in Bastion, M., Jones, O., Moore, N. and Roe, E. (eds) *Participatory Research in More-than-Human Worlds*. London: Routledge, pp. 19–37.

Bekoff, M. and Pierce, J. (2019) *Unleashing Your Dog: A Field Guide to Giving Your Canine Companion the Best Life Possible*. Novato, CA: New World Library.

Berns, G., Brooks, A. and Spivak, M. (2012) 'Functional MRI in awake unrestrained dogs', *PLoS ONE*, 7(5), e38027.

Brambell, F.W.R. (1965) *Report of the Technical Committee to Enquire into the Welfare of Animals Kept under Intensive Livestock Husbandry Systems*. Command Paper 2836. London: Her Majesty's Stationery Office.

Buchanan, B., Bastian, M. and Chrulew, M. (2018) 'Introduction: Field philosophy and other experiments', *Parallax*, 24(4), pp. 383–391.

Charles, N. and Wolkowitz, C. (2019) 'Bringing dogs onto campus: Inclusions and exclusions of animal bodies in organizations', *Gender, Work, Organisation*, 26, pp. 303–321.

Clothier, S. (2017) *He Just Wants to Say Hi!* St Johnsville, NY: Flying Dog Press.

Coppinger, R. and Coppinger, L. (2016) *What Is a Dog?* Chicago, IL: University of Chicago Press.

Despret, V. (2008) 'The becomings of subjectivity in animal worlds', *Subjectivity*, 23, pp. 123–139.

Despret, V. (2015) 'The enigma of the raven', *Angelaki*, 20(2), pp. 57–72.

Farm Animal Welfare Council (FAWC) (1993) *Second Report on Priorities for Research and Development in Farm Animal Welfare*. London: MAFF.

Fudge, E. (2017) 'What was it like to be a cow? History and animal studies', in Kalof, L. (ed.) *The Oxford Handbook of Animal Studies*. Oxford: Oxford University Press, pp. 258–278.

Giraud, E. and Hollin, G. (2017) 'Laboratory beagles and affective co-productions of knowledge', in Bastion, M., Jones, O., Moore, N. and Roe, E. (eds) *Participatory Research in More-than-Human Worlds*. London: Routledge, pp. 163–177.

Greenhough, B. and Roe, E. (2019) 'Attuning to laboratory animals and telling stories: Learning animal geography research skills from animal technicians', *EPD Society and Space*, 37(2), pp. 367–384.

Hobson-West, P. and Jutel, A. (2020) 'Animals, veterinarians and the sociology of diagnosis', *Sociology of Health and Illness*, 42(2), pp. 393–406.

Horowitz, A. (2012) *Inside of a Dog: What Dogs See, Smell, and Know*. New York: Scribner.

Kubinyi, E., Gasvári-Székely, M. and Miklósi, Á. (2011) ' "Genetics and the social behavior of the dog" revisited: Searching for genes relating to personality in dogs', in Inoue-Murayama,

M., Kawamura, S. and Weiss, A. (eds) *From Genes to Animal Behavior: Social Structures, Personalities, Communication by Color*. New York: Springer, pp. 255–274.

Mancini, C. (2017) ' "Animal-computer interaction: A manifesto" (2011) and sections from "Towards an animal-centred ethics for animal-computer interaction" (2016)', in Bastion, M., Jones, O., Moore, N. and Roe, E. (eds) *Participatory Research in More-than-Human Worlds*. London: Routledge, pp. 54–65.

Porcher, J. and Schmitt, T. (2012) 'Dairy cows: Workers in the shadows?', *Society and Animals*, 20, pp. 39–60.

von Uexküll, J. (2010 [1934]) *Foray into the World of Animals and Humans*. Minneapolis: University of Minnesota Press.

Wadiwel, D. (2018) 'Chicken harvesting machine: Animal labor, resistance, and the time of production', *South Atlantic Quarterly*, 117(3), pp. 527–549.

10

How to do social research with... drawing

Catherine Hahn

How I think about museums stems from drawing them. When I was a child, I drew in the Natural History Museum in South Kensington. I would sit cross-legged in front of a Victorian case for hours. As an art student, I used museums as a resource, borrowing ideas and methods from the artworks. In 2005 I began to research museums in South Africa using freehand drawing to record displays. Since then, I have expanded my drawing method to include what museums do; what they have done and what they could be.

I work in the field of museology and would like to see the end of the hierarchy of the Western historic museum and the emergence of the museum as a shared community asset (Sandell and Nightingale, 2012). Social research with drawing in museums helps to achieve this aim. It brings museum issues to the fore; magnifies overlooked areas of practice and illuminates alternatives. My interest in making useful drawings reflects the broader educational turn in art and its critical and communicatory potential (Bishop, 2007; O'Neill and Wilson, 2010). Over the last three years, I have undertaken drawn research with the Global Gender and Cultures of Equality project, see https://www. globalgrace.net/post/british-museum-detour-imperialism-and-other-legacies. GlobalGRACE seeks to understand how equalities are contested and made in different parts of the world through creative, art-based practice. My drawn research focuses on UK and South African museums. Sketches of the British Museum refurbishment show it reinforces imperial tropes and privileges patrons. Whilst pictures made from interviews with South African museum professionals give a visible presence to their concerns. Throughout, my research calls attention to inclusive, collaborative possibilities within museums.

Here, I trace my recent research with drawing in museums. I begin with drawing *in situ* and from secondary sources at the British Museum, followed by drawing from interviews with museum staff in South Africa. I end with drawing from the imagination at the British Museum.

Drawing creates a close connection with the museum, akin to embedded fieldwork. 'Prolonged and total immersion' in drawing produces a 'mute conversation' between draftsperson and subject (Taussig, 2010, p. 172). Once completed, the drawing facilitates a return to the site (through the picture) and a re-activation of one's response. As John Berger describes, images made during research provide an 'autobiographical record of one's discovery of an event' (2007, p. 3). Through this intimate relationship one is drawn into the practice of the museum. My drawing shapes my understanding of the museum and the museum shapes my decisions about what to draw.

Drawing *in Situ* in the Great Court

Most of my drawing in the British Museum takes place in the Queen Elizabeth II Great Court and Enlightenment Gallery, refurbished respectively in 2000 and 2003. I draw often in the museum and feel comfortable on site. When I arrive, I pick up a portable stool and position myself in a corner or against a flat wall. I come ready with an A3 white pad, whose back serves as a board, and a pack of 0.5 black fine liner pens.

I choose to draw in pen because it brings clarity and acceptance of mistakes. Unlike charcoal or pencil, there is no blending in or rubbing out. Once I am committed to a picture there is no turning back. Consequently, drawing in pen incites vigilance but makes me less precious about results. For example, in my drawing of the Great Court (Figure 10.1) I accept my inaccurate, wobbly line drawing of the right-hand Reading Room steps.[1] With a reduced emphasis on output, I can focus on the task.

In the British Museum, my knowledge of the site inhabits and guides the drawing. Before making a mark, I think about what I am going to put in the frame. I wave my hand around rehearsing the lines. If I start too small or unevenly, I will begin again. There is a feral excitement at the outset that gives way to absorption. At some point the image crosses over from picture-in-my-head to the one on the page. My preconceptions are overtaken by

[1]Detour I: https://course.globalgrace.net/british-museum-detour/video/

Figure 10.1 The Great Court (drawing by Catherine Hahn).

the expectations of the drawing – what the picture wants (Taussig, 2010). Through the act of drawing, I gain a clearer understanding of the site.

By drawing *in situ*, I apprehend the substructure that informs the visitor's experience. The first time I draw the Great Court, I situate myself at the main entrance to reproduce the standard 'tourist' view. The magisterial Reading Room, based on the Pantheon in Rome, rises from its centre. The Greek revivalist porticoes at its sides appear small in relation to Norman Foster's tessellated roof. Sketching the pillars and state-of-the-art glass ceiling, I see how the court's architectonic stages the old imperial order as the foundation for the new.

I use drawing to comprehend the way the museum looks *and* illuminate aspects of its practice. When drawing the Great Court, I perceive the need to include the mass of texts across its surfaces. I am impeded as there are many words and my picture is small. I therefore choose examples to stand in for the rest: one sign that asks for donations and two (of around 50) names carved in the Reading Room wall: Queen Elizabeth II and The Weston Family (the majority stakeholders in Associated British Foods). The Weston Family are one of the Court's principal benefactors. Adding their name signals the Court's role as imperial backdrop to capital (Hahn, 2023).

As my choice of texts indicates, research with drawing in museums is not a neutral record but serves a selective view. As Sontag notes, a frame is *always* exclusive (2004, p. 41). Indeed, medical and forensic illustrators use drawing because of its capacity to 'highlight particular aspects of the subject' and avoid extraneous detail (Hagen, 1991, p. 62). Similarly, social researchers deploy drawing to hone in. Their research includes feminist interventions in museums. In the early 1990s, the art activists 'Fanny Adams puts you in the picture' created a series of women-centred museum maps. Using re-interpretations of National Gallery floorplans, their work advertised the handful of works by women artists in the gallery on otherwise blank maps. More recently, Oona Leganovic mapped sexual violence in paintings in the National Gallery, through a series of brush drawings entitled 'National Gallery: The R*pes'.[2] My focus on textual detail in the Great Court more quietly delineates its patron-centred scheme.

My edited drawings provide profitable information, but the loss of detail is fraught. To ensure that my research captures complexity, I produce multiple images of the same site in a sketchbook account. My drawings of the Great Court include: the view from the first floor; the interior of the Reading Room; the names on the wall; sales outlets and visitors. By drawing more, one risks losing less. This maxim retains resonance in established museums, where things appear fixed but are subject to revision.

Drawing from Secondary Sources

During Covid-19, museums in the UK close and I am forced to rely on second-hand sources, including photographs. As an artist, I am aware of the art world's affirmation of drawing from life, imagination and memory, as opposed to drawing from photography. The former share a heritage in the fine art academy, whereas the latter is frequently treated as copyist. Alternatively, as a sociologist I understand the importance of drawing from second-hand sources as a 'strategic re-presentation' and witness (Boyd, 2019, p. 150).

Whilst drawing directly from life creates intimacy, drawing from photographs uncovers spaces and times I would otherwise not see. It also

[2]http://playinprogress.net/masterstudies

reveals the museum's self-styling – the way it seeks to be perceived. Indeed, drawing's capacity to resist the 'iconisation' of the photographic source, its 'pointing gesture, that it is an image of "this, there"', helps uncover its illusions (Boyd, 2019, p. 147).

Looking at the British Museum's photographs of the Enlightenment Gallery, I am struck by their aesthetic embellishment. I find photographs I have taken from a similar view and print them out in black and white on A4 paper, including blow-ups of details. I use this body of images to draw.

The Enlightenment Gallery, created in 2003, is presented as a collector's compendium from the 18th century. In publicity photographs, emptied of tourists, it becomes a place from a previous time. The light source merges walls and ceiling. The busts and information board are luminous – literally enlightened. The angle of the lens accents the balcony. Its parallel walkways signal progress through time. Situated to look up to the balcony, the view valorises the vantage point of the 'Western, masculine, rational universal leader' – the space where he looks down upon his study (Puwar, 2004, p. 39). Though not present, the man evoked is Sir Hans Sloane, whose collection sits in its cabinets.

The romanticism engendered by the imperial vision translates to my picture (Figure 10.2). The worn side of my pen nib picks up the textured parquet floor. Unbidden, the light creates zig zags of the windows. I record tiny details, sensed as treasures. Drawing the Enlightenment Gallery, I imbue its narrative and witness its power to seduce.[3]

Framed as museum history, the Enlightenment Gallery has important sociological implications. Museums are 'designed to impart certain elements of the past – and, by definition, to forget others' (Hoelscher and Alderman, 2004, p. 350). At the same time, they are trusted as authentic custodians of heritage (Jordanova, 1989, p. 31). Their representational style confers truth on their history telling, which makes it difficult to comprehend alternative histories behind their façades.

Undertaking research on the Enlightenment Gallery, I discover images of the room from different periods. The images show that the current gallery is historically anachronistic. Until 2003, it utilised the design conventions of its age. In 1827, it opened as The King's Library – an orderly

[3]Detour II: https://course.globalgrace.net/british-museum-detour/video/

Figure 10.2 The Enlightenment Gallery (drawing by Catherine Hahn).

space dominated by books. In the late 19th century, it was re-purposed for temporary exhibitions with works initially presented in glass cabinets and then in light boxes.

The images of the room show it has undergone significant transformation. But the way they convey this information impedes comparison of the site in different eras. Images of the room have been created in different media: at the outset, small drawings, etchings and prints; then black and white photographs; then colour photographs; and now digital. These different representational registers create confusion in interpretation. Variations in size, composition and angle mean that the images are not immediately identifiable as being of the same room. At the same time, advances in technology mean they relay a strong sense of progress.

To comprehend changes in the room on equal terms, I produce a drawing from each era using the original images as reference. Drawings by the same maker at a similar scale generate 'consistency in the stylistic language', which 'allows for a direct comparison' across time (Anderson, 2014, p. 235). To make the drawings equivalent, I use the Enlightenment Gallery picture as the foundation for the others. Each image is drawn the same size and the basic design features of windows, floor and cabinets are retained. Consequently, each era appears analogous. Differences in the space across time are also clearly defined.

Creating these drawings is messy. It involves taping new pictures onto my original drawing, then photocopying and scanning the change. In the process I spend hours trying to align small bits of pictures, losing images and re-drawing over mistakes. There are also fortuitous errors. The photo-copying makes the balcony line stronger, which reinforces the fact that this is the same space.

Being able to see the past and present museum on equal terms through drawing unmoors it from progressive, enlightenment history. Moving back and forth through my pictures, I experience that same excite-ment I had with books with picture flaps as a child – of concealment, antic-ipation and surprise. This revelatory effect indicates that the current-day Enlightenment Gallery is just one of multiple iterations of the space. By extension it suggests the new 'permanent display' could be used for some-thing else.

Drawing from Interviews with Museum Staff

Before Covid-19 struck, I planned to do a research project in South Africa looking at how staff in museums make change. The intention was to inter-view senior staff in a range of museums and draw at each site. Unable to leave home in London during the pandemic, I do the project online. My initial disappointment makes way for possibilities, as the interviews lead me to draw in response. Whilst anonymity mutes the details of the inter-views – I cannot name respondents or their museums – drawing provides a tangible connection with the interviewees' concerns.

In the second interview, I speak to an Education Manager, who describes a trip she facilitated at her museum with homeless people. The idea lingers after we talk, and I draw a small sleeping bag to record it. The sketch creates the impulse to illustrate each interview (https://exhibition.globalgrace.net/installation/museum-with-walls/).

Drawing in this way, new ideas emerge. Not tied to my view, I see the museum in terms of staff members' interests. We are transported away from the museum floor and into backrooms, archives, activities and travel. Having entered this expanded museum through the staff members' eyes,

I ask more comprehensive questions and listen more attentively to stories. The images grow denser, given flesh by the interviewees and additional research. A respondent's story about a fieldwork trip, that is also an exercise in friendship, produces a picture of the veld. In the image young scientists, one in red gloves, handle specimen containers in front of their tent. The interviewees' descriptions prompt the need for colour. I return to the felt-tip pens of my childhood as a quick means to record.

Felt-tip pens convey the immediacy of the research. Functional and fugitive, rather than fine art, they have an everyday, accessible quality. Mona Chalabi, who uses felt-tips in her data visualisation, says hand-drawn graphics are a reminder 'that a human was responsible for the data gathering and analysis' (Chalabi, quoted by Stone, 2018, n.p.). Felt-tip pens illuminate the human presence, by leaving little hidden. The nibs are thick, the ink stays wet and colours bleed.

The drawings are stylistically dissimilar. This reflects the range of ideas expressed. It is also a response to sensitive subject matter. Thinking that images related directly to rape and homelessness would jar with the bright colours, I use icons, such as the sleeping bag, and add coloured pencils to lower their hue. The pictorial breadth of the project expands further when we invite members of the public to add drawings, as part of the collaborative exhibition 'Dis/locating Cultures of Equality', Goldsmiths (2022). The resultant mass of drawn ideas embodies the notion that there is no single concept of museum equality.

Drawing from Imagination

Drawing from the interviews (beyond what I can see) informs my work at the British Museum, when I imagine the museum's history.

Conducting research at the British Museum, I am interested in the Reading Room at the centre of the Great Court. In the early 20th century, the now locked Reading Room was promoted as a literary workshop. It was home to a wide range of academics, novelists and political thinkers, including those wanting to bring about social reform (Bernstein, 2014, pp. 1–5; Hahn, 2023).

Having made the decision not to limit myself to drawing from life, I think about the best way to convey the Reading Room's past life. I decide to bring together significant people who inhabited the space. I stage Sylvia

Figure 10.3 People in the Reading Room (drawing by Catherine Hahn).

Pankhurst, Virginia Woolf, Mahatma Gandhi and Marcus Garvey as if for a portrait, with Lenin and Marx behind (Figure 10.3). Here, I exploit drawing's creative non-linearity, to introduce people who used the room at different times (Dunlop, 2011).

Creating this sketch, I am shocked by my response. Thrilled about the possibility of drawing these characters, it feels like an adventure. There is a frisson of anticipation before I draw. When I finally create the image, using photographs, cartoons and drawings, it almost draws itself. As if the people were waiting. The drawing mobilises a different, more collaborative, past from the one the British Museum currently promotes. As a result, it feels like a talisman.

Michael Taussig refers to drawing's capacity to bear witness as its ability to hail spirits (2010, p. 177). Bringing characters from the museum's past back into consciousness raises the conjecture that they have the capacity to act in the present. This capacity is demonstrated when I join the picture of Pankhurst, Gandhi, Garvey *et al.* with my drawing of the current-day Reading Room. Faced with its past inhabitants, the Reading Room's blocked doorway reads as a refusal of entry.

Barbara Walker has developed an art practice that recalls hidden histories and critiques their erasure. In her drawing series 'Shock and Awe'

(2015–2020), Walker renders black servicepeople in the British Armed Forces from 1914 to the present day hyper-visible through large-scale drawing. Simultaneously, she removes some of the characters: white-washing and rubbing out. Thus, she alerts us to their 'elimination from our consciousness' at the same time as she summons them.[4] My drawing bears a trace of this unseen/seen approach. The disparate characters, quickly sketched on A4 copy paper, form a fragile montage. Yet they have a strong pull. Their collective presence challenges the current museum to offer greater public opportunity.

What is most significant about undertaking research with drawing in museums is its praxis: its ability to bear witness, claim unseen heritage and produce a vision of what the museum could be.

References

Anderson, G. (2014) 'Endangered: A study of morphological drawing in zoological taxonomy', *Leonardo*, 47(3), pp. 232–239.

Berger, J. (2007) *Hold Everything Dear: Dispatches on Survival and Resistance.* New York: Pantheon Books.

Bernstein, S. D. (2014) *Roomscape: Women Writers in the British Museum from George Eliot to Virginia Woolf.* Edinburgh: Edinburgh University Press.

Bishop, C. (2007) 'The new masters of the liberal arts: Artists rewrite the rules of pedagogy', *Modern Painters*, September, pp. 86–89.

Boyd, J. (2019) 'Patterns of civil imagination: Drawing the unshowable photographs', *Drawing: Research, Theory, Practice*, 4(1), 1 April, pp. 145–157.

Dunlop, A. (2011) 'Hand drawing in a digital age', *Oz*, 33.

Hagen, C. (1991) 'The encompassing eye: Photography as drawing', *Aperture*, 125, pp. 56–71.

Hahn, C. (2023) 'Reclaiming history in the British Museum entranceway: Imperialism, patronage and female, queer and black legacies', *Rethinking History*. doi: 10.1080/13642529.2023.2184966.

Hoelscher, S. and Alderman, D. (2004) 'Memory and place: Geographies of a critical relationship', *Social and Cultural Geography*, 5(3), pp. 347–355.

---

[4]Kingston, A. (2016) 'Barbara Walker: Shock and Awe', www.barbarawalker.co.uk/index.php/info/text/

Jordanova, L. (1989) 'Objects of knowledge: A historical perspective on museums', in Vergo, P. (ed.) *New Museology*. London: Reaktion Books, pp. 22–40.

O'Neill, P. and Wilson, M. (eds) (2010) *Curating and the Educational Turn*. London: Open Editions.

Puwar, N. (2004) *Space Invaders: Race, Gender and Bodies Out of Place*. New York: Berg.

Sandell, R. and Nightingale, E. (eds) (2012) *Museums, Equality and Social Justice*. London: Routledge.

Sontag, S. (2004) *Regarding the Pain of Others*. London: Penguin Books.

Stone, B. (2018) ' "If it's about farts, draw a butt for god's sakes": Mona Chalabi tells us how to illustrate data', It's Nice That, 8 March. Available at: www.itsnicethat.com/authors/bryony-stone

Taussig, M. (2010) 'What do drawings want?', in Curitis, N. (ed.) *The Pictorial Turn*. New York: Taylor & Francis, pp. 166–177.

11

How to do social research with... an exhibition in a university corridor

Nirmal Puwar

Figure 11.1 'Pierre Bourdieu in Algeria' installation, Kingsway Corridor, Goldsmiths (photographer: Doreen Norman).

In the second pandemic lockdown in the UK, while writing chapters for this Methods Lab compendium *How to do social research with...*, as colleagues in the Sociology Department, we came together for online writing sessions, to share and write to specific prompts.

Figure 11.2 'Migrating Dreams and Nightmares' exhibition, Kingsway Corridor, Goldsmiths (photographer: Nirmal Puwar).

I wrote:

Prompt 2: I would suggest ... Sizing up the space.
I would suggest measuring the space in different ways. Take your measuring tape, with a good friend preferably, up and down and across the walls, as well as the floors. Measuring the depth of the glass cabinets, if you have any, though they are not essential to an exhibition (26 March 2021).

How did I as a sociologist end up climbing into cabinets, running around campus hunting for a ladder, and hanging in mid-air trying to centre the black stencil lettering for the exhibition with my students? The focus of this chapter is on how it all started, with my first collaborative inhabitation of the Kingsway Corridor, located in the Richard Hoggart Building, at Goldsmiths, with the exhibition 'Thinking with Pierre Bourdieu: Testimonies of Uprooting', which opened in November 2006 and closed in the summer of 2007. This led to many more installations in the corridor by the Sociology Department, with each having a slightly different configuration. Notably the corridor sits at the back of the large square brick-built main university college building, which was opened in 1907, and jokingly referred to as a mansion. At each end of the corridor two glass doors open to the corridors that line the building, full with administrative offices, café spaces, lecture rooms and the toilets. Thus, people pass through the corridor, can see into it as they walk on the other corridors and students and staff mingle here whilst waiting to get into lectures. There is a very high ceiling and arches running all the way down the length of the corridor. Two glass cabinets interrupt the wall on one side. A few seconds away from the corridor there are two sets of double doors which bring you out on to a large College green. Four large teaching rooms come off the corridor. Several other rooms sit in the immediate vicinity of the corridor. The rhythms of the termly teaching timetable mean that regardless of whether one goes looking for the exhibition in the shape of a gallery punter, the words and images are there every week, waiting for the onlooker to take a closer viewpoint. Students and staff are known to be surprised by supposedly random images that arrest them. There is no start or finishing line. One can start or end in the middle. Or, perhaps more importantly, the viewing never ends. One may return again and again.

Universities are full of hundreds of metres of walls, presenting the possibility of enabling a range of architectures of learning. So often located in our peripheral vision, whilst en route from here to there, walls on campus offer us underutilised spaces for varying our everyday sites of learning within the day-to-day happenings of university life. It is commonplace for universities to have a campus gallery or museum, where works are presented in a recognisable exhibition setting. Or to have art degree shows across campus. It is not so commonplace for social scientists to reflect on working on and through the walls which we walk by every day, as we move from class to office, coffee shop to library, meeting to lecture, as passageways of learning. The walls of the academy can be stretched to provide drawn-out spaces of intellectual encounter through exhibitions in passages, thus habituating a string of interconnected points of learning, alongside lecture theatres and seminars, within the corridors of universities.

Of course, exhibitions in corridors, or elsewhere on campus, can very easily be captured within the education system to become arcades of commodity and audit trails. Against the grain of the corporatisation of the academy, the production of Kingsway Corridor into an exhibition came to claim the location for an alternative inhabitation of the university space, whilst utilising the tools and conventions of the university. Over a span of ten years, I came to realise the kind of, often happenstance, intellectual and social encounters a corridor on campus can offer. Also, working against the grain of speeded-up exhibitions of short duration in gallery spaces and the cultural sector more widely, in the Kingsway Corridor, we have been able to live and converse with images and texts for the longer duration of an academic year.

This chapter reflects on the 'live methods' (Back and Puwar, 2013) of this corridor, relating to the digital records and material ephemera as a 'living archive' (Hall, 1999). Multiple temporalities form this writing, of past-present-future. The reflections also embody an 'archive of feelings' (Cvetkovich, 2003), of intellectual encounter, which has been acutely under attack. Right now, I feel as if I am writing about a bygone age. In this climate, large numbers of longstanding colleagues have left the department.

Photographers' Gallery

Whilst the Photographers' Gallery, in London, was in the middle of planning an exhibition on the Mediterranean, I alerted them to the exhibition 'Pierre Bourdieu in Algeria: Testimonies of Uprooting', curated by Christine Frisinghelli, from Camera Austria and Franz Schultheis, who had been in close dialogue with Bourdieu, before he died in 2002 (Bourdieu and Schultheis, 2001). At this point the exhibition had not travelled to the UK. Bourdieu's work is widely used in the UK by sociologists; but more usually with reference to class than colonialism or racism (Bourdieu and Sayad, 1964). The spatiality of an installation affects how we live with and receive the works. The Photographers' Gallery installed some of the photographs from the Bourdieu in Algeria collection in the then large café space (based in Covent Garden) which doubled up as a gallery space. People sat amongst the photographs as they read, reflected over a cup of coffee and met friends. The shape and atmosphere of the environment impacted on the pace at which one met the photographs. Large audiences came to see the installation and the exhibition-related events were also well attended. After a short period of time, 15 October to 28 November 2004, the exhibition was taken down for the next installation.

The Durations of Our Exposures

The speed of movement limited how one used the photographic exhibition as an extended mode of learning. I was struck by the importance of giving time to the material as an installation in a public space. When one lives with the images and in the company of other observers, one meets the materials very differently to reading them in a book, privately or collectively. Moving our bodies *between* texts and images, words and pictures both immerse and accompany us. With an exhibition, unless it is permanent, one usually plans to see an exhibition in a single visit, rarely returning. I realised that what was required was the possibility of living with the materials over a much longer duration. In other words, a reflection with the images and texts so that learning and viewing are able to move back and forth between walls, images, books, lectures and films, across a long period of time, engendering different ways of approaching them.

The limitations of time and space in a gallery setting led me to look at the walls on campus. We managed to install the whole exhibition of photographs and text selected by Camera Austria in Graz, across two and a half academic terms through an Economic and Social Research Council (ESRC) grant. This was almost a full academic year and we only took the exhibition down to make way for the annual student summer degree shows. Very deliberately we aimed to engage with the exhibition across the duration of the academic teaching calendar. Thus, instead of working to the speeded-up timeline – of exhibition up and down – in the gallery sector, we could galvanise the rhythms of university life to enable prolonged and multilayered learning. In the university, though we pay much attention to the length of our courses and the kind of thinking and learning these temporalities allow, less attention is paid to how the duration of our exposure to an exhibition also facilitates or limits the ways in which we are able to expand and complicate our understanding of and with the materials. Universities have an infrastructure of traditions of learning, with great scope for a multiplicity of dialogues with exhibitions, if time is granted to live with what is installed.

Corridors as Exhibition Spaces

When the boxes of the exhibition arrived from Graz, by courier to Goldsmiths, filling up a substantial portion of my office, there was an air of anticipation as well as a hint of concern that by placing the installation in a corridor, rather than a gallery, we were possibly not granting it the respect it was worthy of. I wonder if Bourdieu would have chuckled at the supposed lack of symbolic authority we were bestowing on his works through their emplacement in a corridor. Corridors are in-between places. The type of corridor it is in impacts on how people orient themselves around an exhibition. Architectural settings and durations come to bear on how we look, especially if we understand looking to be enacted in concert with multiple senses.

Exhibitions can be spatial experiments in meaning making (Macdonald and Basu, 2007). I saw the Kingsway Corridor as a space with vast potential. I imagined the Bourdieu exhibition would actually enable us to bring alive the full breadth of the corridor. A whole raft of events and talks layered how we approached what we displayed on the walls. Reading a publication with the visuals and text inside them invites its own intimacy. Placing them in a public space embodies a more encompassing approach, depending of course on the size of the materials on display. In an exhibition the images and words are amplified. They face us head on, we lean into them. This particular exhibition included a large range of textual excerpts from Bourdieu's publications, which were linked to the themes of habitus, racism, work, home, migration and displacement. A key asset of the university environment is that other texts which are not on the walls, as books and articles, can habitually be expected to be part of the modes of engagement. This is a vital asset of university life, built into the rhythm and time cycles, enabling one to mine the full complexity of related debates and books at hand. We experience the exhibition materials with others, as social encounters with multiple linked textures of learning.

The necessity of building in unexpected and repeated wanderings through a space (of installation) allows for a much more open-ended notion of learning. There certainly was no grand plan or pre-formed teaching and learning objectives that led me to put the Bourdieu exhibition in the corridor. The intention was to simply allow students, staff and visitors to live with the exhibition for longer and to allow it to be a platform for sparking debates in different directions. In a cross-university collaboration, with Les Back and myself at Goldsmiths as well as Derek Robbins (University of East London) and Azzedine Haddour (University College London), we managed to install the exhibition and hold several events and workshops, utilising the full academic year. Viewers and readers also stumbled across the exhibition en route to a meeting or a lecture.

Off the Walls

The 'sense-making paths' (Macdonald and Basu, 2007) between the exhibition, talks and other events encouraged a movement back and forth between the installation and spaces of further conversation, located off the walls. A review in the public London event magazine, *Time Out*, distributed information on the exhibition and events beyond the academic field. We opened the installation with a public viewing of the film *Sociology Is a Martial Art* (2001), an autobiographical film of Bourdieu conducting discussions across very different situations. Due to a reasonable budget from the ESRC Research Seminar Series scheme (a budget the ESRC has now discontinued), we were able to invite a number of scholars who had worked with Bourdieu. This included the curators and film director of *Sociology Is a Martial Art*, as well as T. Yacine who expanded the socio-biography of a French intellectual for an English audience, by foregrounding how Bourdieu worked in collaboration with Algerian scholars right from the start of his ethnosociology in Algeria (Bourdieu, 2003; Yacine, 2004). This exposure had long-standing influences on his scholarship, and upon how he embodied the space of the French academy. Intellectual associations and investments honed in Algeria remained throughout his lifetime, which included scholarly support for Berber intellectuals, such as Mouloud Mammeri, in an overwhelmingly white French academy. All these debates came alive in the corridor, workshops and lectures. The colonial and post-colonial context of Bourdieu's work could not be ignored as we exchanged words and moved with each other between his photographs and images, leading to a Special Issue on *Post-Colonial Bourdieu* (Back *et al.*, 2009). The edited collection only captures a fraction of the life of living and learning with the installation together, through events and gatherings, as well as happenstance encounters and everyday routes through and past the corridor. This chapter too is only a small sample of what we managed to enfold together with the images and texts.

Conclusion

Returning to the online writing sessions, which were part and parcel of the making of this collection, on *How to do social research with...*, whilst reflecting back to the exhibitions in the Kingsway Corridor, I wrote:

Prompt 1: This method allows you to ... live with research materials, encasing your learning surroundings with text and images to offer an embodied sense of learning. Of course reading text and images in a book is also an embodied experience, we pick it up, open the pages, even underline words, place our marker for where to start reading it again. We flick and glance through the images. Placing it on our bedside and carrying it in a bag, waiting for a moment to spring back into where you had left it. Or carrying it around and hardly opening it again. We are also embodied by our books as they sit on shelves around us and behind us. Having the privilege to re-visit them and as a go to prompt while we teach students from [our] study or dining room, or via the screen, as has been the case during the pandemic. Not having the exhibition spaces of the campus during the pandemic, sharpened my attention for what an exhibition on campus and especially one in a corridor with a lot of back and forth movement of staff and students enables. Temporality and space are placed into interaction in a very specific way. ... (26 March 2021).

The photograph located at the start of this chapter (Figure 11.1) was taken by the Sociology Department Secretary, Doreen Norman. It is one of many she took on the night before the installation came down. She knew the exhibition would be taken down in the morning and therefore she would not be passing by it again as she had done for months on her way home from work. Once I had finished the de-installation, I found a CD of photos as a gift in my departmental pigeon-hole in the Warmington Tower, on the ninth floor where the departmental administrators are/were located.

I am humbled by the way colleagues, students and staff from across and beyond the university engaged and collaborated with the Bourdieu exhibition, as well as all the other exhibitions that followed from the Sociology Department. Each one has been forged out of different relationships with people, things, words and images. In solidarity to the spirit of intellectual making in the Kingsway Corridor, we have compiled this collection and written the Acknowledgements.

References

AbdouMaliq, S. (2004) 'People as infrastructure: Intersecting fragments in Johannesburg', *Public Culture*, 16(3), pp. 407–429.

Back, L. and Puwar, N. (eds.) (2013) *Live Methods*. Malden, MA: Wiley-Blackwell.

Back, L., Puwar, N. and Haddour, A. (eds) (2009) Special Issue on 'Post-Colonial Bourdieu', *Sociological Review*, 57(3).

Bourdieu, P. (2003) *Images d'Algérie: Une Affinité Élective*. Paris: Actes Sud

Bourdieu, P. and Sayad, A. (1964) *Le Déracinement: La Crises de L'agriculture Traditionnelle en Algérie*. Paris: Editions de Minuit.

Bourdieu, P. and Schultheis, F. (2001) 'Participatory objectification: Photographic testimonies of a declining world', *Camera Austria*, 75.

Cvetkovich, A. (2003) *An Archive of Feelings: Trauma, Sexuality, and Lesbian Public Cultures*. Durham, NC: Duke University Press.

Hall, S. (1999) 'Whose heritage? Un-settling "the heritage", re-imagining the post-nation', *Third Text*, 13(49), pp. 3–13.

Macdonald, S. and Basu, P. (eds) (2007) *Exhibition Experiments*. Hoboken, NJ: Blackwell Publishing.

Yacine, T. (2004) 'Pierre Bourdieu in Algeria at war: Notes on the birth of an engaged ethnosociology', *Ethnography*, 5(4), pp. 487–509.

12

How to do social research with... ghosts

Martin Savransky

Figure 12.1 Spectral presence (image by Junko from Pixabay).

Introduction: Alas, Poor Ghosts!

A spectre is haunting contemporary social and cultural research – the spectre of … spectres, of ghosts and the spirits of the dead. What might it mean to do social research with ghosts? How might one give shape to a form of social research capable of attending and responding to the presence of ghosts in the world? It is these questions and others like them that have animated my own theoretical practices for some time, wagering on the possibility that changing – even in such seemingly impossible and outlandish ways – the kinds of questions that frame and guide our practices might in turn transform as much our modes of sociality as our understanding of what social thought and research is (for). One might be forgiven for assuming that ghosts belong to the exclusive purview of mediums, horror stories and folktales, but this could not be further from the truth. Even a quick overview of contemporary debates in the social sciences and humanities suggests that, contrary to every expectation, ghosts still lurk everywhere. Indeed, the last 30 years have seen a surge of interest in ghostly presences, experiences and practices of haunting across social, cultural and political worlds. Following the landmark book by Jacques Derrida, *Specters of Marx* (1994), where he sought to explore the phantasmic insistence and persistence of Marxist thought at the end of a millennium that had witnessed the fall of the Berlin Wall and was still coming to terms with the global dominance of capitalism, ghosts and other spectral beings have been invoked to study a whole range of liminal phenomena: forms of social and cultural change; the relationships between history and memory; the intricacies of personal and collective trauma; our complex relationships with diverse forms of data; as well as the uncanny, eerie and phantasmagoric dimensions of contemporary climate change.

In her beautifully composed *Ghostly Matters: Haunting and the Sociological Imagination* (2008), for example, sociologist Avery Gordon sought to reclaim the language and modality of haunting as a social phenomenon that might render us sensitive to the seething absences and shadowy remnants of a past that remains present in the wake of modernity's violences and wounds. Working at the intersection of sociology and literature, she attended to the afterlives of slavery in the United States, as well as to the social echoes that 'the disappeared' during the period of state terror that governed Argentina under dictatorship make reverberate in the present. In this way, she proposed that a socio-historical examination of haunting may render perceptible the shadowy formations of the present and the hazy potentialities that inhabit social life. More recently, ghosts have also been invoked by other researchers seeking to articulate generative means of coming to terms with a radically tumultuous present marked by the catastrophe of anthropogenic climate change, as a way of enabling us to attend to the ways in which landscapes of more-than-human life across the Earth carry with them sediments of other forms of life now extinct (see Tsing *et al.*, 2015).

These are just two of the most thought-provoking examples of what has become a veritable profusion of ghostly figurations, modalities of haunting and spectral forces in the critical imaginations of social researchers, a profusion so remarkable that it has been taken as heralding the advent of a 'spectral turn' (Blanco and Peeren, 2013). But if it cannot be denied that there is a renewed interdisciplinary interest in the phantasmatic, it cannot be accepted that any such 'turn' has incited the *return* of the dead. Indeed, the resurgence of attention to ghostly matters in social research has not involved a reclaiming of the fact that, for a long time, and all over the world, ghosts constituted *actual* presences amongst the living, shaping personal and collective experiences, inspiring folktales and forms of storytelling through which social worlds were woven, and intervening in the relationships between the living and the dead. Nor has any such 'turn' recovered the interest and attention that ghosts elicited even at the turn of the 20th century in the West, when a whole array of practices devoted themselves to the possibility of establishing rapports with strange phenomena that intimated the existence of other worlds in this world: as when psychic photographers would point to light traces that remained visible at the end of the electromagnetic spectrum as proof of everlasting life, and as consolation to the bereaved (Warner 2008); or when the Society for Psychical Research in London would conduct experiments on mediumship, phantoms, telepathy and automatic writing, with the aim of revealing dimensions of the world and forms of being that would otherwise remain hidden (Oppenheim, 1985).

If one can say that ghosts still haunt social and cultural research today, therefore, it is not least because this 'turn' has not so much turned to ghosts themselves as presences with whom the living co-inhabit the Earth, but has turned to the *figure* of 'the ghost' as a conceptual metaphor through which one might come to examine displaced, out-of-place, persistent and shadowy dimensions of social life. These ghostly figurations have proven extremely generative in inspiring researchers to pursue new questions and modes of attention. But if the metaphoric ghost of the spectral turn occasionally 'sets heads spinning', it does not, *pace* Derrida (1994, p. 127), 'cause séance tables to turn'. Indeed, what about ghosts themselves? Social scientists have shown they can do research with ghostly *metaphors*, and they sometimes also do research with *people* so as to find out whether or why they 'believe' in ghosts. But having inherited the modern tale that derided ghosts as mere figments of the superstitious or religious imagination, they would almost never do research *with* ghosts themselves.

What would that entail? This chapter explores precisely this question. By engaging with stories of people who have learned not to 'believe in' but to 'live with' ghosts, and of some social researchers who have accepted the challenge, the chapter addresses the challenge of doing research with ghosts as one which can elicit new questions about *how* social research might be done. Indeed, I suggest that responding to this challenge demands a new ethos or methodology for social research, which I call 'the method of alterity'. In short, the method of alterity consists not in asking what otherness means, or what makes it other, but how others might transform our own ways of understanding and living in the world, were we to take them seriously (Savransky, 2021). This, in turn, transfigures the very purpose of social research. No longer enthralled by the question of what others can tell us about society, social research might instead become a kind of *empirical philosophy*, thinking with 'others' in order to engage in an ongoing experiment with an open question: 'What is reality capable of?'

Beyond Estrangement: Or, How to Do Social Research with Ghosts

Part of the reason why social scientists are often much better at doing social research with ghostly metaphors – or with people who believe in ghosts – than with ghosts themselves, has to do with how they have come to understand the nature of the social world, and their role in it as its students. Irrespective of which specific intellectual tradition social scientists may come from – positivism, interpretivism, Marxism, social constructivism, post-structuralism and so on – most of them tend to agree that social worlds enjoy a bifurcated existence. That is, they often proceed as if reality – not unlike spoiled milk – always came split, divisible into two separate realms: on the one hand, an immediate realm of semblances and appearances. On the other, a *really real* but less evident realm of causes and forces, one that is deeper than the first immediate realm and which, once disclosed, can allow them to understand or explain the reasons that make the immediate realm appear as it does. Of course, different intellectual traditions disagree passionately about what belongs to which realm. For some, it is people's experiences, values and meanings that belong to the first immediate realm, whereas the really real realm of causes would be composed of hard, objective social facts. For others, it is the very claim to objective facts that is the semblance, an apparent realm whose deeper causes lie in the social norms and conventions that have historically pervaded scientific cultures. But however each intellectual tradition distributes the terms, most of them tacitly accept that the task of social research consists in cultivating what I have elsewhere called 'an ethics of estrangement': the task of becoming *estranged* from the realm of appearances immediately available to our experience, in order to gain access to the deeper realm of causes (Savransky, 2016).

Chased away by the expansion of electrical infrastructures and natural gas pipelines, and disqualified by a modern secular culture which relegated them to the realm of superstition, ghosts are primary victims of the ethics of estrangement (Bennet, 1999, Despret, 2018). For regardless of the specific distribution of the terms, the secular assumptions of modern social science imply that (almost) no social researcher would seriously situate ghosts within the realm of the *really* real, appealing to the existence of ghosts in order to understand or explain other dimensions of social and cultural life. By contrast, the tacit assumption is that, even when some people may believe in them, ghosts don't *really* exist. At best, they're metaphors for something else. Whenever ghosts are in question, therefore, researchers assume that it is their presence amongst people that needs to be explained by some other social or cultural phenomenon or cause. Indeed, if asking what it may mean to do social research *with* ghosts seems bewildering, it is because to pose this question is to challenge two basic assumptions of social research. First, that ghosts are at best semblances that have no real existence; and second, that the very task of social research is precisely to explain semblances and appearances in terms of what (we have already decided) *really* exists. Learning how to do social research with ghosts, in other words, demands that we take the risk of moving beyond the ethics of estrangement, and that we learn to think of the means and purposes of social research otherwise.

But how? One way may be simply to follow the path of those exceptional cases in social research that make an alternative perceptible precisely by having embarked on the adventure of taking ghosts seriously: asking not why people *believe in* ghosts, but how they learn to *live with* ghosts. One such exceptional case is provided by the anthropologist Heonik Kwon's (2008) ethnographic research with the ghosts of the Vietnam War: spectres of those who suffered violent and tragic deaths during the war and now roam villages and towns, making regular apparitions amongst the living as they search after the same things the living desire: food and money, clothing and shoes, a house, a bicycle or a motorbike. Much of Kwon's ethnography was carried out among the seaside community of Cam Re, which was built in the 1960s by war refugees and sits on a massive cemetery. 'One evening', Kwon writes,

children returned from playing in the street, shivering from their encounter with the ghost of a one-legged mine victim. Younger boys emulated the ghost's hopping along the ditch without crutches; older ones estimated whether the ghost's mobility was improving as seasons passed. This one-legged soldier was normally alone. Occasionally, he was spotted with an old scholar ghost in full mandarin attire. ... Two American ghosts used to appear under the Areca palm tree, whispering in their unintelligible tongue to each other and making the unpleasant noise of what appeared to be a spoon clinking in an empty can for some villagers or a few bullet shells rattling in an empty munitions box for others. These two huge men were always together. They were shy, reserved, slightly nervous. They were prudent and not at all intrusive to the villagers but very talkative with each other. The wife of an invalid gardener, one of Cam Re's veteran peasant guerrilla fighters, regularly burned two incense sticks under the areca tree. Occasionally, she burned a few notes of paper votive money, in US dollars, for their sake. Another ghost, who people believed was an Algerian conscript during the French War, used to frighten young women by touching their shoulders from behind. Several women claimed that they had seen his hairy arms. The neighbors hired a ritual specialist to chase away this troublesome being.

(Kwon, 2008, pp. 36–37)

While these apparitions are very common across a whole number of villages and towns, they are almost never made public in the media. Like any modern nation, the Vietnamese state disqualifies them as 'remnants of old superstitions and a sign of cultural backwardness and moral laxity' (Kwon, 2008, p. 10). Yet Kwon discovered during his fieldwork that these ghosts are not metaphorical devices, allegorical figures through which people would negotiate the trauma of war and the wounds of the past. On the contrary, ghosts are indeed real and present: 'their existence is perceived to be a "natural" phenomenon rather than a cultural symbol' (Kwon, 2008, p. 16).

When people relay their encounters with them, therefore, what interests their neighbours is not whether those who witnessed them *believe* in what they saw, but the details that may enable them to identify who these ghosts are, and the practical implications of their apparition amongst the living. Indeed, while the desire for land was great amongst Cam Re's inhabitants, they hardly ever sought to convert gravesites for cultivation. Instead, debates were often held about how close to a grave one could plant a particular tree, and people were particularly concerned with the possibility that the roots of trees may perturb the tranquility of someone's afterlife. In Cam Re and elsewhere in Vietnam, people *lived* with ghosts, and these in turn were 'attentive to the social affairs in the living world, just as the latter are fond of telling stories of their existence' (Kwon, 2008, p. 19). As such, Kwon learned that doing social research with these ghosts could not be a matter of estranging himself from their apparitions and stories in order to *explain* their existence (away) by appealing to other aspects of the social world of the living. These ghosts, in fact, were *among* the living. A theoretical rejection of their existence would have rendered social life in these villages incomprehensible. Which is why the approach that Kwon learned to cultivate was much riskier and more adventurous: not to provide an explanation for ghostly apparitions, or to turn them into metaphors, but to allow himself to be transformed by their presence. Which is to say, *to give to the presence of ghosts the power to enable him to learn about the social world.*

The Method of Alterity: Social Research as Empirical Philosophy

Kwon learned much about these post-war Vietnamese worlds, about the relationships between the living and their dead, and the ways in which the dead become part of social life. But he also gained important insights about the mode of existence of ghosts themselves: wandering between worlds, 'they dwell in the traditional cultural habitat in the periphery of ancestors, but this habitat exists within a wider modern and secular political society that negates their naturalist existence altogether' (Kwon, 2008, p. 24). He also learned that ghosts in Vietnam do not always remain such, but can sometimes be transformed into *than*, powerful 'guardian spirits for a community or an individual with whom they have no given connection' (2008, p. 104). Of course, accepting the reality of these ghosts, giving to their presence the power to enable him to learn about social worlds in post-war Vietnam, did not give him licence to establish the existence of every ghost, universally and in general. There are no 'ghosts in general', just as there aren't living beings in general. What his research does intimate is that *some* ghosts *do, in fact, exist* – with their own biographies and necrographies, with their own desires and needs, with their own relationships to the living communities that make worlds with them. As he was told by a member of the community after asking him whether he really believed that Lotus Flower, a young ghost who had long lived in their family, was real: 'if she is not, why are you asking me about her?' (Kwon, 2008, p. 128).

This gesture of refusing to ask what otherness *really* means so as to attempt to *think with* others, to ask how others might transform our own ways of understanding and living in the world, is what I call 'the method of alterity'. This method encourages social researchers to cultivate a radically different set of sensibilities. Instead of associating insightful research with the development of a critical distance, what it requires is learning the art of paying attention to what matters in the situations they're in (Savransky, 2016). Rather than assuming that the task of social research consists in arming oneself with social theories so as to apply them to the worlds we encounter, the method of alterity demands a position of radical exposure and vulnerability: that we enable the worlds we encounter to inspire in us new questions and concepts, ones which no abstract set of theoretical principles could ever anticipate. Above all, the method of alterity requires social researchers to resist the temptation of seeking to explain semblances and appearances in terms of what is supposed to *really* exist. By contrast, it encourages researchers to engage in a permanent experimentation, learning to make perceptible the possible existences that compose a situation, so that they themselves can teach us what the many social worlds in this world are made of.

If doing social research with ghosts asks us to experiment with 'the method of alterity', this method changes some of the basic questions of social research itself. What it demands is that we think *in the presence* of ghosts. Thus, the method of alterity invites social researchers to work under the question *'what is reality capable of?'* Taken in a purely abstract sense, this is a philosophical question, usually pertaining to the purview of metaphysics. But the truth is that, at its best, *social research is philosophy with 'others' in it.* And when social researchers let go of their trained habits of suspicion, estrangement and critique; when they cease asking what others can tell them about society and instead enable others (living or dead) to tell them what matters to them – how their social worlds are woven, who and what inhabits them, what is at stake – social research might perhaps become an *empirical philosophy*: a practice of conceptual and philosophical creation, thinking with 'others' in order to learn how to inhabit a world that is richer, wilder and more multifarious than any theory could encompass, a world capable of transforming our concepts and our ways of co-inhabiting the Earth (Savransky, 2021). A world, in other words, in which ghosts themselves partake in the making of the social.

References

Bennet, G. (1999) *Alas, Poor Ghost! Traditions of Belief in Story and Discourse*. Logan: Utah State University Press.

Blanco, M. and Peeren, E. (2013) *The Spectralities Reader*. London: Bloomsbury.

Derrida, J. (1994) *Specters of Marx*. New York, London: Routledge.

Despret, V. (2018) 'Talking before the dead', *SubStance*, 47(1), pp. 64–79.

Gordon, A. (2008) *Ghostly Matters: Haunting and the Sociological Imagination*. Minneapolis: University of Minnesota Press.

Kwon, H. (2008) *Ghosts of War in Vietnam*. Cambridge: Cambridge University Press.

Oppenheim, J. (1985) *The Other World: Spiritualism and Psychical Research in England, 1850–1914*. Cambridge: Cambridge University Press.

Savransky, M. (2016) *The Adventure of Relevance: An Ethics of Social Inquiry*. Basingstoke, New York: Palgrave Macmillan.

Savransky, M. (2021) *Around the Day in Eighty Worlds: Politics of the Pluriverse*. Durham, NC, London: Duke University Press.

Tsing, A., Swanson, H., Gan, E. and Busband, N. (2015) *Arts of Living on a Damaged Planet: Ghosts and Monsters of the Anthropocene*. Minneapolis: University of Minnesota Press.

Warner, M. (2008) *Phantasmagoria: Spirit Visions, Metaphors, and Media into the Twenty-first Century*. Oxford: Oxford University Press.

13

How to do social research with... i-docs

Ella Harris

I-docs as a Way of Thinking

The Temporary City
www.thetemporarycity.com Password: TTC

This link will take you to the i-doc discussed in the first part of this chapter. I invite you to engage with it before and/or while reading.

My first experiment with i-doc making was during my PhD research into London's 'pop-up' culture. Pop-up is a trend for temporary and mobile places including pop-up cinemas, theatres, shops, bars, supper clubs, etc. It started, after the 2008 recession, as a compensatory urbanism (Harris, 2020) – a second-best way of organising the city in the face of crisis – but it is now a fashionable phenomenon. Pop-ups are defined by their spatio-temporality. They are temporary or mobile and re-purpose existing urban spaces for alternative activities. I decided to use i-docs to explore pop-ups because I was struck by how their spatiotemporal format could mirror pop-up culture's representation of space-time as dynamic and unpredictable.

'I-docs', or Interactive Documentaries, are web-based, multimedia documentaries. As a new media form, they've been gaining prominence in commercial and artistic documentary-making worlds. I-docs are non-linear. Users navigate content via various pathways. I-docs take diverse forms. Some are almost like video games, others are more like websites. Many invite users to upload content, answer questions or leave comments. You can find and explore a range of content about i-docs at www.i-docs.org and I've briefly introduced some examples at the end of this chapter, after the references. Recently, academics have begun experimenting with i-docs as research methods. This chapter explores the methodological values i-doc making can have, drawing on my own experiences making two i-docs.

My research into pop-up culture focused on three types of pop-up: shipping container spaces, supper clubs and cinemas. During site visits I took video footage, photographs and fieldnotes. In preparation for i-doc making, I undertook training in filming and editing using Adobe Premier Pro. I produced short video clips and collaged image and text boxes that I made on Adobe Photoshop. To make the i-doc's interface, I worked with a web-developer, Michael Skelly. I planned how the i-doc should look, its features, interactive capacities and the organisation of content, and discussed with Skelly what would be feasible. I was lucky that Skelly, a friend of mine, was happy to work for a low fee, out of personal interest in the technical challenge as the cost of i-doc making can be a barrier within social research projects.

Much has been written about the methodological values of visual methods (Garett, 2011; Laurier and Brown, 2011; O'Callaghan, 2012). As elements of i-doc making, filming and photography were important, focusing my attention on the aesthetic, sensory and material elements that produce pop-up culture's atmospheres. The editing process was key too. Editing for i-docs is different to editing a standard film because rather than integrating content into one fixed sequence, you're making pieces of content that will stand in multiple relationships to each other, as they can be arrived at via various pathways. This changes the editing process, putting the focus on relationships or conflicts between bits of content.

I saw how linking clips in the i-doc could foreground the significance of seemingly mundane recurrences. For example, a similar bird tattoo on two different pop-up workers revealed the importance of hipster identities and their connection to precarious labour, recession and new iterations of the creative city. The editing process also alerted me to the multiple meanings a clip or image could have, depending on what other content it is experienced in proximity to. Whereas normally an editor to some extent 'fixes' the meaning of each shot by deciding, definitively, what will go before and after it – and therefore which of its potential meanings will be activated – interactive documentary editing includes thinking about how to retain and foreground the many things a clip or image could mean. For example, in editing a clip about a supper club on a residential canal boat, I made sure to keep in footage that linked the event to the wider immersive entertainment cultures of pop-up as well as emphasising pop-up's connection to the worsening housing crisis.

As well as thinking through editing, the decisions I made about the i-doc's design focused my thinking on the nature of pop-up space-time, pop-up's roles in socio-economic issues and its political stakes. Performative transience and transformation define pop-up, so it was crucial that the i-doc illuminated these imaginaries. Its first page features an 'enter' button to reflect the 'immersive' experience many pop-ups try to cultivate. Once inside, my i-doc has two viewing options. One is a category view, giving easy access to any of the videos, but the user is encouraged to use the 'play' option. The 'play' page is a map on which icons appear indicating a type of pop-up (container, cinema or supper club). Crucially, this isn't a static map; places come and go as time passes. The passage of time is marked by a calendar at the bottom of the screen. Its pages turn continuously, evoking urgency. I decided to make the rate at which icons appear and disappear fast enough that not all the clips can be watched in one sitting, mirroring the imaginary of scarcity that pop-ups cultivate. There's no indicator of which clips will disappear or when, mimicking pop-up's unpredictability and possibly generating anxiety and/or excitement for the user. It's impossible to move backwards in time. Users might find that, while they are watching one clip, another they had planned to view has disappeared. Deciding how this combination of i-doc features would work together to evoke the space-time of pop-up culture was a key research process, involving breaking down the component elements that give pop-up its distinctive spatiotemporality.

One way to think about the political stakes of pop-up was considering what agencies i-doc users should have. In one sense, my i-doc gives users power. They can pick which clips they activate, just as pop-up arguably gives communities power in place making. However, I also wanted the i-doc to foreground the burdens of pop-up, where responsibility for rejuvenating urban space during recession is shifted onto small creative groups and businesses. Mirroring this, time doesn't move in the i-doc (and the calendar pages don't turn) unless the user selects a clip; your labour is required to keep the pop-up city going.

Mixing different kinds of media in the i-doc allowed me to engage with conflicting imaginaries of what pop-up achieves. The content about individual pop-ups is all in the form of video clips. These clips predominantly reflect how pop-ups self-represent; a landscape of creative uses of otherwise neglected spaces that bring people together and produce positive change. However, I also used a second medium – the 'outside the pop-up city' collages – to bring out features of the clips that problematise this narrative.

The 'outside the pop-up city' boxes are offered as links at the end of certain clips. They foreground socio-economic and political issues in which pop-up is heavily implicated, like gentrification, labour precarity and the housing crisis. For example, the clip about The Artworks, a shipping container mall, ends with an option to see 'outside the pop-up city'. In the clip, building works are visible in the background but it is unclear what exactly is happening. The outside the pop-up city box explains how the mall occupies the site of the Heygate Estate, a council estate which was controversially decanted, demolished and replaced with expensive flats. Designing the 'outside the pop-up city' boxes helped me to contemplate what is left out of pop-up's stories about itself, and why, and to recover these important narratives.

I-doc making also provoked questions I hadn't pre-empted. For example, the web-developer asked me how I wanted the i-doc to end. Would the user keep exploring until there were no more clips available? Would the i-doc re-start automatically? Or something else? This made me consider how, in real life, pop-up's end would come about. I thought about how pop-up is implicated in its own displacement, because as pop-ups gentrify areas they get replaced by more upmarket, permanent developments. I decided that after ten minutes in the 'play' view, the i-doc should be interrupted by another, larger 'outside the pop-up city' box. Users are unable to access further clips and instead are confronted with images of flats under construction and a notice telling them they must leave the temporary city as re-development is beginning. They are encouraged to visit the 'pop-up city showrooms' and browse luxury apartments. This abrupt, singular, ending illustrates a key fallacy in pop-up. While its imaginaries of flexibility and surprise suggest open possibility, the unwarned ending foregrounds how fixed the trajectories of pop-up are in practice. As this project showed me, doing social research with i-docs is incredibly valuable because decisions about their contents and design are also decisions about how to understand and communicate your topic, making them a great tool for careful, critical thinking.

I-docs as Participatory Method

The Lockdown Game

https://lockdown-idoc.netlify.app/

This i-doc is discussed in this second part of the chapter. Again, I invite you to explore it before or alongside reading.

After experimenting with i-docs during my PhD, I later used them as a participatory method to explore experiences of London's first Covid-19 lockdown.

I worked with a group of 13 Londoners as well as an artistic editor, Jack Scott, and web-developer, Michael Skelly. The group was actually part of a larger cohort recruited for a different project, about class and gentrification, that couldn't go ahead when lockdown was imposed. These 13 people agreed to be part of a revised project exploring experiences of lockdown. They were a diverse group in terms of age, gender, ethnicity, class background and occupation, but were all living in either Deptford in South East London or Dalston in North East London (the areas where the original research was intended to take place). The group agreed to record their lives during lockdown using photography, video, collage, music and writing. We arranged three Zoom workshops where the i-doc design process took place. At the first workshop, the group presented their recordings of lockdown to each other, and I talked through some examples of what an i-doc can look like. At the second meeting, we split the participants into three breakout groups. One group planned the aesthetics of the i-doc including colour schemes, fonts, soundscape and style. A second group planned the infrastructure; how many pages there should be, how content should be divided and connected, whether there should be an entrance page, an about page, etc. The third group made decisions about the i-doc's interactive features including what should be clickable, what prompts and questions the user should be confronted with, if there should be comment options, tasks or mini games and what limits and constraints the users should experience. After a whole-group discussion to amalgamate ideas, I wrote up the design plan and Jack and Michael worked from this to produce the i-doc. At a third workshop, we showed the group the draft i-doc and they suggested final edits before it was completed.

Making content for the i-doc enabled the group members to express their individual experiences of this strange and difficult time. The content they made shows very different realities. For example, one clip depicts washing groceries to keep the virus out, where another shows an illegal party, attended in resistive defiance of lockdown rules. However, the i-doc design process also allowed the group to find what was common in their experiences. They arranged the i-doc as several indoor spaces within a home and outdoor spaces in a local area. These spaces were created by collaging together stills from the group's materials. This means that even the most divergent pieces of content sit against the backdrop of a shared world. Content is accessed by clicking on objects in these spaces and is collated by theme. For example, clicking on a yoga mat in the bedroom gives you content about exercise, whereas clicking on a protest placard in an outdoor community garden gives content about political and community engagement.

As the user navigates the i-doc, they are met with pop-up windows asking them if they will comply with lockdown rules such as washing their hands or wearing a mask. The pop-ups also make suggestions like 'bulk buy loo roll?', 'take a family Zoom call' or 'do you want an injection of bleach? Donald Trump thinks it's a great idea!' (Figure 13.1). Sometimes, if a user tries to move between spaces, they are told that the journey is

Figure 13.1 'Do you want an injection of bleach...?': Parody of Donald Trump's Covid-19 governance written by participants in i-doc making workshop.

Figure 13.2 'Sorry this journey is illegal, unless you're Dominic Cummings?':
Parody of Dominic Cummings saga written by participants in i-doc making
workshop.

prohibited 'unless you're Dominic Cummings?' If they answer, 'I am
Dominic Cummings', they are allowed through; a satirical reference to the
blatant breaching of lockdown rules by UK Government Chief Advisor
Dominic Cummings when he drove 25 miles to a tourist spot while he sus-
pected he had Covid-19 (Figure 13.2). The satirical tone in these prompts
and questions demonstrates the common experience of lockdown as an
absurd situation where rules and recommendations changed constantly,
often seemed nonsensical and were flamboyantly broken by the very people making them. The group also decided to include two meters within the
i-doc, one showing well-being and one showing viral risk. The readings on
the meters change as the user explores content and spaces. Visiting the
park, for example, improves well-being but also raises your viral risk. The
two meters are often in conflict as staying away from activities that carry
viral risk means the well-being meter runs low. This gamified element
reflects the group's shared experience of lockdown feeling like an unwin-
nable game, which might be funny if the stakes weren't life or death.

This participatory i-doc gave voice to my participants, allowing them
to be co-creators of knowledge. The process also showed how participatory

i-doc making can be a tool for expressing difference while simultaneously finding and articulating what is shared.

I-docs, Impact and Imagination

I hope my own experiments with i-doc making show their value in illuminating and communicating complex social issues. In concluding, I'd like to encourage others to work with i-docs, even if just as a thought experiment. I-docs are a brilliant tool for bringing research to publics and stakeholders, because they are interactive and can be easily distributed as a website link. Furthermore, i-docs can engage users in thinking about their own agency and responsibility within social issues because their interactive interfaces require decision making (Miles, 2014, p. 79; Harris, 2016).

I-docs can also collate feedback on research through comment options and even collect data by integrating questionnaires and surveys. For example, the i-doc *onesharedhouse2030* (http://onesharedhouse2030.com/) is explicitly a data collection tool, enlisting users in sharing their ideas about co-living. I-docs can also encourage political and social agency. The i-doc *Prison Valley* (http://prisonvalley.arte.tv/?lang=en) allows users to speak directly to prisoners and encourages research into the prison industry via links to resources.

Making an i-doc is expensive. It requires equipment and software for creating and editing media, purchase of a web domain and, depending on your own skill sets, hiring coders and editors. There are some i-doc-making tools, many of which are listed on i-docs.org (http://i-docs.org/interactive-documentary-tools/), that can bypass coding costs, although they give less flexibility in design. However, even without *making* an i-doc, thinking about how you *would* make one can be a useful method. Creative methods allow particular kinds of thinking to take place (Hawkins, 2015). Much of the particular form of thinking that i-docs enable can still be facilitated by just planning an i-doc; sketching out potential formats, making non-linear storyboards or mind-mapping ideas. Thinking through i-docs in this way can bring illuminating and unanticipated insights to your research. Creating the interface of my i-doc *The Temporary City* required me to identify the component parts of pop-up's spatiotemporal imaginary, so that I could use the interface to evoke those components, as well as identify what is tactically left out of that imaginary (i.e., its role in gentrification).

The participatory process of making *The Lockdown Game* allowed me to see how a group of Londoners made sense of the UK's first national lockdown. In order to design its interface, they had to communicate personal experiences but also reach shared conclusions about the cultural logics of lockdown. Their collective choice to design the i-doc like a game with well-being and viral risk meters and nonsensical rules gave me fascinating insights into changing meanings of freedom, rules, compliance and responsibility. The insights enabled by my i-doc projects could also be achieved by just *planning* an i-doc, even if the resources aren't available to make it. I encourage readers to explore a variety of i-doc projects and to think about what an i-doc about their own research topic(s) might look like.

References

Garett, B.L. (2011) 'Videographic geographies: Using digital video for geographic research', *Progress in Human Geography*, 35(4), pp. 521–541.

Harris, E. (2015) 'Navigating pop-up geographies: Urban space-times of flexibility, interstitiality and immersion', *Geography Compass*, 9(11), pp. 592–603.

Harris, E.R.S. (2016) 'Introducing i-docs to geography: Exploring interactive documentary's nonlinear imaginaries', *Area*, 49(1), pp. 25–34.

Harris, E.R.S. (2020) 'Compensatory cultures: Post-2008 climate mechanisms for crisis times', *New Formations* (99), pp. 66–87. Available at: https://doi.org/10.3898/NewF:99.04.2019

Hawkins, H. (2015) 'Creative geographic methods: Knowing, representing, intervening. On composing place and page', *Cultural Geographies*, 22(2), pp. 247–268. Available at: https://doi.org/10.1177/1474474015569995

Laurier, E. and Brown, B. (2011) 'The reservations of the editor: The routine work of knowing the film in the edit suite', *Social Semiotics*, 21(2), pp. 239–257.

Miles, A. (2014) 'Interactive documentary and affective ecologies', in Nash, K., Hight, C. and Summerhayes, C. (eds) *New Documentary Ecologies: Emerging Platforms, Practices and Discourses*. New York: Palgrave Macmillan, pp. 67–83.

O'Callaghan, C. (2012) 'Lightness and weight: (Re)reading urban potentialities through photographs', *Area*, 44, pp. 200–207.

Examples of i-docs

Gaza/Sderot (http://gaza-sderot.arte.tv/en/time/)

Gaza/Sderot is made up of a series of two-minute video clips that can be filtered by the date they were made, the person they're about, their location and their topic. Each viewing option produces different interpretations, foregrounding the multiplicity of perspectives within the Gaza conflict. However, the i-doc has one fixed element; a line down the middle of the screen dividing Gaza from Sderot, showing the persistent and totalising impact of the conflict.

Universe Within (http://universewithin.nfb.ca/desktop.html#index)

Universe Within is part of an i-doc series about 'hidden digital lives of highrise residents around the world'. To explore its contents, you must pick and follow a 'digital native' who requires you to answer survey-style questions before accessing a clip, mirroring how companies collect data through publics' web-browsing activities. The i-doc therefore evokes how online information is mediated and monetized.

A Journal of Insomnia (www.nfb.ca/interactive/a_journal_of_insomnia/)

Unlike other i-docs, you can't access *A Journal of Insomnia* whenever you want. Instead, you have to request a link that becomes active at your appointment time – in the middle of the night. In this way the i-doc forces the user to join the characters in their world of nocturnal wakefulness.

14

How to do social research with... infrastructure

Sobia Ahmad Kaker

When researching everyday social relations in Karachi, the conflict-ridden Pakistani megacity, my attention was drawn to the rapidly proliferating walls and security barriers across the city's neighbourhoods (Figure 14.1). In the absence of effective policing against crime, residents from all walks of life had turned towards practices of physical enclosure as a form of securing their neighbourhood on the inside from the dangerous city outside. Yet, despite investing in physical infrastructures of security (such

Figure 14.1 An image of a street barrier, placed at an intersection of the main road (photograph by author, 2012).

as boundary walls, gates limiting entry points and guarded security barriers regulating passage), residents continued to suffer from violent burglaries. Moreover, the security situation in the rest of the city continued to deteriorate. One particular incident became a catalyst moment within my research, forcing me to do sociology with 'infrastructures'. It was when I observed how seemingly fixed and inert obstacles such as walls, security gates and guarded barriers could oscillate between being impregnable barriers and porous, osmotic and fluid socio-material objects. In this chapter, I will explain how I studied infrastructures such as walls, gates and security barriers/checkposts as objects of social inquiry.

The Conundrum

I did not consciously intend to do sociology with infrastructures. When I started my research project in 2010, I was interested in studying the relationship between the spatial form of Karachi, the socio-spatially polarised Pakistani megacity, and escalating urban violence. Between 2008 and 2010, the rapid decline in the security situation of the city had meant that more and more citizens – from all walks of life – had started to retreat to what Teresa Caldeira (1996, p. 303) famously refers to as 'fortified enclaves', that is, 'privatised, enclosed and monitored spaces for residence, consumption, leisure, and work'. For upper-middle class Karachiites, to live 'safely' in the city meant to live in heavily guarded (and increasingly enclosed) neighbourhoods. Meanwhile government and private offices, malls, leisure clubs and even parks became more exclusive – only accessible by being allowed passage past security checkposts, and after walking through airport-style security gates. Yet, just as ordinary spaces within Karachi became heavily securitised, violent crime rates continued to escalate. My research project aimed to explore why, despite ongoing securitisation in the enclaved megacity, Karachi continued to become increasingly insecure.

In 2011, I visited Karachi on a preliminary fieldwork visit. By this time, I had scoured through literature on fortified enclaves and urban insecurity in comparable post-colonial cities. Through this literature, I had constructed an idea of what 'fortified enclaves' meant. The term most popularly referred to highly exclusive and heavily secured gated communities. Naturally, I started looking for these 'types' of enclaves in Karachi. I was immediately disappointed. At that time, commercially developed exclusive gated communities did not exist in Karachi in the way that they did in Latin American, African, Middle Eastern or Indian cities (Webster *et al.*, 2002; Falzon, 2004; Durington, 2009; Caldeira, 2020). Karachi's version was a retrospectively developed 'fortified enclave', where either the housing society that developed the land decided to wall and gate the neighbourhood, or the residents of a neighbourhood (developed and managed by public municipal authorities) came together to place security barriers (with government permission) at entry and exit points into the otherwise open neighbourhoods.

In addition to this, despite being walled and gated, or in other cases enclosed with the help of guarded barriers, I found it difficult to categorise Karachi's enclaves as 'fortified enclaves' (Caldeira, 1996; 2020) or 'security parks' (Hook and Vrdoljak, 2002) in the way they had been described in the literature on residential enclaves. These neighbourhoods were hardly isolated spaces cut off from the wider city through the material infrastructures of security and segregation. In fact, given the urban social dynamics of Karachi, it was impossible for these gated and enclosed neighbourhoods to fully function as exclusive spaces that effectively restricted 'undesirable' traffic. This was because the 'undesirables', mostly the racialised and criminalised poor, were essential to the very running of the place (Graham and Kaker, 2014). The movement of municipality cleaners, maids, house guards, drivers, delivery men, etc., allowed daily life inside to function smoothly, while there was also regular movement of others such as tutors, friends, visitors. It seemed impossible for the guards to properly filter entry into enclaved neighbourhoods, as in most cases, there was no proper system of identification which allowed them to ensure that those entering were doing so for legitimate reasons.

What was apparent, however, was how perceptions (and negotiations) of class position helped to determine passage. For example, I never found it difficult to gain entry and move through guarded security barriers. Sometimes, I would get the odd question from guards asking where I was heading, or what my business was in the neighbourhood, but this was usually asked with little real interest or serious follow-up. It was very clear that as a middle-class woman, I just seemed to 'belong'. The people who did find it difficult to cross or enter, however, were the maids, drivers or other 'poor' service workers who came in either to work in the houses within these enclaved communities, or to meet their friends or relatives who worked there. These initial observations made me question the 'form' of the fortified enclave in the Karachi context. What 'constructed' fortified enclaves in Karachi? Was it material infrastructure, such as the boundary walls made of bricks and mortar? Was it the gate, the security barrier, the physical signs next to each stating security warnings and rules of admission? Or was it the socio-technical infrastructures (the private security guards standing at entry and exit points, scanning people with their metal detectors, or with their gaze, and making a judgement on whether to open the gates or barriers for whomever they were encountering) that linked with the material infrastructures to constitute enclaved spaces? In any case, during my preliminary fieldwork, it became clear that to understand the production of securitised spaces in Karachi, I would have to study infrastructures of security in Karachi.

Infrastructure as Object of Inquiry and as Method

Star and Ruhleder (1996) define infrastructure not by 'what' it is, but by asking 'when' it is. They argue that infrastructure is something that develops for people in practice. It is a system that is connected to different activities and structures. In this way, Star and Ruhleder (1996) define infrastructure as a relational concept – it means different things to different people, depending on how they encounter it or what use they get out of it. Reflecting on my initial encounters with the socio-material processes of security along enclave borders, Star and Ruhleder's conceptualisation of infrastructure made perfect sense to me. I realised that I should not be looking at enclaves as taken-for-granted bounded spaces, but as spaces that came into being through systems and practices of bordering.

As a result, I started to study infrastructures of security to understand the materialisation of enclaved spaces. A focus on infrastructure – as a networked material and socio-technical system – led me to understand how the fortified enclave didn't have to exist in perfect form as a walled, gated or enclosed space. Instead, walling, gating and enclosing happened in the coming together of various material, technological and social intersections. Walling, gating and enclosing were infrastructural. As a result, infrastructures became my object of inquiry, while also being my means for approaching my research. For my fieldwork, I took interactional encounters with enclaving infrastructures as my unit of analysis.

How Do You Do Fieldwork with Infrastructure?

For me, the first step was identifying the infrastructure itself. During my preliminary fieldwork, I had made extensive fieldnotes on my personal experiences of crossing into fortified enclaves. I had identified that signs restricting entry, CCTV cameras, security guards, security barriers, gates, graffiti, flags (political/religious) all made me 'feel' that the space I was entering was exclusive. Working together, these symbolic, material or human 'markers' of security operated as 'infrastructure'. Keeping these observations in mind, I selected three places which were 'enclaved' through different socio-material and discursive infrastructures communicating exclusivity and security. I then observed points of passage in each, for a prolonged period. I made notes on my own experiences of encountering these enclave infrastructures at entry points at different times of day – sometimes on my own, and at others, accompanied by different people (middle-class residents and non-residents, non-resident drivers, service workers, male and female, who worked inside). I made some trips by car, others on foot. I also observed some people entering on motorcycles and cycles.

Following each of these visits, I made notes on my interactions with the infrastructures. I made notes on how the infrastructures became 'visible' at sometimes, either when I (or my companion) slowed down intentionally in reactions to socio-material or discursive infrastructures. Or when I/we/they were slowed down by guards to be 'looked at' more carefully; or when I/we/they were completely stopped and questioned by the guards, who were an integral part of gating infrastructures. I carried out reflexive interviews with companions encountering these infrastructures with me. I also carried out interviews with others who encountered these infrastructures without me, as well as the guards who operated security gates and barriers.

What I found fascinating was how enclave entry points, as infrastructures, generated affect and subjectivity. The person standing by it, tasked with 'manning' it, gained power. The person encountering it, to move through it, either went on the defensive or tried to negotiate their power. But most significantly, the feelings and affects the infrastructures produced were also mediated through personal/individual subjectivities of those upholding and encountering the infrastructure. For example, I vividly remember my first experience of entering Askari III with my elderly Pashtun[1] taxi driver. Developed as a residence for retired army personnel, and managed and governed by the Cantonment Board (an institution linked to Pakistan's omnipotent armed forces), Askari III had a reputation of being one of the most 'secure' enclaves in Karachi. It was also the only walled and gated community in the city at that time.

As we got closer to the bright red and white striped security barriers at the gate, my nervousness intensified. It was my first visit to Askari III, and I was hoping we could enter the community without any connection to any resident on the inside. My driver was aware of my lack of connection, and assured me he'd get us through. The security barriers were open, but a visibly young, uniformed guard slowed the vehicle down, and asked the driver what business he had in the neighbourhood in an overly stern tone. The driver, clearly experienced in such questioning, answered with haughty confidence. 'I'm transporting Major Sahib's begum, he'll be upset that you've stopped our car', he said. He then rolled his window up. The young guard gingerly walked back over to the side and waved us through. The driver, who had clearly experienced many checkposts in his past, had used his age and his connection to power (my mythical husband, a major in the army) to negotiate his way in. Further along in my fieldwork, I learned how male, Pashtun domestic workers moving into such spaces on foot and on personal work would never have been allowed in without considerable checks and questioning. They may eventually be allowed in after having to give up their national identity card (NIC) to the guard on the gates for the duration of their visit, or perhaps after a phone call to the house they would be visiting for permission.

[1] Ethnic identity. Outside of the Federally Administered Tribal Area (FATA), Balochistan and the North-West Frontier Province (NWFP), where Pashtuns are from, the ethnic group is popularly racialised as being prone to violence. In Karachi especially, working-class Pashtuns are criminalised for their association with politico-criminal gangs, land mafias and the Taliban.

Figure 14.2 A street entrance into Clifton Block 7 (photograph by author, 2012).

The process of walling and gating as infrastructural went beyond the labour of the guard. Through my observations and interviews, I found how other objects and technologies such as CCTV cameras, street signs, graffiti, guns and uniforms (for guards) made a difference to access and perceptions of access. For example, Minhas,[2] a young Pashtun driver, explained how he used to be able to pass through Clifton Block 7 (an unwalled, privately enclosed neighbourhood, where access was restricted by guards at security barriers at different entry/exit points). This was because one of the security guards at the gate belonged to his village. The cultural association, even though they did not know each other personally, worked to erode the privately hired security guard's professional barriers. However, Minhas said this was no longer the case, and the guard had to 'do his job properly now', because the residents' association managing the 'enclaving' of Clifton Block 7 had set up CCTV cameras at entry/exit points to 'check the guards and surveil people entering the neighbourhood' (Figure 14.2).

[2]Name changed for anonymity.

Similarly, when visiting Sultanabad, a Pashtun ethnic enclave which was popularly considered as a 'no-go area', I realised that despite being physically 'open' and 'unwalled', neighbourhood space could easily be considered a type of 'fortified enclave'. The political graffiti on street walls, and religious and political flags hoisted up on multiple rooftops gave a strong sense of identity to Sultanabad. The enclave infrastructures, in this instance, were largely performative and discursive. I realised this when I asked a rickshaw driver to take me for a drive into Sultanabad, as far as the rickshaw could enter. The driver, a Mohajir (Shia), flat out refused, saying, 'this place is not safe for me, I'm not welcome here'. The political graffiti on the walls and the political and religious flags clearly communicated territorialisation of the space by the Pashtun nationalist Awami National Party and the Jamaat-e-Islami (JI), who were known to be violently opposed to the ethnic Mohajir Muttahida Qaumi Movement and Shia sect Muslims during periods of heightened political violence in Karachi. As a visibly middle-class Pakistani woman, I was clearly out of place in the neighbourhood. Given my gender and class position, and my political neutrality to neighbourhood-level politics, I felt less 'vulnerable' to potentially violent confrontation from local community members known to police the neighbourhood. Even though I was not explicitly questioned by local community watch groups who operated within the socio-politically homogeneous enclave, I did feel very uncomfortable. I was very 'noticeable' as a 'guest', as people would stop the local and ask questions about who I was and why I was visiting.

Using infrastructures as an object of inquiry and method allowed me to question the truth of the material form of a physical space. We know what a wall is, when we see it. It separates and divides. We know a gate is an entry way to a place. But can a wall exist without brick and mortar, and still be a wall? For whom is this possible and at what points/moments? Moreover, using infrastructure as method attuned me to the networked and relational properties of the different technologies, materials and performances that worked to produce exclusivity and security. It allowed me to consider otherwise inert materials to be both lively and agential. As the well-developed literature on the politics of infrastructure explains, infrastructure is about more than networked systems or objects. It is an articulation of urban inequality and struggles over power (Graham and Marvin,

2002; Graham, 2010; Amin, 2014; Angelo and Hentschel, 2015; Coutard and Rutherford, 2015; Simone, 2015).

In Conclusion

When we read other people's accounts of 'doing research', it feels very smooth and put together. However, doing research is a process. Things go wrong, you may not get the answers you expected. You might think your research is flawed. If this happens, take a step back and see what's in front of you. My biggest break came from my first 'problem'. The gated communities I had read about in literature seemed to be put together differently. I didn't find that these existed or operated in the same way in Karachi, a city where urban form and socio-political relations were markedly different from American, South American and African contexts. Could we call a place a gated community if it didn't have walls and gates? That's the kind of question that motivated me to do social research with walls and gates as 'infrastructures'. In using infrastructures as objects of inquiry and as method, I was able to study walls and gates as important social objects – objects that are otherwise largely ignored in social research.

References

Amin, A. (2014) 'Lively infrastructure', *Theory, Culture and Society*, 31(7-8), pp. 137–161.

Angelo, H. and Hentschel, C. (2015) 'Interactions with infrastructure as windows into social worlds: A method for critical urban studies: Introduction', *City*, 19(2-3), pp. 306–312.

Caldeira, T.P. (1996) 'Building up walls: The new pattern of spatial segregation in Sao Paulo', *International Social Science Journal*, 48(147), pp. 55–66.

Caldeira, T.P. (2020) *City of Walls*. Berkeley: University of California Press.

Coutard, O. and Rutherford, J. (eds.) (2015) *Beyond the Networked City: Infrastructure Reconfigurations and Urban Change in the North and South*. New York, London: Routledge.

Durington, M. (2009) 'Suburban fear, media and gated communities in Durban, South Africa', *Home Cultures*, 6(1), pp. 71–88.

Falzon, M.A. (2004) 'Paragons of lifestyle: Gated communities and the politics of space in Bombay', *City and Society*, 16(2), pp. 145–167.

Graham, S. (ed.) (2010) *Disrupted Cities: When Infrastructure Fails*. New York, London: Routledge.

Graham, S. and Kaker, S.A. (2014) 'Living the security city: Karachi's archipelago of enclaves', *Harvard Design Magazine*, 37, pp. 12-16.

Graham, S. and Marvin, S. (2002) *Splintering Urbanism: Networked Infrastructures, Technological Mobilities and the Urban Condition*. New York, London: Routledge.

Hook, D. and Vrdoljak, M. (2002) 'Gated communities, heterotopia and a "rights" of privilege: A "heterotopology" of the South African security-park', *Geoforum*, 33(2), pp. 195-219.

Simone, A. (2015) 'Afterword: Come on out, you're surrounded: The betweens of infrastructure', *City*, 19(2-3), pp. 375-383.

Star, S.L. and Ruhleder, K. (1996) 'Steps toward an ecology of infrastructure: Design and access for large information spaces', *Information Systems Research*, 7(1), pp. 111-134.

Webster, C., Glasze, G. and Frantz, K. (2002) 'The global spread of gated communities', *Environment and Planning B: Planning and Design*, 29(3), pp. 315-320.

15

How to do social research with... insider anxiety

Vik Loveday

Introduction

Recruiting participants can be a daunting process, especially for those embarking on qualitative research projects for the first time. Warnings of 'bias' abound (Chavez, 2008, p. 475), but convenience sampling can be a motivating factor in approaching existing contacts or focusing on familiar contexts; however, so-called 'insider research' is about much more than ease of access. What kinds of subjects draw us in and animate our curiosity? Our own social locations and lived experiences shape our academic interests and paths as researchers; our own trajectories influence how we perceive the world, how we seek to find out more about it and how we choose to tell stories about our findings. In this sense, insider research is closely intertwined with the autobiographical, but this also means it is often fraught with difficult, 'ugly feelings' (Ngai, 2005). Reflexivity is not about avoiding accusations of bias, but about considering how our social locations inform the decisions we make about which subjects to study, how we go about doing our research and how we analyse our findings. Crucially, being reflexive also involves acknowledging how our research makes us *feel*, and the implications of these feelings for the production of knowledge.

In preparing this chapter, I pondered what insights I had gleaned from several years of conducting 'insider' research. Each project has engendered a different type of 'insiderness': being perceived as being 'on the inside' sometimes happened as I worked with participants whom I already knew, or through an understanding that we had shared experiences; more broadly, insiderness has also been a quality assigned to me simply because

I am an academic writing about higher education from within the confines of a university. Interestingly, my insider positionality has also on occasion been elided with 'navel-gazing'; the presumption that looking to our own experience is somehow self-indulgent rather than 'proper' – i.e., objective – social research. However, despite the variety of projects, the unifying experience of insider research for me has been anxiety – much like the 'methodological "panic attacks"' described by Miled (2019, p. 1). Yet far from simply seeing this as an unfortunate side-effect of insider research, I want to suggest here that listening to our own concerns more closely can be both instructive and productive.

This chapter focuses on one dimension of insider positionality: the significance of 'insider anxiety'. Drawing on insights from research projects in which I have been emotionally invested myself, I show why it is important that we listen to our own anxieties and interrogate their wider implications. The chapter draws on three reflections to explore: how listening to our worries can enable us to recognise our ethical responsibilities as insider researchers more clearly; how paying attention to anxious feelings – rather than suppressing them – can help us take our bearings during the course of a project; and why an attention to the anxiety engendered by power dynamics within our research can show the wider sociological significance of anxiety as a relational phenomenon. However, first, I begin by interrogating the notion of the privileged 'insider'.

What Is 'Insider' Research?

Existing literature on insider research has explored some of the interrelated methodological and ethical pitfalls of 'insider' positionality, including 'role conflict' (Toy-Cronin, 2018), over-familiarity (Labaree, 2002) and managing existing relationships (Taylor, 2011). Yet while the idea of being an 'insider' might seem self-explanatory, reflecting on what it means to feel as if we are 'on the inside' has multiple connotations: it might refer to an aspect of our own biography, such as shared experiences, membership of a group/community or an affective state of belonging – 'feeling at home'; equally, insider status can be more of a temporary position – something fleeting based on a specific role, affiliation or relationship. Accordingly, what it means to be an insider should be viewed as fluid and malleable: rather than thinking of 'insiderness' as bounded, we can re-think the insider/outsider dichotomy as being more of a 'continuum' (Mercer, 2007).

It is also important to recognise the danger of making authoritative claims to insider status without acknowledging the operation of multiple overlapping forms of power – both within our research and wider society. Through an exploration of his own status as a Somali scholar researching Toronto's Somali community, Kusow (2003) argues that 'insider/outsider identities should not be seen as predetermined roles' (p. 598). He highlights how a number of factors may coalesce so that 'insider' positionality is contingent on the type of project we conceive, the context of our research and the specificities of our own identities and those of our participants. To attribute insider status on account of one facet of identity belies the complexity of what it means to be an insider; this is never simply about how we see ourselves, but is part of a dynamic and relational process in which we negotiate relationships with others that exist within wider social and historical contexts. Insider perceptions are never monolithic and there will always be more than one type of story in need of telling. Indeed, sociology as a discipline has historically foregrounded and celebrated particular kinds of storytellers whilst silencing others, so from the outset we might ask ourselves: 'For whom is this study worthy and relevant? And who says so?' (Smith, 2012, p. 172).

Research as an 'insider' involves being reflexive about our own role in knowledge production; results are not simply waiting to be 'found out' and research subjects do not exist to be 'mined' for data. The insider perspective eschews the 'God's eye view' (Haraway, 1989) of objectivity and instead values knowledge gained through lived experience. Keeping in mind the danger of reifying this experience rather than examining the discursive conditions in which experience is produced – what Scott (1991) describes as 'the evidence of experience' – the notion of being an 'insider' is premised upon there being value in drawing from insider epistemology, as black feminists have argued for decades (e.g., Collins, 2000).

Keeping these issues in mind, I turn now to three short reflections on 'insider anxiety'. Following Ahmed (2004, p. 4), I consider what anxiety as an emotion *does* when we embark on research projects that are close to our hearts and in which we are personally invested; I show how taking such an approach means understanding anxiety not simply as a side-effect of the research process, but as something intrinsic to the project of *doing* social research.

1 Anxiety and Representation

Perceived insider positionality can help to build trust and foster rapport (see Taylor, 2011); arguably, this complicates the notion of an authoritative researcher speaking *on behalf of* research subjects. This is particularly significant when we consider how marginalised groups have historically and socially been required to account for themselves by providing 'enforced narratives' (Steedman, 2000). Speaking from within a community can be viewed as a shift away from the theft of knowledge to a process of 'co-construction' (Sinha and Back, 2014): a shared endeavour whose results come into being *through* research interactions; as Back (2010, p. 8) notes though, this is a 'socially shaped account' as opposed to an act of exposing 'the authentic voice of truth'.

I want to begin by reflecting on the anxiety inherent in representation from *within*. Before embarking on an academic career, I worked for a grassroots university Widening Participation project, which aimed to support adults from marginalised backgrounds in accessing higher education. The opportunity arose to work as a research assistant on a small-scale sociology project, which aimed to explore perceptions of value and respect amongst working-class people. As an 'insider' on the education project, I became a kind of 'gatekeeper' for the lead researcher and was tasked with recruiting participants and facilitating a focus group. The majority of the men had experiences of incarceration and addiction; since I knew many of them personally, my involvement was akin to a guarantee that they would not be 'stitched up again' (see Skeggs and Loveday, 2012, p. 477).

Listening to participants' anxieties is instructive and might help us to understand reluctance or suspicion; yet paying attention to our own researcher anxieties is also telling. All researchers have a responsibility to ensure that representations are fair, but particular expectations are placed on researchers when they are positioned as 'insiders'. What does it mean to ask participants to give an account of themselves when as researchers we might wield influence and the power of representation? Occupying an 'insider' subject position might lessen the potential for exploitative researcher–researched relations, but – nonetheless – it does not eradicate the need to consider power dynamics inherent in the research process. While more generally I find it helpful to consider how I myself would want to see my life and words represented (even if the interlocutor expresses differing opinions to my own), as an insider, *too much* trust can also be a burden. Acknowledging how we feel about the process of representing others' lives – the worries, uncertainties, blurred boundaries – is a crucial aspect of researcher reflexivity: our anxieties tell us something about our own positionality, relationships and responsibilities, and this informs how we conduct our projects and represent our findings.

2 Taking Our Bearings from Anxiety

One of the perennial issues of being an insider is that personal investment can make it hard to find critical distance: how do we tease out tacit under-standings and begin to *see* the taken-for-granted when it is part of our own embodied experience? Labaree (2002) describes the process of 'going observationalist' as one way of gaining perspective – an active stepping back in order to reveal the unspoken and implicit assumptions we operate with as insiders. Our 'researcher' role is distinct from our role as a friend/ colleague, so setting boundaries is crucial in making this researcher posi-tionality clear (see Taylor, 2011).

Yet I want to flip the conundrum of being 'too close' by considering how proximity to a social problem can be generative, rather than restric-tive. In 2014, I found myself working on a fixed-term academic contract with no guarantee that my position would be renewed. The uncertainty had been causing me considerable anxiety, and I knew through regular conversations with other early career academics that this was a common experience. Yet at that time there was limited research on casualisation in universities or wider awareness of the issue. I decided to channel my own anxieties about employment precarity into a research project: a process of linking my 'private troubles' to 'public issues' as an act of the 'sociological imagination' (see Mills, 2000 [1959]).

Over 22 months, I conducted 100 interviews with 44 fixed-term academics. My contract was eventually made permanent during the course of the project, but my initial positioning as a precariously employed academic helped establish a connection with project participants who seemed keen to speak with a researcher in a similar position; follow-up interviews with most of the participants allowed me to track their changing circumstances but also to exchange stories. Following the end of the project, I received an email from one participant who had written their own blogpost on casualised work in universities after taking part in my project: 'Sending you something which was prompted by talking to you and thinking through those issues because of your study ... Thank you for helping me to see that this is not natural' (see Loveday, 2018, p. 157). Although I had avoided asking questions in the interviews that would merely chime with my views, the act of initially revealing my insider positionality and discussing my personal experience intervened in participants' perceptions about the nature of casualised work. To return to the idea of 'co-construction' (Sinha and Back, 2014), this was a collaborative venture: the project emerged from my own experience of acute anxiety and along the way I collected others' anxious stories as a way of making public a distressing – but often private – emotion.

3 Anxiety as a Diagnostic Tool

In this final reflection, I consider how power dynamics in the research process are infused with anxiety, but also how this can tell us something instructive about the wider context we are researching. As noted earlier, the ethical implications of researching marginalised communities are well-established, but power pervades our access to insider status and researchers may find that their expertise is not always legitimated. Writing on her experience as a Muslim scholar of colour, Ahmad (2003) describes the tensions inherent in occupying the position of an 'insider' researching British South Asian Muslim women's lives from within the confines of British academia. She notes how: 'there may be concerns that our "insider knowledge" is not "good enough knowledge". This may well be reflective of both the nominal status we occupy within academia and the legacy of anthropological traditions that defined us as research objects' (p. 56). Power dynamics do not simply exist between researchers and their participants, but also between researchers and their institutions; 'insider' research can trouble and disrupt taken-for-granted hegemonic norms about what constitutes valid research and who is seen as legitimately occupying the identity of 'researcher'.

I provide one final reflection here on a project I conducted in 2017 with senior university managers to consider how anxiety can act as a 'diagnostic tool'. Gunasekara (2007) describes the multiple identities a researcher occupies in any given project; these are both attributed by participants and self-ascribed, and can exist harmoniously or in tension with one another. In my own research, I felt this conflict acutely: I saw myself as a well-informed researcher of higher education and in some interviews, I was legitimated as an expert insider; yet in others, I was left in no doubt about the importance of my participants – and accordingly, the relative insignificance of my project. 'Insiderness', then, was not a concrete attribute but one that was variously granted or withheld; the denial of recognition followed me out of the interviews as my confidence slowly eroded and my anxieties swelled.

However, the context in which the project unfolded was crucial for understanding these ensuing anxieties: I had embarked on the research to understand how managers were making sense of wider policy changes occurring in the UK's higher education sector, but this happened to coincide with a period of unusual public scrutiny of university management after a well-publicised expenses scandal. I found myself interviewing a set of participants who were acutely anxious and perceived the sector as being 'under attack' (see Loveday, 2021). This anxiety then fed through into my project: several participants were clearly concerned about their anonymity, and I became increasingly worried about how I would represent their views from my comparatively junior position. Rather than viewing anxiety as an obstacle in the path of the project, I chose to focus on the sociological significance of my own anxieties and those of my participants, which were both situated and relational: anxiety was not only my individual burden, but symptomatic of a wider context in which universities have become subject to increasing scrutiny and where managers are responsibilised for their institutions' survival. Acknowledging anxiety – both our own and that of our participants – is an important part of researcher reflexivity, but examining the wider *significance* of those anxieties can also be sociologically instructive.

Conclusion: Listening to Our Anxieties

I began this chapter by noting that insider research is entwined with the autobiographical: by researching contexts in which we are ourselves implicated, we are taking personal risks. In her work on LGBTQ+ researchers, Nelson (2020) notes that researcher introspection 'can result in a range of emotions and outcomes including retraumatisation, euphoria, querying oneself and a change in researcher identity' (p. 911). In this sense, it is important to acknowledge the emotional toll of researching difficult subjects as 'insiders'. While considering the ethical implications of our research strategies for project participants is an integral part of the process of conducting social research, I have noticed over the years that students are sometimes quite blasé about the emotional effects of their research on themselves as *researchers*. I am not suggesting here that experiencing anxiety is positive, but it can be instructive: when 'ugly feelings' arise, we should *listen* to them. What do they tell us about the subject we are researching, or our relationships with participants? How are our own feelings implicated in the process of knowledge production? And how might we take better care of ourselves as researchers?

Anxiety is a common emotional experience for insiders, yet rather than only seeing it as a difficult side-effect, I have been arguing that paying attention to our anxious feelings can make us more attuned to our role as researchers in knowledge production. Each stage of the research process – from the conception of an initial idea to the messy process of *doing* social research, from making sense of our findings to deciding how we will present them – engenders worry. The trick is to listen to our anxieties and pay attention to what they are telling us.

Top Tips

Feeling anxious? Listen to your own concerns

- Consider exactly what is worrying you and why: pinpointing your concerns can help you address them more clearly.

- You have an ethical responsibility to your participants, but it is also important to look after yourself!

Consider the wider significance of your anxiety

- Rather than only seeing anxiety as an unpleasant side-effect, consider the wider sociological significance.

- Anxiety is both situated and relational; it does not exist in a vacuum. Your own anxieties might tell you something about wider power dynamics at play in your research context, so they should not simply be dismissed.

Don't be tempted to erase the messy parts of research!

- Acknowledging 'ugly feelings' is an important dimension of reflexivity.

- Writing your own anxious feelings into your project can help make your research design, methodology and findings more transparent.

References

Ahmad. F. (2003) 'Still in progress? Methodological dilemmas, tensions and contradictions in theorizing South Asian Muslim women', in Puwar, N. and Raghuram, P. (eds) *South Asian Women in the Diaspora*. Oxford: Berg, pp. 43–65.

Ahmed, S. (2004) *The Cultural Politics of Emotion*. Edinburgh: Edinburgh University Press.

Back, L. (2010) 'Broken devices and new opportunities: Re-imaging the tools of qualitative research', ESRC National Centre for Research Methods, NCRM Working Paper Series 09/10. Available at: https://eprints.ncrm.ac.uk/id/eprint/1579/1/0810_broken_devices_Back.pdf

Chavez, C. (2008) 'Conceptualizing from the inside: Advantages, complications, and demands on insider positionality', *The Qualitative Report*, 13(3), pp. 474–494.

Collins, P.H. (2000) *Black Feminist Thought: Knowledge, Consciousness, and Empowerment*. London: Routledge.

Gunasekara, C. (2007) 'Pivoting the centre: Reflections on undertaking qualitative interviewing in academia', *Qualitative Research*, 7(4), pp. 461–475.

Haraway, D. (1989) 'Situated knowledges: The science question in feminism and the privilege of partial perspective', *Feminist Studies*, 14(3), pp. 575–599.

Kusow, A. (2003) 'Beyond indigenous authenticity: Reflections on the insider/outsider debate', *Symbolic Interactionism*, 26(4), pp. 591–599.

Labaree, R. (2002) 'The risk of "going observationalist": Negotiating the hidden dilemmas of being an insider participant observer', *Qualitative Research*, 2(1), pp. 97–122.

Loveday, V. (2018) 'The neurotic academic: Anxiety, casualisation and governance in the neoliberalising university', *Journal of Cultural Economy*, 11(2), pp. 154–166.

Loveday, V. (2021) ' "Under attack": Responsibility, crisis and survival anxiety amongst manager-academics in UK universities', *The Sociological Review*, 69(5), pp. 903–919.

Mercer, J. (2007) 'The challenges of insider research in educational institutions: Wielding a double-edged sword and resolving delicate dilemmas', *Oxford Review of Education*, 33(1), pp. 1–17.

Miled, N. (2019) 'Muslim researcher researching Muslim youth: Reflexive notes on critical ethnography, positionality and representation', *Ethnography and Education*, 14(1), pp. 1–15.

Mills, C.W. (2000 [1959]) *The Sociological Imagination*. Oxford: Oxford University Press.

Nelson, R. (2020) 'Questioning identities/shifting identities: The impact of researching sex and gender on a researcher's LGBT+ identity', *Qualitative Research*, 20(6), pp. 910–926.

Ngai, S. (2005) *Ugly Feelings*. Cambridge, MA: Harvard University Press.

Scott, J.W. (1991) 'The evidence of experience', *Critical Inquiry*, 17(4), pp. 773–797,

Sinha, S. and Back, L. (2014) 'Making methods sociable: Dialogue, ethics and authorship in qualitative research', *Qualitative Research*, 14(4), pp. 473–487.

Skeggs, B. and Loveday, V. (2012) 'Struggles for value: Value practices, injustice, judgment, affect and the idea of class', *British Journal of Sociology*, 63(3), pp. 472–490.

Smith, L.T. (2012) *Decolonizing Methodologies: Research and Indigenous Peoples*. Second edition. London: Zed Books.

Steedman, C. (2000) 'Enforced narratives: Stories of another self', in Coslett, T., Lury, C. and Summerfield, P. (eds) *Feminism and Autobiography*. London, New York: Routledge, pp. 25–39.

Taylor, J. (2011) 'The intimate insider: Negotiating the ethics of friendship when doing insider research', *Qualitative Research*, 11(1), pp. 3–22.

Toy-Cronin, B. (2018) 'Ethical issues in insider-outsider research', in Iphofen, R. and Tolich, M. (eds) *SAGE Handbook of Qualitative Research Ethics*. London, Thousand Oaks, CA, New Delhi, Singapore: SAGE, pp. 455–468.

16

How to do social research with... knitting

Katherine Robinson

'I'm so lonely', says Rithika,[1] suddenly.
'Depressing, very depressing', murmurs Pearl, concurring.
'Where do you live?', asks Rithika. Pearl gives her address. Rithika doesn't know it and states hers, saying, 'it's near Tesco. Come round my house any time. Come and visit. It'll be nice.' Turning to me, she exclaims, 'You come too!'
'That'd be nice', I say.
'What's your name?' Rithika asks Pearl. Pearl says her name then spells it out as Rithika writes it in a little notebook. They swap their home phone numbers. I hover beside them, listening, watching.

Introduction

In the early summer of 2011, I started doing ethnographic research in a South London public library, and later that year, I joined its knitting group. Material from my time knitting with the group became a chapter in my PhD thesis and then a journal article (Robinson, 2020). Rather like a knitting project that refuses to get finished, over time I have continued to return to my experiences from joining in with the knitting group, and to carry on thinking with the voices and gestures of the women there.

I've opened the chapter with Rithika and Pearl's brief exchange as it seems to encapsulate some of the ideas I want to explore in this chapter. For these women, each of them living with grief and loneliness, the knitting group offered a cover story, a reason to be in the library, among others. In a quiet moment, at the end of the knitting session, having recognised their

[1]All names have been changed for anonymity.

shared vulnerabilities, their brief exchange marks an accelerated process of making contact with each other.

In this chapter, I suggest that the tactile gestures and physical closeness of knitting fostered forms of intimacy and connection among a group of people who were strangers to each other. I'm also thinking about the role that joining in with this group played at an early stage in my research, how it opened the door to a different way of participating in and understanding the daily life of the public library. In this way, the chapter is also a reflection on making a beginning to research. I want to ask, what concepts and preconceptions do we take with us into the field, and how do they shape what we start to look for? And what does joining in allow us to do, as researchers? I'll also explore joining in with the knitting group as an embodied research method, asking, how might we work with the unspoken, the gestural and the felt?

Getting Started

'I'm feeling very self-conscious today, flicking through a book and not able to see or overhear very much, and very unwilling to make any kind of notes.' ... 'Need a strategy for my behaviour. Need to improve my listening'.
(Fieldnotes, 2011)

When I started my library research I would travel to my fieldwork library several times a week, and spend a few hours sitting in different spots, observing what was happening around me. My presence in the library was ostensibly no different to that of anyone else, but bathed in an aura of self-consciousness, I felt like a spotlight accompanied my every move.

As my fieldnote shows, I found the state of heightened embodied awareness that was needed to 'make the familiar strange' (Neyland, 2008, p. 102), awkward and exhausting. These feelings are not unusual at the start of ethnographic fieldwork, as Allaine Cerwonka and Liisa Malkki also acknowledge (2007, pp. 81, 87). Fieldwork can feel overwhelming as its mundanity and open-endedness butt up against the weight of hopefulness and expectation – an exhausting combination.

Moreover, the anxieties, loss and disappointments that are constitutive of fieldwork experiences, as Ruth Behar observes in her introduction to *The Vulnerable Observer* (1996, p. 3), are smoothed away in published ethnographic work. In contrast, in their book, Cerwonka and Malkki share an extensive collection of fieldnotes, draft reflections and emails gathered as Cerwonka navigated entry to her fieldsite during her PhD and started to carry out her research. Their text, rich with the generally invisible and unacknowledged 'backstage' material of ethnographic research and its attendant worries became an important resource for me as I began my own research.

Looking for Concepts

Having read a raft of academic work which positioned public space as a forum for civic encounter (Amin, 2002; Sennett, 2002; Watson, 2006; Neal *et al.*, 2015), I spent the early weeks of my library fieldwork watching out for 'encounter' which I imagined as people falling into conversation with each other, perhaps even debating with each other as the public agora worked its magic.

But these encounters didn't appear to be happening. I started to recognise a set of regular library users, but whether they were browsing the crime fiction shelves, sitting at a table with a book in front of them or using one of the computers, they seemed to keep themselves to themselves. My early observations seemed rather to reflect how, in the library, people 'weave an individual net around themselves that does not invite communication with others' (Aabø and Audunson, 2012, p. 143). I was left feeling anxious.

My expectation of recognising 'encounter' from what I'd read reflects a desire to find 'the answers' to what we're looking for in academic texts, what Les Back calls bibliophilia (2007, p. 175). Based on what I had been reading, I had imagined encounter as something spirited and obvious, as vocal, even voluble, and I found it hard to reconcile this with the quiet and individualised behaviour I observed in the library.

I can see now how my anxiety and self-consciousness in my role of observer perhaps inhibited me from recognising the potential in the things I did see. For instance, one Friday morning, a few weeks after I had begun fieldwork, I came across Sarah, one of the librarians, sitting with a group of women in the library's front space by the large window. I had inadvertently come across the inaugural session of the knitting group. I sat nearby, listening in. I was disappointed with the chat: 'the talk is all technical, knitting-related,' I wrote in my fieldnotes later, dejectedly.

But perhaps I needed a bit of distance. During fieldwork there is a fundamental and sometimes uneasy gap between what is happening in the moment and what this might turn into eventually. In this way, the experience of fieldwork might even be analogous to knitting:

> it always looks wrong
> At the place you work
> the yarn stretched between
> Needles coming together,
> The pattern pulled...

(Sonnenschein, 2009, p. 129)

The process of ethnographic research is to live with the partiality of the close-up while also creating space through which to absorb a bigger picture; it's a question of perspective, zooming in and out. I needed time to tune in to the knitting group, which helped me to absorb and understand what was happening.

Figure 16.1 Working from the perspective of knitting ('knit blanket' by functoruser is licensed under CC BY 2.0. www.flickr.com/photos/functoruser/2272444834/)

I can see now how joining the knitting group helped me to re-assess my understanding of encounter and how it manifested in the library. As Helen Wilson observes, 'encounter' is complex and multi-faceted (2017). As I learned to sit with the knitting group's polite conversation and technical chat that I had been quick to dismiss at first, I started to appreciate how these exchanges created a space of common ground that paved the way to more intimate and touching encounters between some members of the group.

Joining In and Playing Along

Joining in with the knitting group and other library activities marked a shift in my relationship with the library and my research. My previously awkward and self-conscious visits became purposeful, anchored by the legitimating rhythms of the library's activity schedule. As I chatted with others at the session, I realised that they had also experienced joining in as giving legitimacy to their presence in the library. Pearl said she came to the knitting group because she needed a reason to get out of the house; Smita said that she had found the library boring before she had joined the knitting group. For older women living with loneliness, attending the fortnightly sessions allowed them to meet others in a dignified and purposeful way.

Joining in as a research method is common in ethnomusicology, where, during fieldwork, researchers learn an instrument or join in with musical rehearsals and performances. In her research on classical music and social class, Anna Bull writes how her musical training gave her 'insider status' in her fieldsite, giving her the skills and experience to shape her role, whether as orchestral player, accompanist or observer (2019, p. xxv). The capacity to join in thus depends both on the research context and the positionality of the researcher. I had learned to knit as a child and while I remained a beginner, this was enough for me to feel I could join in with the group. I knitted very slowly, trying to listen and be attentive to what was going on around me. After a while, I realised that several women regularly dropped in on the group without ever knitting; they would sit and join in with the chat and look through the knitting books and patterns on the table, playing along. The knitting group was like a social umbrella that sheltered different forms of participation. This openness allowed me to play along too.

Requiring my 'embodied engagement and presence' (Thanem and Knights, 2019, p. 47), encountering the knitting group marked a turning point in my fieldwork. Joining in shifted me out of the role of self-conscious observer and allowed me to thread myself into the group as a participant. (This is not to give the impression that I slid smoothly from one methodological pole to another; as Behar notes, participant observation is inherently an oxymoron [1996, p. 5]; always an awkward mode of encounter). In her research, Emma Jackson found that joining the bowling league in her fieldsite 'offered insights ... into bowling as a practice of belonging that works back on the body of the bowler' (2020, p. 522). Knitting, while so different to bowling, also involves a learned repertoire of physical movements and patterned gestures. These legible rhythms made the knitting group approachable for people to join because they knew what to expect. Participating in the group, I perceived how the shared rhythms and embodied movements of knitting became the foundation for gestures of closeness and moments of understanding between the people there.

Embodiment – Hands, Gestures, Touching

Bernice, Ursula, Shauna and I gather around the table, leaning over to look at the moss stitch pattern on a scarf. Ursula and Shauna explain how to 'read' the stitches, pointing out which is a purl and which is a knit. 'There's the bump! Now the bump's on the other side', Shauna says, flipping the piece over to show us.

Moments like these often happened during the knitting sessions. The knitting was gently stretched out on the table, turned over and inside out to extract information about its construction. We would lean in close to each other, peering closely at the knots and loops we'd made and deciphering their patterns. Engagement with the materiality of knitting was embodied and collective; we passed our knitting among ourselves for everyone to examine and admire. People turned towards each other or stood behind each other to closely watch a new technique. The more expert knitters would take the knitting out of a person's hands to demonstrate a new stitch and would sometimes even place their hands on top of someone else's to guide their movements. Touching each other's knitting, touching each other's hands, these tactile gestures of showing and sharing are embedded into knitting.

How might we think about touch sociologically? Tuning in to touch and gesture is to move away from methodological standbys such as the interview (Back, 2012) and the predominance of the visual, to engage with forms of sociological knowing that are sensory, experiential and embodied (Bull, 2019). Gabriel Josipovici understands touch as perceiving each other through our embodied selves (1996, p. 4), a sense of encounter with the materiality of experience that goes beyond words.

Practically, what might we perceive when we attend to touch? In their research on a knitting group in a Canadian public library, Elena Prigoda and Pamela McKenzie observed knitters' hands (2007, p. 97), making connections between knitting's gestures and the flow of conversation in the group. As the weeks went by, and my piece of knitting gradually grew longer, I learned to listen in different ways (Back, 2007), and not just to the chat, trying to pay attention to what was unspoken, registering how knitting's gestures of touch and proximity created an affective atmosphere. Sitting so close our elbows touched, soothed by the warmth of the room and the repeated rhythms of knitting, we were lulled into a sense of connection. In this space of quiet trust and tacit companionship that was held together by knitting, people started to open up, sharing intimate hints of grief and vulnerability (Robinson, 2020).

Touch as Tactfulness

In thinking closely with these tactile and haptic experiences of knitting and their affective resonance, I've found myself reflecting on the role played by tactfulness in these encounters. Understood as a sense of perception that is likened to touch (Josipovici, 1996, pp. 140–141), I started to recognise tactfulness in how people in the knitting sessions responded to the intimations of vulnerability that occurred there. After the final knitting session I attended, I was hanging around in the room, which had gradually emptied of people, apart from Pearl and Rithika. Pearl was standing, ready to go, but then sat down again near Rithika, who was still looking through knitting patterns and commenting on them, turning the pages towards us so we could see. Earlier on in the session, she had spoken briefly about being lonely since her husband had passed away the previous year. It became obvious to us both that Rithika was playing for time, trying to keep us in the room.

'Don't sit down here by yourself' said Pearl, taking charge of the situation, 'come upstairs'. Pearl's social tactfulness, rooted in her being, as she put it, 'accustomed to the crowd' and practised over her lifelong commitment to church (Robinson, 2020, p. 564) bridged us out of this vulnerable moment. Back upstairs, as I said goodbye, Rithika took my hand and briefly pressed her lips to the back of it. Years later, her gesture, with its mixture of confidence and trusting vulnerability, still resonates with me. And now, from the vantage point of a time in which the vestiges of social distancing are still retained in institutional settings, when I think back to Rithika's mouth touching the back of my hand, this gesture seems almost unimaginable. It's not only this gesture but also the closeness of our bodies as we knitted together during these sessions – such proximity among strangers now seems like an experience from another world. And I wonder how, as researchers, we might be attentive to touching and tactful gestures in spaces of distanced sociality in the 'new ordinary' of Covid-19 (Sheldon, 2021). Perhaps in a situation where touch is not possible, its relation, tact, comes to the fore; you don't have to touch to be moved.

Conclusion: Returning to Encounter

In this chapter I've shown how doing sociology with knitting presents a challenge to some of our assumptions of what doing research can look, sound and feel like. Joining in with the knitting group became my legitimating cover story for being in the library, helping me to shift to a more participatory role in my fieldwork. It also shifted my understanding of encounter in this social space as, through knitting together with others, I started to work towards an understanding of encounter that threaded together the material practices and embodied gestures of knitting.

Knitting's tactile gestures and embodied proximity allowed people who remained strangers to each other to share moments of connection and vulnerability. I have shown how paying attention to quiet forms of closeness and tacit companionship, to movements and gestures and tactful moments, generates a more textured understanding of the encounters that were made possible through the library's knitting group.

References

Aabø, S. and Audunson, R. (2012) 'Use of library space and the library as place', *Library and Information Science Research*, 34, pp. 138–149.

Amin, A. (2002) 'Ethnicity and the multicultural city: Living with diversity', *Environment and Planning A*, 34(6), pp. 959–980.

Back, L. (2007) *The Art of Listening*. London: Berg.

Back, L. (2012) 'Tape recorder', in Lury, C. and Wakeford, N. (eds) *Inventive Methods: The Happening of the Social*. London: Routledge, pp. 245–260.

Behar, R. (1996) *The Vulnerable Observer: Anthropology That Breaks Your Heart*. Boston, MA: Beacon Press.

Bull, A. (2019) *Class, Control and Classical Music*. Oxford: Oxford University Press.

Cerwonka, A. and Malkki, L. (2007) *Improvising Theory: Process and Temporality in Ethnographic Fieldwork*. Chicago, IL: University of Chicago Press.

Jackson, E. (2020) 'Bowling together? Practices of belonging and becoming in a London ten-pin bowling league', *Sociology*, 54(3), pp. 518–533.

Josipovici, G. (1996) *Touch*. New Haven, CT, London: Yale University Press.

Neal, S., Bennett, K., Jones, H., Cochrane, A. and Mohan, G. (2015) 'Multiculture and public parks: Researching super diversity and attachment in public green space', *Population, Space and Place* 21(5), pp. 463–475.

Neyland, D. (2008) *Organizational Ethnography*. London: Sage.

Prigoda, E. and McKenzie, P. (2007) 'Purls of wisdom: A collectivist study of human information behavior in a public library knitting group', *Journal of Documentation*, 63(1), pp. 90–114.

Robinson, K. (2020) 'Everyday multiculturalism in the public library: Taking knitting together seriously', *Sociology*, 54(3), pp. 556–572.

Sennett, R. (2002) *The Fall of Public Man*. London: Penguin.

Sheldon, R. (2021) 'A new normal? The inordinate ordinary of COVID times', *Journal of Psychosocial Studies*, 14(3), pp. 173–186.

Sonnenschein, D. (2009) 'Knitting', *Feminist Studies*, 35(1), pp. 128–130.

Thanem, T. and Knights, D. (2019) *Embodied Research Methods*. London: Sage.

Watson, S. (2006) *City Publics: The (Dis)enchantments of Urban Encounters*. London: Routledge.

Wilson, H. (2017) 'On geography and encounter: Bodies, borders and difference', *Progress in Human Geography*, 41(4), pp. 451–471.

17

How to do social research with... music

Les Back

Sociologists are often secret musicians. These musical lives shape how social researchers think, even if it is unacknowledged. It is true of myself because for most of my career as a researcher and teacher, I have had a parallel life as a journeyman guitarist performing in clubs and bars and often turning up to give weekend keynote lectures bleary-eyed after a late night travelling back from a far-off gig. In this chapter I want to explore the relationship between sociological craft and music making and the part that music has played in shaping the ideas of sociologists in often unacknowledged ways.

My experience is far from exceptional and the story of musical sociologists goes all the way back to W.E.B. Du Bois and Max Weber in the 19th century – musical life was always woven into their sociological thinking. These founding figures had strong attachments to music and both men had fine singing voices. As biographer David Levering Lewis (1993) comments, 'Willie' Du Bois, as he was known during his student days at Fisk University, was an enthusiastic member of the student organisations, acting as literary editor of its magazine and a regular public speaker at its events and debates. He was also a member of the Fisk Mozart Society. The mastery of the highest forms of music Europe had to offer the young African American were in many respects a statement of African Americans' equal faculty and capacity for the mastery of the musical canon from Mozart to Wagner. Studying in Berlin between 1892 and 1894, Du Bois deepened his appreciation of European music and particularly Schubert's symphonies, operas by Weber and Wagner and also the German tradition of folk music (Beck, 1996).

Born in Great Barrington, Massachusetts, it was when he moved to the South in the 1880s that 'Willie' Du Bois encountered the songs that truly carried the full historical load of slave experience. In the second of his biographies, he wrote:

I heard the Negro folksong first in Great Barrington, sung by the Hampton Singers. But that was second-hand, sung by youth who never knew slavery. I now heard the Negro songs by those who made them in the land of their American birth.

(Du Bois, 1968, p. 120)

He taught in a country school as a student and he attended church. From across the field, he heard 'a rhythmic cadence of song – soft thrilling, powerful, that swelled and died sorrowfully in our ears'. As he approached the 'little plain church perched aloft', he saw the intensity and excitement of the congregation: 'A sort of suppressed terror hung in the air and seemed to seize them – a Pythian madness, a demonic possession, that lent terrible reality to song and word' (Du Bois, 1968, p. 120).

That 'terrible reality' was most manifested in the embodied medium of music, first through spirituals and Jubilee singers but also reverberating through the whole history of black popular song as it changes and takes on new forms. The songs, he wrote, are the 'sifting of centuries' with melodies 'more ancient than the words' (Du Bois, 1989 [1903], p. 180). Du Bois' use of music comes from more than just a listener's appreciation. He minimises his musical skill in his classic *The Souls of Black Folk* (1989 [1903]) when he writes with, I would argue, false humility: 'I know little of music and can say nothing in technical phrase...' (Du Bois, 1989 [1903], p. 179). As a singer, who sang in choirs and understood harmony and could read and write musical notation, he comes to understand the embodied social aspect of musical expression and is able to link this to the affordances of slave song and struggle for freedom. This is why he is able to write in a few lines this deep historic insight: 'I know that these songs are the articulate message of the slave to the world' (Du Bois, 1989 [1903], p. 179).

Weber's concerns with music were very different from those of Du Bois. Contrary to Weber's austere sociological image, he was a profoundly musical person. He sang the songs he learned in patriotic male choirs of his youth in Germany with his brother Richard, with whom he had a torrid sibling rivalry, right up to the end of his life. For him the history of Western music is one of limiting rationalisation. The emergence of the piano and keyboard harmony and its incorporation into domestic bourgeois life constrained rather than expanded the human faculty for making and hearing music. The emergence of the piano as the pre-eminent Western bourgeois instrument limits rather than extends the capacity for hearing. The technological developments that led to this rationalisation included everything from the construction of musical instruments and their tuning, to the 12-note scale and the emergence of written musical notation. Always the comparative and historical thinker, Weber felt by contrast that other human cultures display a much higher fidelity of hearing than those in the West.

Weber could play the piano, although during the hard financial times his pianos were often sold and there were long periods when he did not own one. In 1911 he bought a Steinway piano for his wife Marianne as a birthday present. In his intimately revealing biography, Joachim Radkau (2009) recounts a story of someone who visited Weber's home around this time. When asked to give an impromptu lecture about his sociological treatise on European music he surprised the visitors by sitting at the piano and demonstrating his argument about theory and harmony by playing for them. The visitors, Radkau writes, were 'greatly surprised' and left thinking that the great sociologist had 'never done anything more phenomenal' (Radkau, 2009, p. 367). Radkau argues that his musical life was also linked to his complex emotional relationships and erotic life, arguing that it was through his extra-marital relationship with pianist and muse Mina Tobler that Weber developed an interest in writing a historical sociology of music. His long essay *The Rational and Social Foundations of Music* was written in 1911, but it didn't appear in German until a decade later in 1921 (Weber, 1958 [1921]).

Weber's emphasis on the relationship between technology and music set the course for the study of music throughout the 20th century. It was in turn picked up by the Frankfurt School Marxists, most prominently in Theodor Adorno's writing. Adorno was himself an accomplished pianist and composer. As a young person, Adorno even dreamed of being a professional musician (Müller-Doohm, 2005, p. 38). He famously argued that the commodification of music exacerbated this rationalisation or what Adorno referred to as standardisation. This for him produces a 'regression of listening' (Adorno, 1991, pp. 40–41) that results not only in aesthetic and sonic limits, but also produces a moronic conformity amongst the masses and a masochistic submission to capitalism (Adorno, 1989/1990 [1936]).

What is interesting here is that both of these sociological analyses of Western music would not have possible without Weber and Adorno being trained musicians. Their critique is only possible because they understand how the organisation of music works.

There are many examples of contemporary musical social researchers too and almost every social science department has a hidden and unformed band of guitarists, trumpeters, DJs or banjo players. I would suggest this relationship with music is the backdrop or soundtrack to their sociological imaginations, even if they no longer play their instruments. For example, Professor Evelyn Ruppert is an authority on 'Big Data' and an actor–network theorist (Isin and Ruppert, 2015). It is less known that Evelyn, who grew up in Toronto, Canada, is also a jazz trumpeter (although now she rarely plays). 'For the last thirty years I have had different fits and starts to return and it somehow never quite happens' she commented in the summer of 2018 (Evelyn Ruppert, personal communication, 21 August). And yet her experience of learning to play music has had a deep effect on her life. She picked up the trumpet because 'I wanted to be heard ... I wanted that loud shiny thing ... it was a gender thing'. She grew up in a large working-class family, had a difficult home life and in a way the trumpet was her way of being noticed and of 'getting through school'. Playing in jazz orchestras helped her understand how the music was enacted through all the elements interacting, from the instruments to the social dynamics of feeling together, tuning to other people and improvisation when playing music together. There were also injustices and inequities in this world as the boys broke off to form smaller bands and develop their capacity.

When we met to talk about her life in music in 2018, she brought a prop to the interview (see Figure 17.1). Evelyn explained:

My prop is a sock which comes from my High School years ... that's like thirty years ago. And it was always in my trumpet case and I used to shine my trumpet with it. And it has lots of stitches in it and inside is my pride and joy my trumpet, which has a custom-made mouthpiece. Which is gold plated.

(Personal communication, 21 August 2018)

For trumpet players, the mouthpiece is the most precious part of the instrument and – as in Evelyn's case – it is often adapted to the particular

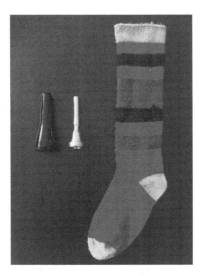

Figure 17.1 Evelyn's mouthpiece and trumpet sock.

needs of its player. Evelyn's mouthpiece was gold-plated as a special birthday gift to her by her partner.

Evelyn comments that playing music taught her how social differences can be bridged through making music together and being 'in tune' with others (see also Schütz, 1951). But perhaps the most significant lesson that Evelyn's trumpet offers is as a reminder that material things matter in the social world. Evelyn explains:

It's not just the material [quality] ... it's easy to say and it's really lovely, I love the material and I spent hours shining that thing and cleaning it in the bathtub and taking it apart and re-assembling, oiling and there is that kind of care of it too and it['s] almost like it's a friend that you take care [of] ... So there's that – the object matters immensely but it is what comes out that is between you and the object that I feel is important. The sound, which is the two of you, you know together, would be impossible for either to exist. That I think you know is amazing. That I think is maybe a good metaphor for what many of us write about as the more-than-human relations we have [–] that one could not produce that without the more-than-human relation. And there is that agency of the trumpet.

(Personal communication, 21 August 2018)

Evelyn also talked about the pressures on her time from her academic job and also the broader vocation of intellectual work that make it hard to dedicate the time needed to practise her instrument. The trumpet in her flat is a reminder of these limitations. She captures this beautifully when she personifies her trumpet speaking to her from its stand, issuing her a challenge:

'Are you [going to play me]? Seriously...? Ok come on ... are you gonna really? Or, are you just gonna play with this?' [Laughing] 'Are you serious or not? Or are you going just [to] spend five minutes and put me away again? Or are you really serious[ly] going to re-establish this relationship because relationships are work?'
(Personal communication, 21 August 2018)

I love the idea of the trumpet talking back to her and questioning her commitment and seriousness. The time pressures of academic life make it harder to do the embodied work – in the case of the trumpet, strengthening the embouchure and practising scales – to be an active musician. Yet the lessons Evelyn has learned from music – from tuning social life to the relationship between the human and material world – endure as a resource for her thinking. The trumpet on the stand in her flat symbolises this lesson, whether or not she actually picks it up and holds it to her lips to play.

When I reflect on my own life, I can see that my own involvement in music making has been a kind of hinterland for my sociological thinking, teaching and writing. I was a member of Earl Green's touring band for over ten years (2003–2013). Earl was Britain's first black British blues singer and garnered many awards and we played hundreds of gigs together from London clubs to international festivals. That experience informed my research and teaching interests in so many ways. Now I use music often at the beginning of a lecture to set the key and mood of the session. I also get students to make 'playlists' as a way of engaging them, including choosing 'alternative national anthems' or their own 'personal protest songs'. More than this, I was alongside Earl through his struggle with Alzheimer's disease that ultimately forced him to retire from music. Through that decade I drove Earl to gigs and we spent hours travelling together. Towards the end, Earl would be lost in the fog of his illness and be unable to communicate or speak to the fans who would want to talk to him. Promoters would be astonished by the fact that I could often anticipate what he was trying to say from the fragmented and sometimes incoherent things he said. This was because we had spent so many late-night drives travelling together on the road and I had heard many of his stories before. The reason why I mention this here

Figure 17.2 Earl Green performing at The Bronte Blues Club, Laycock, Yorkshire (photograph by John Ashton).

is because I witnessed first-hand the restorative and therapeutic power of music for people suffering from Alzheimer's. Even when Earl couldn't speak, the sound of the band would often restore him to himself and he could go to the microphone and sing and the lyrics would come back to him. This experience led me to design and teach an undergraduate course on 'Why Music Matters for Sociology' that includes sessions on the therapeutic power of music to treat people with dementia or Alzheimer's or anxiety or pain.

The musical life of sociologists offers, then, *an interpretative device* or practical form of insight. I think this is true of W.E.B. Du Bois' reading of the politics of slave song as well as Max Weber's insight into the constraints of modern rationalisation. Du Bois, Weber and Adorno are not isolated cases and I could have chosen many other examples ranging from Roland Barthes and cultural theorist Stuart Hall who both played the piano. When you start to look, music seems everywhere in the sociological tradition although there are times where caution is needed. In July 1947, C. Wright Mills wrote a letter to his friend Dwight Macdonald from a ranch in Sutcliffe, Nevada where he was staying temporarily. Mills told his friend cheerfully: 'I am playing the guitar now, about an hour a day in the sun, with the lizards running around on the rocks' (Mills and Mills, 2000, p. 108). Reading this letter provoked fantasies of discovering that Wright Mills had a secret guitar-toting life. However, when I asked his daughter Kate Mills about it via email she was surprised and told me no one in the family had ever heard him play although he did play the harmonica as a boy (Kathryn Mills, personal communication, 18 July 2018). So, it is important not to jump to conclusions and be cautiously precise over the exact nature of the relationship between musical and research craft.

I am not suggesting that being a musician is the only way to understand society better. There are other kinds of practices that can offer a productive hinterland to the craft, be it theatre, sport or art. Part of our opportunity now is to do social research *with* these other crafts. I have argued that that opportunity has been there all along. The pressure placed on academics – particularly young scholars – from the twin forces of specialisation and professionalisation bear down on these possibilities. Do we have time for this, they might justifiably ask? The pressures are considerable as Evelyn Ruppert pointed out. Satisfying campus priorities to teach, write and publish books means we certainly do not have the time to put in enough practice time. But like Evelyn's trumpet that sits silently in her flat, an unplayed instrument can continue to act as a resource for thinking differently. The power of music is that it alerts us to the inchoate, not-yet or utopian movements of imagination. Music also has the power to evoke not only *what is* but also *what might have been*.

To end, compared to the professional instrumentalism and status obsession that pervades academia, music is a reminder of the things that inspired us to think, research and write in the first place. Many social researchers I have spoken to use music as a spur to be brave and bold in their work, allowing them to find new forms and modes for research itself. Living with music here is inextricably linked to keeping their imaginations alert and attentive to the unfolding nature of society. In a time when universities around the globe are often under attack – be it from political pressure, auditing of academic worth or ever-increasing commercialisation – thinking with music is also a reminder to let our ears tingle with the things that really matter.

References

Adorno, T. (1989/1990 [1936]) 'On jazz', *Discourse*, 12(1), pp. 45-69.

Adorno, T. (1991) *The Culture Industry*. London: Routledge.

Beck, H. (1996) 'W.E.B. Du Bois as a study abroad student in Germany, 1892-1894', *Frontiers: The Interdisciplinary Journal of Study Abroad*, 2(1), pp. 45-69.

Du Bois, W.E.B. (1968) *The Autobiography of W.E.B. Du Bois: A Soliloquy on Viewing My Life from the Last Decade of Its First Century*. New York: International.

Du Bois, W.E.B. (1989 [1903]) *The Souls of Black Folk*. New York: Bantam Books.

Isin, E. and Ruppert, E. (2015) *Being Digital Citizens*. London: Rowman & Littlefield International.

Lewis, David L. (1993) *W.E.B. Du Bois: Biography of a Race (1868-1919)*. New York: Henry Holt and Company.

Mills, K. and Mills, P. (eds) (2000) *C. Wright Mills: Letters and Autobiographical Writings*, Berkley, Los Angeles, London: University of California Press.

Müller-Doohm, S. (2005) *Adorno: A Biography*. Cambridge: Polity Press.

Radkau, J. (2009) *Max Weber: A Biography*. Cambridge: Polity Press.

Schütz, A. (1951) 'Making music together – a study in social relationship', *Social Research*, 18(1), pp. 76-97.

Weber, M. (1958 [1921]) *The Rational and Social Foundations of Music*. Carbondale: Southern Illinois University Press.

18

How to do social research with... outrageous propositions

Monica Greco

I became interested in outrageous propositions as methodological devices while researching the history of psychosomatic medicine for my doctorate. Working in the tradition of Michel Foucault, my aim in turning to the past was not to contribute to the history of medicine as such, but rather to 'step outside' the present – that is, to find a vantage point from which I might learn to think critically about health, illness and contemporary forms of medical knowledge. The history of psychosomatics did not disappoint: I soon started to come across ideas that seemed outlandish from today's perspective, and had duly been relegated to the status of historical curiosities or obsolete beliefs. Chief among these were the ideas of the German physician Georg Groddeck (1866–1934). In this chapter I will share what I learned from my encounter with the lectures he delivered to patients at his Marienhöhe clinic in Baden-Baden between 1916 and 1919, among his other writings.

An encounter with Groddeck raises important methodological questions for any researcher who is interested in understanding knowledge practices in contemporary society and the political struggles associated with them. The first question might be: why take any notice of Groddeck at all? As we shall see, his ideas and clinical methods appear not just implausible but ethically questionable from a 21st-century perspective. Born into a prominent family of the German upper bourgeoisie, Groddeck generally enjoyed a life of privilege. At first glance he might therefore be considered quintessentially 'male, pale and stale', not the sort of figure whose history needs re-discovering or re-claiming. Indeed, dwelling on the importance of Groddeck's ideas carries a certain risk for a contemporary researcher – of losing credibility by association. It is certainly safer to ignore his work altogether or to approach it, as others have done, as something firmly lodged in the past, of no relevance for the present. Such responses should be expected and respected, for they are entirely reasonable. And yet ... we risk missing out on significant insights through such hasty dismissals, despite their reasonableness.

The concept of *outrageous proposition* allows us simultaneously to acknowledge the disturbing character of a set of ideas or practices, and to distil their specific value for the present as tools for critical reflection, and for developing a sociological imagination of possible alternatives. This double function is reflected in the ambiguous character of the word *outrageous*. Etymologically, *outrageous* derives from the Latin *ultra*, literally meaning 'what goes beyond'. To say that something is *outrageous* conveys the sense that it exceeds what is usual, expected or appropriate, whether in a negative sense (e.g., 'wildly improbable', 'shocking and morally unacceptable') or a positive one (e.g., 'bold and unusual'). While the negative connotations of an outrageous proposition can be obvious enough, we can use the feelings aroused by such propositions to interrogate the assumptions that tacitly inform our research, and to learn to think beyond them.

Groddeck's Outrageous Propositions

In his writings and in his clinical practice, Georg Groddeck rejoiced in provocation. An example is his contention that '[i]t is always better to produce an interesting disease than a mediocre painting' (1988, p. 540). Aside from comparing diseases to works of art, in 1918 he named his clinic's new house magazine *Satanarium* (a pun on 'sanatorium'), inviting his patients to think of the clinic as a sort of hell: for hell, he claimed, was the only place where a man [*sic*] could scream his agony 'unimpeded, without shame or reserve' (1992, p. 15). Groddeck encouraged his patients to think of their illness as atonement for their criminal or sinful impulses. He acknowledged that they, the patients, might disagree with his pronouncements – but he instructed them not to disagree. As he put it,

You must make an effort to believe, you must silence all doubts in yourselves. It makes no sense to refute what I say through reasonable arguments. It is easy to find this or that false, but that is not the point of the exercise. You have come here to be helped. What I deliver is a remedy, a medication

(Groddeck, 1987, p. 95)

Groddeck was aware that, even in his day, his propositions sounded outrageous: they clashed with what his patients expected of a doctor and were at odds with modern medical science, which was at its most advanced in Germany at the time. Modern scientific medicine is premised on a clear separation between (objective) facts and (subjective) values, and on the notion that disease is a natural and biological phenomenon of no intrinsic moral or aesthetic significance. Groddeck's provocations playfully unhinged and re-shuffled the customary relations between nature and culture, medical facts and aesthetic or moral values, and in so doing they worked their healing magic. By all accounts he was highly sought after as a doctor, known for his 'astonishing success with patients suffering from chronic symptoms long since abandoned as non-curable by others' (M.C., 1951, p. 6).

A proposition is not a matter of fact. A proposition announces something that *might be*. It refers to something whose mode of existence is of the order of potentiality rather than actuality. In grammar this is expressed by the *subjunctive* mood of verbs (e.g., something *might be* the case) as distinct from the *indicative* mood (e.g., something *is* the case). The philosopher Alfred North Whitehead described propositions as 'lures' for feeling (1978, p. 263), and this is well illustrated in Groddeck's practice. Groddeck's propositions did not state facts but – in a very specific context, to which we shall return – they *lured* his patients to imagine something strange, something that went beyond their understanding of their illness as a matter of fact. He suggested not simply that they might have produced their disease, but that they might take some pride in having produced an interesting disease, something of greater value than a mediocre painting.

An outrageous proposition unsettles expectations, often in unwelcome or frightening ways, and can therefore be found scandalous by those lured to entertain it. Handled with care, however, such propositions can also focus our attention on unexpected possibilities, and thus help to facilitate transformations. In this sense, engaging with outrageous propositions is a tool in the methodological kit of researchers and practitioners who are interested in *speculative* research; that is, in exploring possibilities rather than actualities, and in articulating alternatives to what appears likely, established or inevitable from the perspective of the present (see Wilkie *et al.*, 2017).

Research Practice and Clinical Practice

Groddeck's writings and his medical practice exemplify the value of carefully engaging with outrageous propositions in two ways: first, he himself was a wielder of outrageous propositions which, as we have seen, he described as 'a remedy, a medication' (1987, p. 95). This invites us as researchers to ask how such propositions 'worked' in the context of his practice as a physician, and what we might learn from this about (the limitations of) contemporary forms of medical knowledge practice. Is there any possible basis for agreeing with Groddeck about the medical value of his propositions? What forms of knowledge might help us understand the efficacy of his practice? We can see how taking Groddeck seriously by momentarily suspending our disbelief might serve to re-orient our attention as researchers: not *against* mainstream knowledge practices in the present – those that feature prominently in public discourse, and also as funding priorities – but *beyond* them, towards traditions of thought and practice that are potentially important but remain relatively neglected. Obvious examples here would be the traditions of research on the relevance of the imagination in medicine (see Harrington, 2006; Kirmayer, 2006).

Second, we are prompted to ask to what extent the practice of social research may resemble clinical practice, in so far as it seeks to produce a different future by effecting a radical shift in perspective. I have chosen Groddeck's propositions as an example because they resonate strongly with polemics that characterise the political context of contemporary healthcare, particularly in relation to the growing number of so-called contested illnesses and 'medically unexplained symptoms' (Greco, 2017). Engaging with Groddeck's work affords a measure of distance from these polemics, and the possibility of considering them in a broader socio-historical context.

'Truth' versus 'Efficacy'

Groddeck's own practice may be described as a form of speculative experimentation with possibilities, mobilising an array of lures for feeling, as other practices of healing have done since time immemorial (see Hinton and Kirmayer, 2017). What appears distinctive about his practice, at least in the context of modern Western medicine, is that Groddeck put outrageous propositions into play *as such*; that is, he took deliberate care to maintain their speculative character and to make it explicit. Groddeck did not attempt to systematise his ideas into theoretical claims, indeed he actively resisted doing so. Likewise he refused to qualify himself as a scientist, at a time when achieving scientific status was already held as a key aspiration by clinical innovators. Instead, he introduced himself as a 'wild analyst' before the Psychoanalytic Association in 1920, prompting remarks that he had, in this and other ways, 'endangered the carefully earned esteem of psychoanalysts with his carefree behaviour' (Storfer quoted in Tytell, 1980, p. 93). Sigmund Freud, who credited Groddeck for inspiring aspects of his own psychoanalytic theories, was critical of Groddeck's wish to distance himself from the 'rigours of pure science', describing this as a form of personal vanity (1984, p. 362). But Groddeck's gesture of refusal expressed a form of coherence with the obligations inherent in his practice first and foremost as a *healer*, rather than an aspiring scientist (or knowledge producer). While Freud was busy developing techniques designed to safeguard the objectivity of his method, Groddeck happily conceded that '[a] certain harmony of feeling on the animal level between doctor and patient is the fundamental basis of medical treatment, which is, in essence a *reciprocal* activity', adding that

[t]he term 'animal' is meant to indicate that this important factor in treatment has ... nothing to do with the knowledge and skill of the physician, but arises from the contact of two human worlds and from their mutual human sympathy and antipathy.

(Groddeck, 1949, p. 46)

For Groddeck, therefore, the possibility of healing did not depend on the application of an objectively 'true' theory, a theory whose truth would be predicated on an operation of separation between the subject of knowledge and its object. It depended exactly on the opposite; that is, on the recognition of a fundamental continuity that obtains between human beings, and indeed across all beings, such that they necessarily affect each other, for better or for worse. We can thus see how Groddeck, while being biomedically trained, had good reasons to refuse to submit his propositions to the 'rigours of pure science', to stabilise them into generalisable claims: doing so would have compromised their ability to connect with his patients in the most responsive way possible.

The emphasis on reciprocity speaks of the paramount importance Groddeck attributed to the *relation* between doctor and patient in facilitating (or obstructing) the healing process, over and above the quality of a doctor's 'knowledge and skill'. Something similar obtains in social research: whether we acknowledge it or not, the quality of our presence as researchers is never neutral and never disembodied. We become part of the system of relations that characterises the phenomenon we are studying, and as such we affect it and transform it, minimally or maximally, for better or for worse. Whatever its scientific value, a concern with methodological rigour informed by abstract principles should never become a distraction from our ability to be sensitive to the situation we enter, and to the effects we might produce within it.

The Efficacy of a Proposition Arises from the System of Relations in Which It Occurs

In his practice, then, Groddeck put outrageous propositions into play, explicitly subordinating their truth-value to the value of their capacity to generate a change of perspective in those whom he lured into resonating with them. He did this by making a home for such propositions at Marienhöhe, a medical clinic, where they formed, as he put it, part of his treatment. Alongside physical therapy mainly based on massage and diet, this treatment routinely included asking patients questions about the purpose of their illness, regardless of the type of condition they suffered from, be it a broken limb, heart disease or a tumour:

it is my custom to ask a patient who has slipped and broken his arm: 'What was your idea in breaking your arm?' ... [W]e can always find both an inward and an outward cause for any event in life. In medicine the external cause has received so much attention ... that there can be no great harm if a few doctors here and there seem to exaggerate the importance of the neglected inward cause, and maintain as I do that man creates his own illnesses for definite purposes...

(Groddeck, 1951, p. 81)

Groddeck's question, 'What was your idea in breaking your arm?' sounded very different in the context of Marienhöhe from how it might sound today. What accounts for this difference? It is significant, for example, that Groddeck's question was asked *as part of the treatment*, and not as a condition of admittance into treatment. The same question, asked today, is likely to sound distinctly *outrageous* in the negative sense of this term – not in the sense that it might provoke curiosity, stimulating an effort of comprehension that might produce a new perspective, but in the sense that it might provoke outrage and polemical entrenchment, or the familiar, 'How *dare* you suggest that I have brought this on myself, that it is my fault!'

In the lectures he delivered during the last two years of the First World War, Groddeck himself pointed to why the type of questions he had routinely asked of his patients would come to sound outrageous in this way. He claimed that the medical profession had been irrevocably compromised by the Great War, when doctors had been called upon to perform functions of policing (1988, p. 515). From then on, asking a patient, 'What do you want to obtain with your illness?' would be associated with questioning the authenticity of the illness, and implicitly accusing the sick person of lying. In Groddeck's practice, this had been a question to be asked of *every* patient and *every* type of illness. Today, by contrast, questions about the intentionality of illness tend to be asked only as part of a process of *differentiating between* more or less authentic or legitimate illnesses. The potential interest of Groddeck's question in relation to the possibility of producing a change of perspective has become unintelligible – it is pre-empted by the probability of judgement, disqualification and exclusion.

Conclusion

What can we learn from thinking with Groddeck about the value and risks of engaging with outrageous propositions in social research? The possibility of learning from Groddeck's propositions depends, as Foucault taught us (1969), on removing the filters that would prevent us from taking them seriously. In Groddeck's case, this is the filter of historicisation that would have us dismiss him as a maverick of his time, with nothing to offer to contemporary sociologists. Other forms of disqualification are possible; for example, along criteria of reasonableness, practicality or scientificity. Once we remove such epistemic filters, the world appears full of outrageous propositions pointing to wondrous possibilities. One conclusion to be drawn here, therefore, concerns simply the importance of learning to recognise outrageous propositions that are good for the purpose of thinking with them, in relation to the problems we engage with in research.

Groddeck's propositions draw our attention because, taken at face value, they are simultaneously so similar and yet so different from propositions that are ubiquitous and that tend to cause outrage today. Today we can fully appreciate how the notion that 'man creates his own illnesses for definite purposes' (1951, p. 81) might be one that anyone who is wary of stigmatising the sick or blaming the victim would want to steer clear of. We have learned to distrust attributions of personal agency in producing illness, for good reasons; but Groddeck offers the opportunity of reading similar statements in the context of an entirely different system of relations, where they point to a completely different and surprising set of consequences. Taking the possibilities latent in his propositions seriously means hesitating, where previously there might have been a knee-jerk reaction of dismissal. Learning to hesitate allows us to gain a deeper insight into the contextual, situated value of contemporary (as well as historical) propositions. It also means becoming capable of entertaining the thought that, in a different system of relations, a given proposition might produce rather different effects.

What we also learn from this example is that, while it is useful to think with outrageous propositions in order to re-activate latent possibilities, we must take very great care in how we re-propose them. In this respect, Groddeck is interesting because of the explicit care he took in relation to the efficacy of his words: he forfeited the status of a *knower* in order to preserve his capacities as a *healer*, in the special environment he had created in Marienhöhe for this purpose. While it is impossible to turn his strategy into a general prescription, it points to the importance of evaluating what the imperative of 'taking care' might mean in the specific context of relations within which we hope to intervene.

References

Foucault, M. (1969) *The Archaeology of Knowledge.* London: Routledge.

Freud, S. (1984) *On Metapsychology: The Theory of Psychoanalysis.* London: Penguin Books.

Greco, M. (2017) 'Pragmatics of explanation: Creative accountability in the care of "medically unexplained symptoms", *The Sociological Review*, 65(2), pp. 110–129.

Groddeck, G. (1949) *Exploring the Unconscious*. London: Vision Press.

Groddeck, G. (1951) *The World of Man*. London: Vision Press.

Groddeck, G. (1987) *Vorträge I*. Basel, Frankfurt-am-Main: Stroemfeld/Roter Stern.

Groddeck, G. (1988) *Vorträge II*. Basel, Frankfurt-am-Main: Stroemfeld/Roter Stern.

Groddeck, G. (1992) *Satanarium*. Basel, Frankfurt-am-Main: Stroemfeld/Roter Stern.

Harrington, A. (2006) 'The many meanings of the placebo effect: Where they came from, why they matter', *Biosocieties*, 1(2), pp. 181–193.

Hinton, D.E. and Kirmayer, L.J. (2017) 'The flexibility hypothesis of healing', *Culture, Medicine, and Psychiatry*, 41, pp. 3–34.

Kirmayer, L.J. (2006) 'Toward a medicine of the imagination', *New Literary History*, 37(3), pp. 583–605.

M.C. (1951) 'Georg Walther Groddeck, 1866-1934', biographical introduction to Groddeck, G., *The World of Man*. London: Vision Press, pp. 5–11.

Tytell, P. (1980) 'Un précurseur des fictions théoriques', *L'Arc*, 78, pp. 92–103.

Whitehead, A.N. (1978) *Process and Reality*. New York: The Free Press.

Wilkie, A., Savransky, M. and Rosengarten, M. (eds) (2017) *Speculative Research – The Lure of Possible Futures*. London: Routledge.

19

How to do social research with... performance

Katalin Halász

Introduction

Performance art is a unique means to do social research with bodies. Sociology has long been engaging with 'the body/bodies', but up until the present, research tends be *about* bodies rather than *with* bodies. Unlike bodies represented in other media, the body in a live performance is unique: through the live performer's strong physical presence, the performed and enacted culturally coded body can step outside of the story and confront audiences with the juxtaposition of the socially inscribed body, that which is muted and cannot speak back, with the real, thinking and feeling body of the performer (Blackman, 2008).

Live sociology implies expanding the sensory dimensions of sociological attentiveness to capture 'the fleeting, distributed, multiple, sensory, emotional and kinaesthetic aspects of sociality' (Back, 2012, p. 28). In this chapter I propose that this involves using performance art as an embodied method that is capable not only of representing but of creating realities in the location where it is staged, even if only temporarily (Law, 2004). From my performance *I LOVE BLACK MEN* (2011) I argue that creating performative situations through artistic research methods permits gaining access to those registers of human experience that cannot be adequately expressed through words. The staged performance enables the investigation of the co-constitution of social discourses with lived experience (Gunaratnam, 2003). Employing the body of the performer alongside texts, it becomes possible to demonstrate that meaning does not only reside in language (which itself is embodied) but in the body as a whole.

I begin by discussing my performance *I LOVE BLACK MEN*, which I used as a research method in a visual sociology doctoral research project on the making of anti-racist white femininities. After explaining how I planned for the piece – paying particular attention to the ways in which the design of the performance allowed me to activate concepts the research engaged with – I move on to discuss how a very close attention to the performer's bodily experience has thrown up an unexpected 'critical incident' (Butterfield *et al.*, 2005) and shifted the research into a new direction. This 'accidental incident' required the body to be taken seriously not only as a research tool but as a theoretical argument. I then move on to situate performance art as a live sociological method that is particularly suitable for doing research with bodies, on bodily and lived experiences and embodiment. I conclude by reiterating that performance art as a research method is distinctly placed in accessing knowledges of bodies and 'the meaning of being human' (Leigh and Brown, 2021, p. 81).

Bodies and Text in *I LOVE BLACK MEN*

I designed the performance in the framework of a visual sociology doctoral research piece on the production of anti-racist white femininities. As a PhD researcher, I too started off with a review of the literature and a mapping of existing research that worked with the concepts of visual practices in racialisation and visibility in relation to whiteness and white womanhood (Halász, 2019). In 2010, at the start of my PhD, critical whiteness studies were dominated by a claim of the invisibility of whiteness (for a view of how this has changed radically to a hyper-visibility of whiteness today, see Hunter and Van der Westhuizen, 2021). The historical construction of white femininities has a rich literature, which works with racial ideologies, discourses, representations (Hall, 1992; Ware, 1992; Frankenberg, 1993; McClintock, 1995; Dyer, 1997; Harris, 2000; Byrne, 2006; Nava, 2007). My aim was to contribute to and expand on this literature by theorising the production of white femininities through the body.

Since a practice element was an integral part of my visual sociology PhD research, I used my first experiments with artistic research methods to activate theories and concepts I had engaged with in my readings in order to see how bodies respond to them. The two central holding components of *I LOVE BLACK MEN* are (1) a key racial text of the persistent stereotype of the alleged sexual attraction of white women to black men; and (2) black and white bodies that are attached to this racist stereotype. The theoretical concepts I wanted to mobilise were the invisibility and performativity of whiteness, and the relational construction of white womanhood through racial discourse and racialised seeing practices. I also wanted to test if using performance art as a research method would enable me to dislodge knowledges of the white female body and observe how it not only reacts to these concepts, but actively takes part in accepting or resisting them.

I took inspiration from the long tradition of black performance art and theory, especially the works of Coco Fusco (Halász, 2012), Adrian Piper, Eleanor Antin, Anna Deavere Smith and Nikki S. Lee (see Smith, 2011). Drawing on aesthetics of feminist video and performance art of the 1970s, I designed the performance to be visually very plain, so that the focus stays on the act of the performing body. It took place in a studio, without audience and with only the performer, a white female artist and me present. I designed the room to resemble a classroom and put the camera at an angle that only shows a big blackboard against a white wall. I asked the performer to implement a very simple act of writing one sentence on the board until there was no space left (Figure 19.1). I remained

Figure 19.1 *I LOVE BLACK MEN.* Video still (black and white, sound).

Figure 19.2 *I LOVE BLACK MEN*. Video still (black and white, sound).

invisible throughout the act. The role of the invisible instructor becomes highly relevant in the performance, as it is the one who enacts white power and creates the classroom as a racialised white space. As such, I position myself similarly as white in the racial hierarchy and provide a detailed description of my positionality and reflexivity in the accompanying written thesis (Halász, 2019).

I recorded the performance from two camera angles: at the start of the video, we see the full length of the board and a woman writing from edge to edge, but what she writes becomes only legible with the change of the camera angle midway through the video, when a part of the board, the shoulders and head of the woman and her writing hand come closer (Figure 19.2). She writes the sentence 'I LOVE BLACK MEN' in capital letters until the last row, where the writing becomes confused, loses its track and reads 'MEN I LOVE MEN I'. The video documentation is four minutes long. At the very end the woman moves out of the frame while the camera is still fixed on the board and we hear an exasperated sigh. The sigh of the performer became the unforeseen 'critical incident' that has opened up a new, affective dimension that I then engaged with both theoretically and methodically. I knew that I was 'onto' something (Leigh and Brown, 2021, p. 80). Without this performance, and the very close attention to the different bodily states the performer has gone through in the piece, my research would maybe not have engaged with the role of affects in the making of white womanhood. In my consequent performances I directly designed and staged for affective circulation to happen between bodies and bodies and texts.[1]

Performance Art as an Embodied Live Sociological Research Method

Particularly since 'the affective turn' (Clough and Halley, 2007), bodies and embodiment have become an explicit focus of social research. Still, as Jennifer Leigh and Nicole Brown argue in their review of embodied research, it remains the case that 'although the physical, material practice of doing research is not at all disembodied or unembodied, the body is regularly written out of research articles' (2021, p. 90). Les Back and Nirmal Puwar (2012) provide an opening to the hitherto '"innovative" and risky' (Leigh and Brown, 2021, p. 92) forms of embodied research and to doing a more 'artful'[2] sociology. My argument is that by using performance art as a live sociological method, registers of human experience that cannot be expressed through language and words can be accessed and made relevant to sociological research. By producing performance art as a research method not only can the embodied nature of doing research find its place in research articles that provide social critique, but alternative social realities can be enacted (Law, 2004). Performance art is exceptional in that it enables the social scientist *to do research with bodies*: to pay very close attention to the multiple movements, sounds, smells, sensations, vibrations and resonances of bodies and to excavate their potentialities

---

[1] The consequent artworks I produced as part of my research were staged in various art contexts in the UK, Germany, Denmark, Brazil and Bolivia. For more information, please see: www.katalinhalasz.com

[2] I understand art here as an ensemble of practices, performances, experiences and artefacts rather than as a singular object (a painting or a sculpture) (Dixon, 2008; Hawkins, 2010). This attentiveness to art practices in addition to the finished object points to understandings of art as a site where 'new multi-dimensional knowledge and identities are constantly in the process of being formed' (Rogoff, 2000, p. 20, quoted in Hawkins, 2011, p. 465).

in creating meaning and envisioning a critically different social world – within the confines of the time and place of the artwork. To be precise, I am arguing for social scientists themselves to design and stage performance art as part of the research process, right from its initial stages. Creative collaborations between social researchers and artists can expand the social research toolkit and can bring about 'the innovation of the research process itself' beyond only for dissemination purposes (Puwar and Sharma, 2012, p. 49). As I demonstrated through *I LOVE BLACK MEN*, planning for the performance, and being not only present but taking an active role in the performance event, enabled me to enter into a close inter-corporeal relation with the performer, to sense the changes and movements in their body from within my own, and consequently led to the research engaging with new theoretical fields that I had not considered before.

When using performance art as a research method in social research, methodological questions emerge: what are we social scientists doing when we bring artistic research into our methods? Why do we want to incorporate art practice into social research? Doesn't it water down our robust methods? Do we want to be artists? To the latter two questions my answer is a definitive no. In contrast, I would argue that using artistic methods can enable the social scientist to expand the attentiveness and sensitivity of the researcher (Back and Puwar, 2012); to be open to 'learning to be affected' and 'being affected to learn' (Gunaratnam, 2012, pp. 117, 119); to create situations where social questions can be answered through accessing registers other than talk and texts; to share a relationship to research with audiences who consume the work (Leavy, 2015); to present new ways to think about traditional research practices, about making/generating data (Leigh and Brown, 2021) and analysing and presenting findings; and finally, to access worlds to facilitate seeing, thinking, feeling differently. What we are doing as social researchers by incorporating art practice into our research is to open ourselves to the messiness of life, to the uncontained and unarticulated knowledges of bodies. By doing so, we are making art's unique capacities productive for tapping into layers of human experience in our social research projects. As Patricia Leavy puts it: 'The arts can uniquely educate, inspire, illuminate, resist, heal, and persuade ... it is for these reasons ... that innovative scholars across the disciplines have harnessed the power of the arts in their social research' (2015, p. ix.).

I have argued elsewhere for doing sociology through the intensive, the performative and affective dimensions of art (Halász, 2017). Here I want to dwell more on the epistemological questions of doing research with bodies and the knowledges they hold, on the question of what arts-based approaches can reveal and represent that cannot be captured with other methods. The knowledge that is acquired through the methods of arts-based research challenges the dominant model of a scientific concept of 'objective' and 'impersonal' knowledge. The major critiques of arts-based research relate to validity and trustworthiness, which stems mainly from positivist science relying on objectivity and conceiving of reality as consisting of knowable truth. In contrast, 'artistic knowledge seems to have more potential in relation to the human individual, their experience, their emotions and their embodied relationship with the world' (Biggs and Karlsson, 2010, p. 2). Embodied knowledge as the outcome and the artworks that embody and communicate this knowledge as the outputs of artistic research methods demonstrate the potential for arts-based research to have an impact far beyond the arts. The basic assumption here is that social research questions are addressed in an holistic and engaged way in which theory and practice are intertwined (Leavy, 2015), and that art produced is made to be answerable to the research questions. Feminist epistemology has put subjective knowledge to the forefront of social research, but as Leigh and Brown argue, criticism of bias, and a lack of rigour and validity can be fair because embodied research can be particularly disposed to 'a projection of our own values and ideals than an open inquiry into others' (2021, p. 76). Therefore, these authors put particular emphasis on positionality and reflexivity, which they sum up as: 'we need to know what we are looking *from* in order to critically analyse what we are looking *at*' (2021, p. 76, emphases in original).

Conclusion

This chapter outlined the basic parameters of performance art as a live sociological method to counteract the absence of the body/bodies in social research. It provided an example of a performance art piece in the context of a visual sociological research on anti-racist white femininities, offering some initial thoughts on how *I LOVE BLACK MEN* opened up new dimensions for the research to thoroughly engage with affects and bodily experiences. The chapter argued for a wider use of performance art as a social research method uniquely placed to do research that takes the body, bodily experiences and the embodiment of researcher and performer seriously, a method that 'has an emphasis on the felt, the unspoken and the hard to capture as much as it does on words that are spoken.' (Leigh and Brown, 2021, p. 84)

Acknowledging the 'open-endedness of interpretation', that we 'as classed, raced, sexed and gendered (fully socialised and embodied) subjects ... are imbricated within any potential determinations of meaning' (Jones and Stephenson, 1999, p. 1) and that as an artwork, *I LOVE BLACK MEN* can be perceived and understood differently by viewers, it has allowed me to develop an argument on the centrality of affective sensitivities of bodies in producing meaning of varied white femininities. In theorising the making of white womanhood, I used the performance to demonstrate how language and sensuous, embodied meaning-making processes are connected and productive of subjectivities and social relations. In my reading, racial discourse in the form of the racist stereotype and the affective experience of the sigh and the broken writing at the end of the performance work together in producing potentially new embodiments of white womanhood, ones which have the capacity to actively resist taking part in the essentialising colonial project of whiteness (Halász, 2021).

Acknowledgements

The author received financial support for the research and authorship of this chapter from the Leverhulme Trust.

References

Back, L. (2012) 'Live sociology: Social research and its futures', in Back, L. and Puwar, N. (eds) *Live Methods*. Oxford: Blackwell Publishing Ltd, pp. 18–40.

Back, L. and Puwar, N. (eds) (2012) *Live Methods*. Oxford: Blackwell Publishing Ltd.

Biggs, M. and Karlsson, H. (eds) (2010) *The Routledge Companion to Research in the Arts*. London, New York: Routledge.

Blackman, L. (2008) *The Body: Key Concepts*. Oxford, New York: Berg.

Butterfield, L.D., Borgen, W.A., Amundson, N.E. and Maglio, A.S.T. (2005) 'Fifty years of the critical incident technique: 1954-2004 and beyond', *Qualitative Research*, 5(4), pp. 475-497.

Byrne, B. (2006) *White Lives: The Interplay of 'Race,' Class and Gender in Everyday Life*. London, New York: Routledge.

Clough, P.T. and Halley, J. (eds) (2007) *The Affective Turn: Theorizing the Social*. Durham, NC, London: Duke University Press.

Dixon, D. (2008) 'The blade and the claw: Science, art and the creation of the lab-borne monster', *Social and Cultural Geography*, 9, pp. 671-692.

Dyer, R. (1997) *White*. London: Routledge.

Frankenberg, R. (1993) *White Women, Race Matters: The Social Construction of Whiteness*. Minneapolis: University of Minnesota Press.

Gunaratnam, Y. (2003) *Researching Race and Ethnicity: Methods, Knowledge, and Power*. London: Sage.

Gunaratnam, Y. (2012) 'Learning to be affected: Social suffering and total pain at life's borders', *The Sociological Review*, 60(1), pp. 108-123.

Hall, C. (1992) *White, Male and Middle-Class: Explorations in Feminism and History*. Cambridge: Polity Press.

Halász, K. (2012) 'Decentering images: An interview with Coco Fusco', in Engel, A. and Dorrance, J. (eds) *Bossing Images: The Power of Images, Queer Art and Politics*. Berlin: Neue Gesellschaft für Bildende Kunst, pp. 55-66.

Halász, K. (2017) 'Performing sociology at a music festival: Art's agency', *Academic Quarter* (e-journal), 16, pp. 133-148. Available at: https://journals.aau.dk/index.php/ak/issue/view/246 (Accessed: 25 September 2021).

Halász, K. (2019) *A Visual Sociology of White Woman: Investigating and Creating Affective Performances of Anti-Racist White Femininities*. Unpublished PhD thesis. Available at: http://research.gold.ac.uk/id/eprint/26403/ (Accessed: 25 September 2021).

Halász, K. (2021) 'Affects in making white womanhood', in Hunter, S. and Van der Westhuizen, C. (eds) *Routledge Handbook of Critical Studies in Whiteness*. London, New York: Routledge, pp. 54-66.

Harris, H. (2000) 'Failing 'white woman': Interrogating the performance of respectability', *Theatre Journal*, 52, pp. 183-209.

Hawkins, H. (2010) 'The argument of the eye: Cultural geographies of installation art', *Cultural Geographies*, 17, pp. 1-19.

Hawkins, H. (2011) 'Dialogues and doings: Sketching the relationships between geography and art', *Geography Compass*, 5(7), pp. 464-478.

Hunter, S. and Van der Westhuizen, C. (2021) *Routledge Handbook of Critical Studies in Whiteness*. London, New York: Routledge.

Jones, A. and Stephenson, A. (eds) (1999) *Performing the Body/Performing the Text*. London, New York: Routledge.

Law, J. (2004) *After Method: Mess in Social Science Research*. London, New York: Routledge.

Leavy, P. (2015) *Method Meets Art: Arts-Based Research Practice*. Second edition. New York: Guilford Press.

Leigh, J. and Brown, N. (2021) *Embodied Inquiry*. London, New York: Bloomsbury.

McClintock, A. (1995) *Imperial Leather: Race, Gender, and Sexuality in the Colonial Contest*. New York: Routledge.

Nava, M. (2007) *Visceral Cosmopolitanism: Gender, Culture and the Normalisation of Difference*. New York: Berg.

Puwar, N. and Sharma, S. (2012) 'Curating sociology', in Back, L. and Puwar, N. (eds) *Live Methods*. Oxford: Blackwell Publishing Ltd.

Rogoff, I. (2000) *Terra Infirma: Geography's Visual Culture*. London: Routledge.

Smith, C. (2011) *Enacting Others: The Politics of Identity in Eleanor Antin, Nikki S. Lee, Adrian Piper, and Anna Deavere Smith*. Durham, NC, London: Duke University Press.

Ware, V. (1992) *Beyond the Pale: White Women, Racism and History*. London, New York: Verso.

20

How to do social research with... performative experiments

Michael Guggenheim

No method has more influenced our conception of science than the experimental method; no method makes the contemporary sociologist more suspicious.

(Zelditch, 1961, p. 528)

Here are two experiments I have conducted with colleagues:[1]

For the first experiment, we were interested in learning about how people taste food, and how we can make people taste them differently (Voss *et al.*, 2022). We were interested in what happens if people learn to create dishes not according to tradition, but according to various socio-logics. For this experiment, which we ran as an exhibition at the Museum of Natural History in Berlin, we tasked visitors with sitting at a table with various bowls on it with small amounts of food. The experiment unfolded in two steps: first, there was a sequence of five experiments which decomposed the practice of tasting into its constituent elements. For example, participants had to taste an ingredient, and imagine they were other creatures, such as snakes or tigers to understand how taste is an outcome of an interaction between ingredients and specific bodies. Or they were invited to taste other ingredients as if it were an honour or shameful to eat this food, to understand how taste is shaped by expectations. There were

[1]My thanks go to all the people with whom I had the privilege to create these experiments. For the taste experiments, this is first and foremost Jan-Peter Voss, who was the Co-Principal Investigator of the overall Taste! Project, and Nora Rigamonti, Aline Haulsen and Max Söding, who helped create experiments, but also all the citizen scientists of the Taste!-Project. For the sandtable experiments, these are Bernd Kräftner and Judith Kröll, with whom I have worked for a decade, and Gerhard Ramsebner and Isabel Warner, who were part of the sandtable team. Recently, with Nicholas Bussmann I have taken the sandtables in new directions for a project called Wandering Dunes. We are most deeply indebted to all participants.

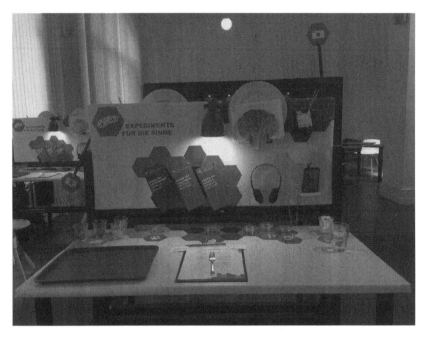

Figure 20.1 Taste! Exhibition setup. Museum of Natural History Berlin (photograph: Michael Guggenheim).

similar experiments for memory, atmosphere and information. In the second stage, participants were asked to use the ingredients they had tasted, and their tasting notes from the experiments, to create and name a new dish. Thus, every participant created a unique dish, which was not based on culinary traditions, but based on their specific tasting experiences.

For the second experiment, we were interested in creating alternative disaster scenarios (Guggenheim *et al.*, 2013, 2016). We were aiming to find an alternative to government 'risk registers', where government experts define what future risks we might face (such as earthquakes, terrorist attacks or pandemics). For this experiment, we created a sandtable with figures and objects. We asked the participants to first 'build a world' by placing objects into the sandbox and explaining to us what these objects represent for them (they were not informed what would come later). Objects could represent humans, animals or other objects, but also emotions or actions. Once they had finished building their world, we asked them to 'turn the world upside down'; that is, to create a disaster. Again,

Figure 20.2 Sequential photo from the three steps of sandplay (photograph: Kräftner, Kröll, Guggenheim, Ramsebner).

they should use one object at a time to represent the disaster. In the final third step, we asked them to think about a form of preparedness that would have changed the course of the disaster.

Why Performative Experiments?

Sociologists, as per Zelditch's epigraph above, are suspicious of experiments. It has to suffice to mention cursorily the history of cruel experiments on humans that cumulated in the Tuskegee experiments and human experiments in Nazi Germany, but also later experiments such as the Milgram experiment and the Stanford prison experiment, which were criticised for misleading participants and submitting them to cruel and demeaning actions. Further, sociologists have been suspicious of the artificiality of experiments and the difficulty of extending the knowledge gained from them to the world outside. So why do experiments?

There are at least three reasons for doing performative experiments. The *first* reason is that if sociologists are 'enacting the social' (Law and Urry, 2004), then re-enacting the existing is not particularly interesting. Sociologists need to mobilise participants to produce *surprises*.

The *second* reason follows from this: other research that intentionally aims to enact the social with human participants, such as participatory action research, necessitates that participants identify with the goals of the project. It imagines participants as lacking expertise, power and agency (otherwise there would be no need for the researchers in the first instance). The implicit assumption of this buy-in clause is that participants should not be made to do something when they do not or cannot know its outcome. But as Christoph Paret has argued (Paret, 2021), to experiment with participants can also mean to liberate them from social constraints and to open up possibilities that do not exist somewhere else in their lives. To be part of such a making of unknown events does not mean to be duped, to be taken hostage or denied freedom.

The *third* reason is that experiments allow us to produce knowledge about the future. Recently, many sociologists have called for a sociology of the future. Other disciplines such as climate science or demographics create data about the future, by extrapolating from past data sequences. For qualitative sociologists, there are no methods that would generate such extrapolations, because the obstinacy of social forms will not conform to extrapolation. Performative experiments, uniquely, allow us to create novel, unforeseen and therefore future social forms. I suggest calling such experiments, which answer the three reasons for experiments outlined here, performative experiments, to distinguish them from representational experiments, which claim to operate in a representational register (Wehrens, 2019).

A Guide for Doing Performative Experiments Based on Our Experiences

Once we have figured out why we might want to do such performative experiments, we may also want to understand some heuristics to conduct them:

1 **Materialise a question by creating an experimental system:** first of all, we need an 'experimental system', which is 'a device to materialise questions' as Hans-Jörg Rheinberger calls it (Rheinberger, 1998, p. 287). *Asking* a question, such as 'how do apples taste if it were an honour to eat them' is something very different from *making people taste apples* as if it were an honour to eat them. The materialisation of a question immediately brings with it a plethora of issues as to how we might want to materialise a question. In what room are they going to eat the apple? Which apple? Who is giving the instructions and how?

2 **Allow the experimental system to co-generate:** when I stressed the fact that we materialise the question and design a device to do so, this does not imply that the experimenter is in control. From actor–network

theory we can learn that if people do things with things, then these objects are agents themselves (otherwise, the stress on *materialising* a question would not make much sense). An experimental system is thus a 'socio-material' network and therefore 'cogenerates ... the phenomena' (Rheinberger, 1998, p. 287). We need to work along with the device. We need to be able to tinker with it and observe how specific elements of the experimental system create changes in the experiment. For example, in the case of the sandbox, we first tried interviewing people about future risks. Interviewing people led nowhere, because participants would simply tell us about whatever disaster was most recently in the news. But we were interested in *as yet unknown risks*, not those in the news. Only materialising the question with the sandbox produced surprises. We began without sand. But without sand, there was no terrain, and the world created remained literally flat. Adding sand created another layer of complexity, and surprise, and made the playing out of disasters far more precise, as well as surprising to the players. Thus, decisions such as using objects, adding sand, even the precise amounts of sand *change the answers we obtain.*

3 **Think in design logics:** this requires a very different kind of practice from the representational practices of descriptive text or photographs. Creating an experimental system means to *invent and implement* a new social world. It is fundamentally a design practice, but not as objects for use, but to materialise a question. Design here is not beautiful or useful, but enhances the operation of the experimental system. For example, the sandbox needs to have a specific size: too small and it cannot simulate a large variety of worlds. It will be impossible to lose oneself in it, and to get an idea of a world that is built. It will not create its own maelstrom of play. Too big and players can't reach the middle of the sandbox, and the flow is interrupted. In the taste experiments, the complex choreography of knowing which food item to taste next needs to be clearly sequenced on the table and through references between the table, the food and the written instructions. In this specific case, the hexagons on the table are coloured differently from left to right, with each colour corresponding to the colour of a page of the instruction booklet to indicate which foods belong to which experiment.

4 **Work with the singularity and strangeness of the experimental system:** from this it also follows that we need to accept the agency, *singularity and strangeness* of the experimental system and its role in the co-construction of phenomena: '[e]xperimentation has a life of its own' (Hacking, 1983, p. 150). The experimental apparatus produces its own logic, to which both the experimenters and the participants need to attune themselves. The experimental system needs to make participants feel comfortable in its strangeness (when did you last play seriously in a sandbox without children or when did you last focus on eating unknown food?). In both experiments, the experimental system had its own duration (approximately 45 minutes), which it needed to run. In the case of the taste experiment, we had to shorten the overall experiment, because participants would not sustain interest for more than five tasting experiments. In the case of the sandbox, it turned out that most participants took about 20 minutes to build a world, and then another 10 minutes each for disaster and preparedness. This life of its own takes over the community of those who are involved in an experiment and they cannot easily extricate themselves from it. In both experiments, our participants very often commented at the end how strange *and* satisfying the experiments were.

5 **Think about recording devices:** to produce data, an experiment needs to be recorded. If performative experiments produce fleeting new social forms that only exist within the experimental system, then these social forms need to be preserved and made intelligible. Most sociologists are used to recording interviews or maybe using photographs, where the recording is the end-product to be displayed. But experiments often produce a type of audio-visual data that resembles the data of natural scientists. I have called these data 'tight (visual) translations' using mechanical recording technologies, where the recording is merely an unintelligible interim point (Guggenheim, 2015): these recordings are not used for the representation of the complexity of the social world (as in documentary photography), but as representation of some underlying logics. In the case of the sandbox, the materials are annotated video recordings of the sandplays. In the case of the taste experiment, these are written answers to the experiments and drawings and photographs of the final dish. Such materials are sequential and repetitive.

The individual image has no meaning in itself, but only gains it in its relevant difference to other similar images. The production of such data requires situated recording setups, that are attuned to the experimental system. For the sandbox, we developed our own computer program that allowed us to annotate a video-stream of the sandbox with live transcripts. For the taste experiments, we developed an intricate clipboard with answer sheets that visually corresponded to the design of the table to guide the participants through the experiments.

6 **Instruct the participants:** experimenters instruct participants to do something that they would otherwise not do, which is at odds with the observatory gesture of qualitative sociology. Unlike participatory action research, where researchers and participants share a goal, in performative experiments, a shared goal cannot be assumed. Therefore, any kind of instruction must be both simple, so as not to restrict the pool of participants and surprising to make the experiment worthwhile for them. Thus, in the sandbox experiment, the first instruction is simply: 'build a world'; and in the taste experiments, the first instruction is: 'taste the food in front of you and describe your memories.' Both instructions familiarise the participants with the surprise of focusing on something that they usually do not do. They allow the participants to accept the artificiality of the setup and understand it as a challenge. From there, the instructions become more challenging and perplexing, while also drawing participants further into the experiment.

7 **Liberate the participants by restricting them:** the goal of a performative experiment is to create new social forms, both as an experience for the participants *and* as data. In the case of the sandbox, these are new risks and forms of preparedness. In the case of the taste experiments, these are new dishes. But to directly instruct participants to create new social forms will not work. They would be clueless and overwhelmed. It is precisely the initial absence of a shared goal, the lack of emancipatory promise that liberates the participants. Only because they are *forced and instructed to do something that they otherwise would not do, are they able to create something new.* Freedom is not the absence of constraints, but the presence of *liberating constraints.* Freedom results from giving participants tools and instructions that allow them to operate in ways they could not imagine before.

8 **Understand the experiment as a performance:** the unnaturalness of the setting and the instructions given to participants require that we understand the experiment as a performance for the production of facts (Lezaun *et al.*, 2013). Even an interview is a scripted performance, except that the performative aspect is rarely acknowledged and mobilised for the improvement of research. As a performance, it forces the researchers to become attentive to the situation and its atmosphere. In both experiments, it was crucial that we did not design a test, nor did we dupe the participants. We were staging an interaction that should be playful, full of surprise and reflexivity, by making people think about what we made them do. Making people stage worlds and risks in a sand-table requires them to accept their role as storytellers. For this reason, we highlighted this role to them, and explained that they should think about their identity as a narrator. We also offered them the chance to wear an animal mask to become a different narrator in case they were uncomfortable with themselves. Even if they did not use the masks, the offer indicated that this was not a form of psychotherapy (in which sandplay has a long history), but was about the interplay between a narrator and a world.

9 **The experimenter is a performer:** from the previous point it follows that the instructors are co-performers. They have to be transparent about what the experiment does, and where this is not possible, they have to explain the overarching setup. For example, in the sandbox experiment, we could not tell people that this was about risks and disasters from the outset, as they would have started to build a world attuned to risks. Thus, the experimenter had to make clear that 'building a world' really was a prompt that would resolve its logic in a second step, and not a ruse.

Conclusion

The above examples of and instructions for performative experiments should suffice for you to attempt your own. The most important lesson for me has been to stop thinking in terms of the dualism of representation versus intervention. On paper, all of this is not very difficult, except that our acquired disciplinary habitus and the skills we have learned make it difficult to move away from it. Performative experiments require you to accept that you intervene and represent *at once* and that an alternative idea of society emerges out of this intervention and not before it. Most importantly, experiments require you to accept the burden of working with participants on something when neither you nor them know what the outcome will be. This militates against the descriptivist instincts of ethnographers and statisticians as much as it militates against the critical instincts of critical theorists, and this is precisely why you should try it.

References

Guggenheim, M. (2015) 'The media of sociology: Tight or loose translations?', *British Journal of Sociology*, 67 (June), pp. 345–372.

Guggenheim, M., Kraeftner, B. and Kroell, J. (2013) ' "I don't know whether I need a further level of disaster": Shifting media of sociology in the sandbox', *Distinktion: Journal of Social Theory*, 14(3), pp. 284–304. Available at: https://doi.org/10.1080/1600910X.2013.838977

Guggenheim, M., Kräftner, B. and Kröll, J. (2016) 'Creating idiotic speculators: Disaster cosmopolitics in the sandbox', in Wilkie, A., Rosengarten, M. and Savransky, M. (eds) *Speculative Research: The Lure of Possible Futures*. London: Routledge, pp. 145–162.

Hacking, I. (1983) *Representing and Intervening: Introductory Topics in the Philosophy of Natural Science*. Cambridge: Cambridge University Press.

Law, J. and Urry, J. (2004) 'Enacting the social', *Economy and Society*, 33(3), pp. 390–410.

Lezaun, J., Muniesa, F. and Vikkelsø, S. (2013) 'Provocative containment and the drift of social-scientific realism', *Journal of Cultural Economy*, 6(3), pp. 278–293. Available at: https://doi.org/10.1080/17530350.2012.739972

Paret, C. (2021) *Fabrikation der Freiheit: Über die Konstruktion emanzipativer Settings*. Berlin: Wallstein Verlag. Available at: https://doi.org/10.5771/9783835397378.

Rheinberger, H.J. (1998) 'Experimental systems, graphematic spaces', in Lenoir, T. (ed.) *Inscribing Science: Scientific Texts and the Materiality of Communication*. Stanford, CA: Stanford University Press, pp. 285–303.

Voss, J.P., Guggenheim, M., Rigamonti, N., Haulsen, A. and Söding, M. (2022) 'Provoking taste: Experimenting with new ways of sensing', in Voss, J.P. and Rigamonti, N. (eds) *Sensing Communities*. Bielefeld: Transcript, pp. 199–218.

Wehrens, R. (2019) 'Experimentation in the sociology of science: Representational and generative registers in the imitation game', *Studies in History and Philosophy of Science Part A*, 76 (August), pp. 76–85. Available at: https://doi.org/10.1016/j.shpsa.2018.10.003

Zelditch, M. (1961) 'Can you really study an army in the laboratory?', in Etzioni, A. and Lehmann, E.N. (eds) *Complex Organizations: A Sociological Reader*. New York, London: Holt, Rinehart and Winston, pp. 528–539.

21

How to do social research with... plastic

Caroline Knowles

Figure 21.1 A scene from an underground station in Seoul.

Scene I: Oyster Dinner

The night gets more raucous as the milky liquor soju circulates and the pile of oyster shells grows. The laughter and the talk gradually amplify and we huddle around the central burner and the bubbling ramen pot on the table. An after work meeting of men. The team. With only one woman - the team secretary. The young man who is about to get married tells me his girlfriend has an important job in the control room and he wants her to keep working. They tease the only unmarried man saying he is a 'homo'. Having moved on from serious conversations, like the likelihood of North and South Korea combining, they ask me about Princess Diana, the Queen, the Dr Who TV series, the premier football league and actor Hugh Grant. Their grasp of UK popular culture is impressive and I struggle to answer their questions. I doubt that a similar gathering in London could point to Korea on a map. The team boss, Mr K is mystified – why do I consider humdrum repetitive lives like theirs worth writing about? Who would be interested in reading about their daily routines, which even they find boring? The men tell me their lives revolve around work, even at weekends when they don't need to be at the petrochemical plant in Daesan they come to work, because there is always something to do; and when they are not working they drink. By 8pm it is all over and the team secretary, who like me dipped sparingly into the soju, drives me and Berkeley[1] back to the guest house.

Scene 2: Cockle Pickers

The window of my room at the Sea and Tel guest house looks out onto the Yellow Sea. The sea front is lined with restaurants and fish process-ing, mostly shelling and preparing, for restaurants. The little town of Sam Gil Po, near Daesan, lives from the sea. There are small fishing boats off-shore and holding tanks of fish. People visit from Seoul at the weekend. The buildings are small concrete blocks with commercial logos in bright colours. The sea is steely grey and calm. The cockle pickers are part of the commercial activity of the sea. They sell their pickings from a small blue flat-bed truck with a grey awning for cover. The pavement side is opened to create a makeshift counter. He is 80, she is 72. She is bundled-up against the cold in a purple jacket, a red tartan scarf over its hood for extra warmth. Her hands are red with cold and ice and shellfish, the bounty of the sea, dug out of the sand at low tide. She scrapes and prepares cockles with a knife and places them in a plastic colander, ready for bagging up. The couple tell me that they collect cockles because they don't want to be a burden to their son, who owns a hairdressing salon. He has a fam-ily of his own to support. But there is no old age welfare system in South Korea, so the elderly go on working. There are jetties jutting into the sea, but fishermen and women must share the sea with the long oil jetties and the hundred berth points for tankers that move oil in and out for making plastic. Fishing and plastic tussle over the sea, which they share, but not on equal terms. Plastic rules.

[1]Name has been changed for anonymity.

Scene 3: The Woman at the Supermarket

The GS-25 store is next to the company apartments and the 'happy center' [social club]. 'Friendly, fresh, fun' it says on the window. Piles of empty cardboard boxes are haphazardly stacked outside beside a wooden table attached to benches. The store doubles as a makeshift café. Inside, I buy sealed cans of hot coffee from the machine for the young woman, Berkeley and myself, which we drink in the warmth of the store at the only table, a rickety old thing in Formica (more plastic). Berkeley, a sociology student at a famous American university, is indispensable as my assistant/translator. Warmed junk food options are available from the cash desk, but no one wants them. They look like they are made from chemicals too, so we settle down among the soap-powder with our coffee. The young woman speaks hesitantly to start with, but later warms to the topic of company wages, and how she is paid half what a man of her age (she's 30) and education gets. I can see how this works as an inducement to marry – the expected course – but she stands firm. She lives in the company apartments for single people – mostly men. She has a car and enjoys the freedom of it. Next weekend she is driving a group of girlfriends to a ski resort. She's not particularly interested in having a boyfriend – the men in the company are younger than her, or married, or getting married. She is quietly spoken, pretty and content with her life as it is. Marriage, on the other hand, she thinks presents all sorts of hazards alongside its evident material rewards. We finish our tinned coffee and she takes off.

Designing Plastic Research

I call these vignettes *scenes* because I think of them like the sequences in a film. Each scene condenses bigger stories extending beyond it, leaking at the edges. The scenes above are of everyday life gathered in and around a petrochemical plant making plastic granules. I'm doing sociology with plastic,[2] and this allows me to wonder how plastic configures the social and material life of this place. I didn't begin with plastic, I came across it sideways. I borrowed from the anthropologist Igor Kopytoff (1986) the idea of writing an 'object biography'. His object was a car in an African village: he

---

[2]There is an admirable stream of material sociology dealing with plastic; for example, Jennifer Gabrys, Gay Hawkins and Mike Michael (eds), *Accumulation: The Material Politics of Plastic*, Routledge, 2013; and Alice Mah, *Plastic Unlimited: How Corporations Are Fuelling the Ecological Crisis and What We Can Do About It*, Polity, 2022.

suggested the car could provide a point of access to situations that are difficult for researchers to understand. The car, Kopytoff reasoned, would provide a way of investigating how a particular place actually worked. Who owned the car? How did they raise the money to buy it? Through questions like these, he would piece together the social relationships and forms of authority that he wanted to understand.

My object was a pair of flip-flops, chosen for their simplicity and their social significance. Flip-flops are the world's cheapest shoe: a billion people globally still walk barefoot and flip-flops are a first step into footwear. This is how I arrived at plastic – flip-flops are made from it, and they have only two parts, a sole and a toe strap. Simplicity is important, as I intended to unfold their life story (biography) from beginning to end. I planned on tracking the key scenes of plastic production, consumption and disposal, along with what I was calling the 'flip-flop trail'. Where the shoe went, I would follow; and with the shoe, plastic moved into the centre of my research.

My mission was part of a bigger story. In following the flip-flop trail I was tracking one of globalisation's humble 'backroads'. Globalisation is the overall arc of these stories – the scene that links the other scenes. I was using plastic flip-flops to trace how globalisation *actually works*, on the ground, in contrast to the abstract ways in which sociologists like Saskia Sassen (2001) had written about it as 'flows' across borders. I learned that nothing flows, that flip-flops move with great effort and difficulty through people's lives and the landscapes in which they live. The research was made into a book, *Flip-Flop: A Journey through Globalisation's Backroads* (Knowles, 2014, Pluto) and a website www.flipfloptrail.com.

The flip-flop trail took me first to oilfields and drilling operations in the deserts of Kuwait. It then transported me to the vast petrochemical enterprises of Daesan in South Korea, where oil is turned into plastic granules. In Daesan a whole world of plastic is fabricated and lived in some of the ways hinted at in the scenes above. Moving with the cheap kinds of plastics that are made into flip-flops took me to small factories in Fuzhou in South East China. At each point along the trail, I followed the *rules of the road*, which I made up to provide consistency in what felt like a project I had little control over: the plastic led and I followed. My rule was to follow the biggest volume of everything – oil, chemicals, plastic granules, flip-flops. There were literally hundreds of flip-flop trails and each of them splintered in all directions, creating a confusing array of paths, so the rules of the road kept me on a consistent track. South East China was the biggest manufacturer of cheap flip-flops. The biggest market is Ethiopia: and so I followed the flip-flops through a cascade of wholesale and retail markets and onto the feet of Ethiopians going about their everyday business. At each point, plastic flip-flops provided me with a vantage point from which I could observe everyday life as it is lived on the ground. My story ends on a landfill site on the outskirts of Addis Ababa, where I met the 'scratchers' who sort through the trash for recyclables. Some plastics are recycled, and some lie gently decomposing for more than 100 years. This isn't really the end of the story because some plastics are recycled, taking off again in all directions. But on Addis's landfill site I ran out of the energy, creativity and effort that it takes to do this kind of research.

A Looser and More Speculative Approach

In re-visiting scenes from my original research in order to write this reflection on doing sociology with plastic, I noticed that my focus on tracking plastic's global connections through cities and across borders, trying to understand what was happening in each place, narrowed my research to plastic's technical and social dimensions. My fieldnotes were full of questions designed to reveal particular kinds of information and overlook other kinds. 'What does a typical working day for you involve? Can I see the machine that makes the plastic pellets? What does it do exactly? Where do you live?' And so on. Looking back, I am struck by the highly focused way in which I excavated everyday scenes of social and chemical production. This was driven by my intention to map micro-scenes of everyday life onto stories of connections across borders – an analysis of how globalisation works as it moves through people's lives in plastic shoes. In excavating small places for bigger, theoretically oriented and multiscalar insights, in being over-focused and instrumental, I missed out on the benefits of a looser and more speculative approach in evoking the worlds I wanted to understand.

The three scenes above are my attempt to address these limitations with a more speculative approach to doing sociology with plastic. By this

I mean an approach that allows for uncertainties, unanswered questions, incomplete understanding, rumination and a focus on small things in and of themselves, rather than for their broader significance. In developing a looser and more speculative approach, anthropologist Kathleen Stewart (2007, 2011) provided vital insights. Stewart (2011, pp. 445–447) suggests that theory can be built through stories and descriptive detours, as she explores the layered *plasticity* of lived compositions of the ordinary. She calls these lived compositions 'pockets', and suggests unfolding them, 'slowed and amplified' to see what might be in them (2011, p. 447). I think of what Stewart calls 'pockets' as the scenes of my research: a tableau slowed down temporarily, like those above.

Alchemies of Plastic

Where to begin. Alchemy – a term that in the past combined a form of chemistry and speculative philosophy – seems like a promising beginning. Alchemy invites a speculative exploration of plastic's entwined elements, its physical properties as a material and its social chemistries in the lives and landscapes of its making. This approach is inspired by Primo Levi's (2000) *Periodic Table*, in which he describes the properties of the chemical elements composing matter, alongside stories about what matters in his experiences of Auschwitz and life in fascist Italy. Sometimes he draws direct parallels between members of his family and the properties of particular chemical elements: a playful creativity.

The chemical alchemy of plastic describes a world of chemical variation produced through arrangements of hydrogen and carbon, which are extracted from oil by cracking it – taking large hydrocarbons and breaking them into smaller ones – into a substance called naphtha, a flammable oil containing hydrocarbons. Different types and strengths of plastic are produced through creating polymer chains of different combinations of hydrogen and carbon and additives like chlorine, nitrogen and sulphur. These emerge from reactors as a raw material that can be subjected to treatments with additives – like antioxidants and colorants – which further change their physical and chemical properties. Social alchemies are, perhaps, not dissimilar. My research notes are full of chemical formulae, as I struggled to understand what plastic is. As a material, plastic is, well, *plastic* in the sense of being malleable, like people's lives. It is made into different shapes, colours and densities, and has a range of uses. The plastics made into cheap flip-flops are polyethylene (PE) and ethylene-vinyl acetate (EVA), a co-polymer product of ethylene adjusted with the chemical vinyl acetate. PE and EVA – like the corrugated metal from which much of the world's housing is constructed – form the material textures of poverty in everyday life in much of the global south. And the fabrics of everyday life exert important influence on how life is lived: they are an important, if often overlooked, element in sociological research and analysis.

Plastic Landscapes

I reasoned that the alchemy of plastic would be woven into its landscapes of production, and I wanted to visit these landscapes and take a close look at its material and human textures. In Daesan, we drove round the perimeter of chemical plants. I took photos and made notes. This is a landscape scattered with giant securitised plants and vast domed white holding tanks of imported oil treated in clusters of refineries. Barbed wire atop high chain-link fences and security cameras, which occasionally sent security teams to see what we were doing, meant we only saw the plants, belting out white steam, from a distance, across the bleak winter landscape. At night – plants operate 24/7 – the same landscape was magically transformed by brightly lit metal stacks and chimneys reaching for the sky, enormous white storage silos and networks of pipes, glowing in brilliant amber and white. Strewn around on the ground where we stood by the wire fences were traces of these distant worlds: an abandoned white plastic safety helmet, giant shipping containers elegantly rusting and bits of plastic bags.

Plastic Production

Inside, the plant is unpeopled and eerie. We walk around long low sheds the size of several football pitches combined. These specialise in different parts of the production processes and different kinds of plastic – PE and EVA. Machines rule and men are the minders who keep them running while female secretaries mind the men. Machines apply heat and pressure, while men sit in control rooms watching monitors. Plastic pellets are invisibly propelled along pipes by blasts of air. There are storage areas with vast silos. Little yellow driverless trains transport stuff about. Over the next little while we are allowed to interview workers. They all wear identical mandarin-collared jackets with their names embroidered on them, black trousers and black trainers. They move about in formation, like the team they clearly are, just as they ate together at the oyster dinner. I began to understand that plastic was a way of making lives, as our work extended beyond the plants, as workers invited us into their homes to meet their families. Routines in production segued into routine lives lived in step in company apartments.

Why Plastic Matters

Plastic matters because the world in which we live is fabricated in it. Clothes have plastics woven into them; and everyday objects on which people rely – pens, plugs, electrical cable coating, spectacles, cars, computer parts and so on – are made of plastic. Microplastics have entered food chains and human bodies – we are part-plastic constructions ourselves. As a consequence of the accelerated incursion of plastic over the last hundred years, bodies and everyday lives are literally entangled in it. Life with deadly viruses has amplified demand for plastic facemasks and shields. But at the same time as plastic fabricates the social and material life of the planet, it destroys it. Plastics are a major environmental hazard. Dumped in landfill sites, some take hundreds of years to decompose. Today we produce 300 million tonnes of plastic waste every year, roughly equivalent to the weight of the world's entire population.[3] Plastic is part of the Anthropocene – the earth's re-shaping by human occupation – incorporating the earth in the geological layering of landscape (Amin and Thrift 2017).

Plastic material and social worlds are intricately entwined as this chapter on doing sociology with plastic has shown. Threaded through people's lives and the operation of everyday scenes, plastic could not be more central to social life. Our lives are made of it and wound around it, and this is amplified for those involved in plastic production. In the three scenes at

---

[3] www.unep.org/interactive/beat-plastic-pollution/

the beginning of this chapter, worlds shaped by plastic production are delicately explored for their social relationships – between workers, between men and women, between old and young – textures and atmospheres. We catch glimpses of lives lived in and through plastic by slowing a stream of activity down into scenes so that we can take a close look, as Stewart suggests, so that stories and actions – which are also stories told by other means – have time to unfold. Plastic could not be more relevant to social life and to sociological reflection. Surprising, then, that it is rarely given the attention it warrants.

References

Amin, A. and Thrift, N. (2017) *Seeing Like a City*. Cambridge: Polity.

Knowles, C. (2014) *Flip-Flop: A Journey through Globalisation's Backroads*. London: Pluto.

Kopytof, I. (1986) 'The cultural biography of things: Commoditisation as process', reprinted in Apadurai, Arjun (ed.) (2014), *The Social Life of Things*. Cambridge: Cambridge University Press, pp. 64–91.

Levi, P. (2000) *Periodic Table*. London: Penguin.

Sassen, S. (2001) *The Global City*. Princeton, NJ: Princeton University Press.

Stewart, K. (2007) *Ordinary Affects*. Durham, NC: Duke University Press.

Stewart, K. (2011) 'Atmospheric attunements', *Environment and Planning D: Society and Space*, 29, 445–453.

22

How to do social research with... podcasts

Michaela Benson

Between 2017 and 2020, I podcasted my way through a live (and lively) sociological project about Brexit and its consequences for British citizens living in the European Union's 27 member states (EU-27). At the outset, I imagined these podcasts as engaging the people taking part in the project and meeting the funders' requirements for public and stakeholder engagement. Over the course of the project, the podcasts became a central pillar of the research in ways I had not anticipated at the outset. Now the project is over, they are an invaluable archive of the research. They document how my understandings and analysis unfolded alongside the twists and turns of the Brexit negotiations. Drawing on my experience of producing and presenting *Brexit Brits Abroad*, this chapter offers some tentative reflections on the prospects for sociological podcasting, not only for broadcasting research findings but as integral to the knowledge production at the heart of a research project.

The BrExpats Research Project

The 'BrExpats' research project was one of 25 projects funded through the Economic and Social Research Council's (ESRC) Brexit Priority Grant scheme (ESRC, 2017).[1] Its focus lay in understanding what Britain's exit from the EU meant for the British citizen population living outside the UK in the EU-27. Freedom of movement within the EU had been a significant factor in facilitating the mobility of this population, estimated at

[1]'BrExpats: Freedom of Movement, Citizenship and Brexit in the Lives of British Citizens Resident in the EU-27' was funded by the Economic and Social Research Council (Grant Number ES/R000875/1) through the UK in a Changing Europe Initiative.

the time of the 2016 Referendum to be somewhere in the region of two million people. Yet, the UK Government's insistence that through Brexit they would 'end Free Movement' had the potential to change their rights and entitlements. Running from May 2017 to 31 December 2020, the project coincided with the Brexit negotiations between the UK and EU (2017–2018), Britain's exit from the EU (31 December 2019) and the Brexit transition period (2020). By the end of this period, no longer EU citizens eligible for Free Movement within the bloc, British citizens across the EU had their rights to live and work in their country of residence protected, while losing continued rights to Free Movement (for a more detailed analysis, see Benson, 2021).

The 'BrExpats' project was an exercise in what Les Back and Nirmal Puwar, (2012; see also Back, 2007) describe as 'live sociology', an approach that addressed our funders' mandate to undertake public and stakeholder engagement activities while feeding these into the project. As my co-investigator Karen O'Reilly and I have written elsewhere, working with new platforms and technologies to conduct and communicate the research offered opportunities to disturb 'linear and static understandings of the research process to call for an agile, contingent and collaborative reflexive practice' (2022, p. 181).

The project included an internet-mediated Citizens' Panel of 200 British citizens living across Europe; and two longitudinal case studies, informed by an ethnographic approach, which built on Karen's and my respective research in southern Spain and rural France (see, for example, O'Reilly, 2000; Benson, 2011). These elements of the research ran over the duration of the project. Part-way through the project, we received further funding for a case study focused on British citizens in Ireland. In total, over 600 people took part in the qualitative dimensions of the project. Our engagements with those taking part in the research included face-to-face interviews, participant observations, email conversations and other internet-mediated research. We regularly returned to those taking part, via diverse media of communication, to discuss and learn with them about how Brexit as an ongoing process continued to shape their lives. The scale of the project was made possible by working with a team of researchers who included Katherine Collins, Chantelle Lewis and Michael Danby.

The *Brexit Brits Abroad* Podcast

The podcast was one of a set of multimedia outputs from the project, including the project website which now serves as an archive of the research (https://brexitbritsabroad.org). My initial pitch had been for a podcast series aimed at raising awareness of the key issues that British citizens living in the EU-27 were facing in consequence of the UK's decision to exit the EU. I anticipated that the content would be informed by the research as it unfolded, making accessible our analysis to wider publics that included those taking part in the research, other stakeholders and interested parties. The only catch was that this was a format and genre of which I had no first-hand experience. It became clear that I would need to enlist some help.

Through my conversations with podcasters and producers it became clear to me that while I had the skills for developing the content and narrative of the series and episodes – indeed, these are skills most proximate to the process of academic writing – these could only get me part-way to my goal. Producing content was only one part of a much bigger process that included, among other things, curation and editing, navigating various online platforms and technologies, building and developing audiences. While preparing the content of an episode or series is the equivalent of researching and writing a journal article, the production and post-production work involved in podcasting is more like what happens after writing, the arcane processes and the publishing platforms that few academic authors fully comprehend through which an article (or book) makes its way into the world (and reaches its intended publics). As the podcast was just one element of a fast-moving and multispoked project, I took a decision at an early stage that this was not going to be a DIY effort, and contracted Emma Houlton and her production company, Art of Podcast, to help me out.

Over a period of nearly three years, I released fortnightly episodes. These 30-minute episodes included interviews with British citizens living in the EU-27; members of grassroots and civil society organisations; local community group leaders; interviews with other academics, those also working with British citizens living abroad and on related topics; interviews with project partners and episodes dedicated to the research and its findings including different members of the project team.

Making Sociology Sociable through Podcasting

From the heightened politics around Brexit to the contemporary politics of social research, we were concerned about the potential for research on Brexit – undoubtedly a 'hot' political topic – to lose its critical and analytical focus in the rush to generate knowledge, *including through the funders' requirement to undertake impact-generating activities from the get-go.*

(Benson and O'Reilly, 2022, p. 180, emphasis added; see also Benson, 2021).

The focus of live sociology on re-imagining and re-claiming the craft of social research in the context of a shifting political landscape of social research – where the tools that sociologists could once claim as their distinctive contribution to making sense of the world have been co-opted to generate data on an unprecedented scale, and in the process decoupled from the critical evaluation and ethical judgement integral to the sociological craft — appealed to me and Karen. Working with the affordances of new platforms and technologies, as Back and Puwar (2012) advocate, became a way for us to navigate the tensions we felt in doing research under these conditions and in the context of a major political transformation.

In a recent article, Chantelle Lewis, Tissot Regis and George Ofori-Addo – the presenters and producers of the anti-racist podcast *Surviving Society* – emphasise: 'sociological podcasting has the capacity to offer alternative ways of rejecting presentist accounts of society, and clearly demonstrates a live mode of doing sociology. It does this through providing engagers with fluid and interconnected analyses about society and politics' (Lewis *et al.*, 2021, p. 96).

They present podcasting as a space for resistance and what, following Patricia Hill Collins, they describe as dialogical knowledge production, learning with and alongside their guests and making audible alternative ways of understanding politics and society. In his new book, anthropologist Ian Cook (2023) documents insurgence as the predominant theme when scholarly podcasters explain why they podcast. Podcasting here becomes an act of rebellion against the normative structures and communicative repertoires of academic practice, in this way reminiscent of what David Beer (2014) refers to as 'Punk Sociology'.

These understandings of scholarly podcasting make clear why the medium is a good fit for a distinctively public sociology. From my experiences with the *Brexit Brits Abroad* podcast, the prospects for sociological podcasting also lie in its prospects for the research process. This is in terms of what Shamser Sinha and Les Back (2014) refer to as 'making methods sociable' (p. 473), challenging explicitly some of the more extractive practices of social research by extending the dialogue between researchers and those taking part in the research into analysis and the production of outputs. Conceived in this way, sociological podcasting animates and intervenes in the process of knowledge production (see also Cook, 2023). Such methodological affordances of podcasting fit to an understanding of the research process as iterative, the researchers engaged in an ongoing and dialogical process of reflexive practice (Benson and O'Reilly, 2022).

As a space where the liveliness of the research could be crafted, cultivated and communicated, the *Brexit Brits Abroad* podcast was vital to the dialogic production of knowledge through the research. In the context of the project and its other outputs, the podcast became one of the sites where the development of our analysis was on show, made audible in ways that are more often obscured in the written work of social scientists (Cook and Udupa, 2019).

Podcasting Our Way through Brexit

My claim about the prospects for podcasts to make sociology sociable lies in how we used the podcast to engage those taking part in the research and members of our primary public, British citizens living in the EU (see also Benson and O'Reilly, 2022). Making the project public in this way invited commentary and feedback, bringing people into our conversations on a continuous basis. I should stress here, that this also meant being attentive to silences, noticing whose voices were not being heard or present in these (online) conversations and thinking about ways to amplify these through the research and through our presence in these conversations. Other correspondence included that from people asking us for advice on their particular situation – drawing our attention to where there were gaps in the provisions being developed and who might fall through them as the Withdrawal Agreement was implemented. This opened up areas that we might want to look into in more detail through the research. Others wrote to us to share their reflections and experiences or suggest alternative interpretations.

However, the prospects for making sociology sociable through podcasting also lie in its rhythms and frequency. The frequency of the *Brexit Brits Abroad* podcast and its duration – broadcasting fortnightly, mapping onto the project from start to finish – were significant to the podcast's integration into the research process as a site for the development of ongoing sociological analysis. On the surface, the frequency of podcasting might seem to contradict the critique of the 'frenzied rhythm' of the audit-led research environment that drives Back and Puwar's (2012) call for 'live sociology'. While producing *Brexit Brits Abroad* with such frequency did make it prone to 'frenzy' – arguably the consequence of researching a 'frenzied' issue – to my mind, for podcasting to deliver on its prospects for *live sociology*, questions of rhythm and frequency are crucial. It is through this that communities build up around podcasts, and with these, increasing prospects for making sociology sociable.

Within this, the approach we took to format and production was also significant. Each episode was organised around a conversation, with interviews and discussions offering space for some brief sociological reflections. Foregrounding dialogue – within the project team, with other academics, with British citizens living in the EU, with campaigners, advocates and policy-makers – amplified the dialogic production of knowledge. In the spirit of not looking through rose-tinted glasses, just as we consider the politics of knowledge production within the research interview or other research encounters, I want to highlight here that there is work to do on considering questions of positionality, power and inequality in the podcasting encounter (see also Cook, 2020). But that is for another day.

In respect to content, I never planned very far in advance. At any one time, I might have two or three episodes ready to go live, but I left space to think about who and what else might be brought into the conversation in the context of a fast-changing environment. This meant that if something came up in the research or in the unfolding (and unpredictable) Brexit negotiations that was of relevance to the project and its publics, I would bring someone in who could speak to the issue or theme. When it came to podcasting conversations with British citizens living in the EU, the direction of the conversation and analysis would be led by our guests and their concerns.

Finally, as a communicative repertoire, the podcast allowed us as a project team to present our sociological analyses as tentative, as in process, and created the space to make audible the conversations through which this analysis was produced. Indeed, when members of the project team got together to record episodes, when we interviewed academics working on related topics, when we spoke to those participating in and contributing to the research – whether the wider publics or stakeholders concerned with the issues at the heart of the research – what stood out to me was how these conversations became fundamental to the process of analysis. In other words, the podcast centred the role of dialogue in analysis, rather than seeking to present the project team as singular authorities on the topic of Brexit and its impact on British citizens living in the EU. The resulting back catalogue reveals the persistence and development of some of the themes through the conversations at the heart of the podcast – notably, questions of identity, belonging and citizenship; relationships to Britain and Europe; the diversity and stratification of the British citizen population living in the EU.

Within the context of re-imagining the craft of sociological research, the *Brexit Brits Abroad* podcast became a way for the project to demonstrate sociology's vital role in the broader project – with its multiple stakeholders and publics – of making sense of Brexit as it unfolded.

Concluding Thoughts: The Afterlife of *Brexit Brits Abroad*

Although the project and the podcast have come to an end, *Brexit Brits Abroad* has had an afterlife. At the time of writing, there have been nearly 48,000 downloads of the podcast. This means that on average each episode has in excess of 500 downloads. I could never have imagined that the podcast would reach that many people. Even now there are no new episodes, and episodes are no longer promoted through the project's bespoke social media ecosystem, they continue to be downloaded. Other unexpected outcomes included the listing of the podcast in the US website Politico's review of the top 25 podcasts on Brexit, a special mention in the category 'best academic podcasts on Brexit' by RTÉ, and more recently, being named one of the top 20 best podcasts on the EU by *Welp* magazine. The series has also had an afterlife in the classroom when, during the Covid-19 pandemic, colleagues at the University of Newcastle used the series as the basis for a virtual field trip for undergraduate students. These outcomes are important to me, not because they indicate (quantifiable) engagement, but because they show the potential of scholarly podcasts to travel beyond our immediate publics.

The podcast and the associated transcripts offer a rich archive of the project as it unfolded, showing how our analysis developed over time. It reveals what could be communicated in the moment, and where we might take this as we developed the outputs from the project further. From a personal point of view, it also helped me to develop confidence in my knowledge and ideas, leading my co-author Karen O'Reilly to tell me that in my written work my voice is now more confidently and clearly expressed.

To conclude, the question of how to do sociology with podcasts is one that is deeply entangled with the ongoing question of how we might cultivate the liveliness of sociology, and where podcasting might sit in the expanded communicative repertoire of a re-imagined sociology.

Podography

Brexit Brits Abroad: https://brexitbritsabroad.libsyn.com

Surviving Society: https://soundcloud.com/user-622675754

References

Back, L. (2007) *The Art of Listening*. Oxford: Berg.

Back, L. and Puwar, N. (2012) 'A manifesto for live methods: Provocations and capacities', *The Sociological Review*, 60(S1), pp. 6–17.

Beer, D. (2014) *Punk Sociology*. London: Palgrave.

Benson, M. (2011) *The British in Rural France*. Manchester: Manchester University Press.

Benson, M. (2021) 'Brexit's hidden costs for Britons living in the EU', *Current History*, 120(824), pp. 118–120.

Benson, M. and O'Reilly, K. (2022) 'Reflexive practice in live sociology: Lessons from researching Brexit in the lives of British citizens living in the EU-27', *Qualitative Research*, 22(2), pp. 177–193. Available at: https://doi.org/10.1177/1468794120977795

Cook, I.M. (2020) 'Critique of podcasting as an anthropological method', *Ethnography*, publication online ahead of print. Available at: https://doi.org/10.1177/1466138120967039

Cook, I.M. (2023) *Scholarly Podcasting: Why, What, How*. London: Routledge.

Cook, I.M. and Udupa, S. (2019) 'Talking media with "online Gods": What is academic podcasting like?', *EPW Engage*, 29 January. Available at: www.epw.in/engage/article/talking-media-online-gods-what-is-academic-podcasting-like

ESRC (2017) UK in a changing Europe: Brexit priority grants call specification. No longer available online.

Lewis, C., Regis, T. and Ofori-Addo, G. (2021) 'Can "sociological podcasting" offer radical hope, care and solidarity in times of crisis?', *Soundings*, 79, pp. 94–109.

O'Reilly, K. (2000) *The British on the Costa del Sol*. London: Routledge.

Sinha, S. and Back, L. (2014) 'Making methods sociable: Dialogue, ethics and authorship in qualitative research', *Qualitative Research*, 14(4), pp. 473–487.

23

How to do social research with... recalcitrance

Marsha Rosengarten

Recalcitrance: *refusing to obey authority, custom, regulation, etc.; stubbornly defiant. (C19: via French from Latin* recalcitrāre, *from* RE- + calcitrāre *to kick.)*

In this brief chapter, I propose that recalcitrance by our research subjects may enable us to decolonise our thinking and, consequently, enable new modes of thought and practice. By actively or passively putting research authority to the test, recalcitrance invites us to reflect on what we have decided in advance of a problem and how it matters or should matter to those who are affected by it (Savransky, 2014; Stengers, 2018). To illustrate, I offer two contrasting stories where the rules of inquiry were refused. The first story is from Michel Serres' (1997) book *The Troubadour of Knowledge*. It captures much of what I want to convey: first, about a mode of rationality that has colonised (infected) thought to suggest that there is only one way of viewing reality; second, that those whom we research may provoke us to question what we have assumed is the only way to approach a problem or, indeed, how to understand a problem. The second story concerns the area that my research is largely focused on, and is considerably less optimistic. It is about research designed to correct the problem of HIV infection. Here I suggest that recalcitrance provided a crucial opportunity for learning what might matter to those at risk of HIV infection, but was elided by research convention. Later in the piece I consider what these stories might offer to other problems, notably 'Covid-19 vaccine hesitancy'.

Story One

A group of sailors from a supply ship find themselves shipwrecked on a Polynesian island in a strange but wonderful paradise. Intense exchanges take place between contrasting cultures. As Serres describes this:

The natives nourished a strange passion for words: they asked for the precise translation of their terms and were tireless in their explanations. ... They [the shipwrecked and the natives] wore themselves out on parallels: the constraints differed, but each was subjected in his country to equally complicated rules, incomprehensible to the point of laughter to his interlocutors, but on neither side were these rules neglected.

(Serres, 1997, p. 127)

Eventually the shipwrecked sailors were rescued but chose to return to the islanders. They were welcomed with a large feast and an almost never-ending soccer match. Each time the game finished with an uneven score – precisely what we would regard as signalling an end winner and loser – the game was re-played. Only when the score was even, did the Islanders stop playing and celebrate. The game was played according to the usual rules of soccer with only one single rule change: the absence of a 'conqueror and a conquered'. The Islanders explained the alteration through the example of a pancake that would usually be divided according to the numbers needing to eat it: 'This pancake, did it occur to you not to share it?'

'That wouldn't mean anything,' the sailors protest.

'But yes, as in soccer. Someone will eat the whole thing and the others won't eat anything, if you don't share it' (Serres, 1997, p. 130).

The sailors continue their queries to which they receive the following reply:

THE ISLANDERS: We do not understand that which is neither just nor human, because one gets the upper hand. So we play the game for the time you taught us. If at the end the result is nil, the game ends on true sharing ... If not, the two teams, as you say, are decided between, which is something unjust and barbaric. What is the point in humiliating the vanquished if one wishes to pass for civilized like yourselves? So, one must begin again, for a long time, until sharing returns. Sometimes the game lasts for weeks. Some players have even died from it.

THE SAILORS: Died from it? Really?

THE ISLANDERS: Why not?

(Serres, 1997, pp. 130–131)

Serres concludes his story with a type of postscript. He says the sailors again left, but now with the question of what it means to win. It led them to wonder if they had truly 'won' the Second World War, given the event of Hiroshima. In turn, one sailor offers the following insight as the group reflected on their experience:

Are you trying to determine the true conquerors? ... I know them well, from having taken them sometimes in my boat ... Ethnologists, sociologists, I don't know their title, but they study the natives of the islands ... and in general take men for the subject of studies, that is, for objects.

(Serres, 1997, p. 131)

And a final comment from another: 'They sing of victory: who can conceivably be above those who explain and understand others who, from this point of view, will never again be their fellow creatures, what is more their neighbours?' (Serres, 1997, p. 131).

Serres' narrative invites its reader to ponder on the stakes of play and reveals how, by changing one rule only, that what matters to a community may be vastly different to that of another. In this case, taking some forms of dying for granted (those for conquering) in contrast to others (those for sharing). It also alludes to a willingness or an ableness by all the characters - and potentially its reader - to be exposed to other possible modes of existence. The sailors' response proffered by Serres' imaginative play may be tentative but, in his telling, they became privy to the investment we - those of us who do not live in a paradise-like world - have in the act of conquering or, as I want to understand it, claiming victory by erasing the kind of thinking that may come from exposure to the experience of others.

Story Two

Biomedical scientists travel to distant lands to enrol 14,000 research subjects in randomised control trials (RCTs) to test the efficacy of a pill called PrEP (pre-exposure prophylaxis). Because of this research, it is now established that if you take PrEP as prescribed and have sex with someone who has HIV, you are extremely unlikely - almost guaranteed - not to acquire the infection. Even so, the research that has led to this fine evidence did not go smoothly. Whereas some of the RCTs found PrEP to be efficacious, others did not. Those that enrolled gay men, trans men, men who have sex with men (MSM) and those that enrolled heterosexual couples (one HIV positive and one HIV negative, with men and women of both categories) provided sound scientific evidence that PrEP was safe and efficacious. But two other RCTs, respectively called Fem-PrEP and VOICE, with 'young single women' resulted in the same number of participants becoming infected in both arms of the trials: the arm that included giving a placebo pill, indistinguishable in appearance from the PrEP pill; and the arm that provided the 'real' PrEP pill. Not surprisingly, these latter trials were deemed to have 'failed'. The explanation for failure was found not in the pill but in the women. Although the women reported that they had been taking PrEP, blood tests showed that they had not.

The scientists were thus able to exonerate themselves from the fact that unexpectedly high numbers of women, already deemed vulnerable to HIV infection, became infected. That is to say, they were not to be held responsible for the 'failure'. Their research, as borne out by the other RCTs, promised a benefit to the participants and to their future sexual partners who would also have been at risk of HIV infection. But, more specifically, the scientists were able to exonerate themselves from the women's recalcitrance or 'changing a rule' (the requirement to take the pill), because they followed the conventions of what has been agreed in their community as ethical or 'bioethical' research. Indeed, they did all and more than was required. In practice, they employed local outreach workers to make personal contact with possible participants in order to explain the potential risks and benefits before gaining the participants' consent. This included attending women's groups, sex-worker 'hot spots' and conducting formalised meetings amongst the participants' communities (Mack et al., 2013).

I shall not presume to tell the story of the women research subjects in the 'failed' trials. Rather, I will suggest that we do not need to read their publications – which, of course, do not exist because publishing research findings is a practice esteemed by 'us' – to appreciate that what mattered to them diverged from the problem assumed by the researchers. Instead, I want to dramatise the affordances of their recalcitrance.

In Place of Victory or Failure

If recalcitrance is understood according to the definition I have provided above, it requires a situation where certain 'rules' are imposed or, less explicit, where a certain conduct is expected. That is to say, recalcitrance does not come from nowhere. Its emergence forces an alteration in the dynamic of the nature of the encounter (Savransky, 2014). In the first story, the sailors learned from a change to the rules of football that seeking victory over others may not be what matters and that their own culture rather than that of others might be mistaken in its conduct. In the second story, the scientists remained closed to such learning and, as I have recounted from their publications, were able to feel justified in being so according to their rules of conduct that held the women in the Fem-PrEP and VOICE trials as responsible for 'failure'. However, not only did the scientists fail in their attempts to conquer a situation of HIV infection. They unintentionally increased the average rates of HIV infection expected in their research participants. While we might agree that the research showing PrEP's efficacy in some of the trials matters to those who have since taken up using PrEP and to public health authorities who seek a decline in the epidemic, there remains the question of its relevance to others who are also at risk of HIV but for whom PrEP was not found relevant – at least in the Fem-PrEP and VOICE trials.

A further trial called 'SMART' (Sequential Multiple Assignment Randomised Trial) involving the testing of PrEP with women also 'failed'. In this case, there was high uptake of the drug in the first few months, but it declined over the 12-month study (Celum *et al.*, 2020). By contrast with the Fem-PrEP and VOICE trials, the trial design did create a situation where recalcitrance to dosing could be actively expressed and appreciated. I do not want to underplay the possible significance of this change, although there remains the question of whether it, in itself, addresses the question of what mattered to the women. Indeed, again, many acquired HIV during the trial, leading me to suggest that the force for alteration in the rules required more than enabling an overt recalcitrance to PrEP. However, it has since occasioned a change to the 'rule' of demanding dosing adherence. In place of a pill, scientists have developed a long-lasting injectable form of PrEP. Here we might ask whether this mode of intervention will be found relevant by those affected by HIV? Have the researchers developed, as Serres' story suggests, a sensibility to the insistent presence of plural realities or, again, prioritised their study *of others* without taking the time to know them as 'fellow creatures' (1997, p. 131)?

None of what I have covered means that we should jettison scientific or, indeed, social scientific research. Nor am I suggesting that we should simply disregard conventional ethical codes of conduct intended to protect research subjects from known risks or ill intentions (see Washington, 2008). On the contrary, I am proposing that as researchers we need to continue to reflect on the underlying assumptions that inform our approach, including what constitutes 'victory' or, more usually phrased, 'ethically' achieved 'success'. If, having encountered recalcitrance, we return 'home' without a genuine difference in our thinking, we can ask what it is that we have dodged for our world to seem as when we left it (Whitehead, 1929, p. 66).

To give a little more weight to my proposition, I want to diverge a little and suggest that it is not only human subjects that exhibit recalcitrance to the rules. So, too, do the pathogenic substances that are held by science as causally responsible for infection. Biomedical efforts to mitigate an infectious disease do not always hit their mark. If we turn to the situation in which I am writing, we would find that the promise for preventing Covid-19 infection is currently carried by vaccines. Yet the virus held responsible for Covid-19 is also mutating and thus is, to some degree, recalcitrant to the specificities of available vaccines. As such, it is putting science and public health policy to the test. Arguably, fuelling the potential for new strains of the virus is the 'social' problem of 'Covid-19 vaccine hesitancy'. It is also putting science and public health policy to the test. A growing body of literature suggests that the 'hesitation' is multifactorial, reflecting concerns such as the unusual speed of vaccine development and unknown potential side-effects (Danchin and Buttery, 2021; Subbaraman, 2021) and, not unrelatedly, 'conspiracy claims' about science and government that take root from different social and historical experiences (Prasad, 2022). Against this backdrop, many ask: when will we return to normal? But might there be something to learn about what is assumed of the past and the imagined progress made by a culture that is premised on seeking victory? The Islanders in Serres' story might well laugh at this nostalgia for a world that has not alleviated our ills (Chakrabarty, 2019; Roy, 2020).

An Alternative Beginning

If, at this point, it may seem that I am proposing that as researchers we should visit 'foreign lands' while leaving our assumptions behind, I want to be clear that doing research is never a matter of constructing oneself as if one were an empty slate. If it were, there would be no possibility of coming up with a topic or, as I am proposing, identifying a problem that we think matters but, in doing so, remaining open to the possibility that this may not be so for others. Nor am I proposing that recalcitrance should be judged as either right or wrong. It is never a matter of simply taking 'the other side' but, rather, paying attention to the differences that a situation may cultivate (Despret, 2018). Research is a process and requires conceptual tools. Usually it builds on the work of others, notably journal articles or books, possibly blogs and other media sources, to identify what has not already been investigated and to fill a gap. But when turning to the work of others we might also decide that a different style of investigation is called for. My recourse to Serres' story may seem a long way from my own study of infectious diseases, but it enabled me to re-visit the second story with an appreciation for the women 'as fellow creatures'.

Whatever criteria we assume at the outset of visiting a 'foreign land' (whether it be to learn about culture or, for the natural sciences, the body encountering infection), there is no guarantee that it will or, to re-phrase, we should remain the same. Research is an adventure. It has no absolute guarantees. Rather, it is an experiment whose demands need to be taken seriously *if* the difference it makes is to be found relevant by all those situated by the formulation of the problem (Savransky, 2018; Rosengarten, 2021). I have proposed recalcitrance as a possible counter to what the speculative philosopher Alfred North Whitehead (1929, p. 66) refers to as 'the atrophied' decay that becomes of thinking that a changing world is there for knowing while, paradoxically, requiring it to remain the same. As if, even after leaving familiar shores, we and the world we encounter will conform to what is already known.

References

Celum, C.L., Gill, K., Morton, J.F, Stein, G., Myers, L., Thomas, K.K., McConnell, M. *et al.* (2020) 'Incentives conditioned on tenofovir levels to support PrEP adherence among young South African Women: A randomized trial', *Journal of the International AIDS Society*, 23(11), e25636. Available at: https://doi.org/10.1002/jia2.25636

Chakrabarty, D. (2019) 'The planet: An emergent humanist category', *Critical Inquiry*, 46(1), pp. 1–31. Available at: https://doi.org/10.1086/705298

Danchin, M. and Buttery, J. (2021) 'COVID-19 vaccine hesitancy: A unique set of challenges', *Internal Medicine Journal*, 51(12), pp. 1987–1989. Available at: https://doi.org/10.1111/imj.15599

Despret, V. (2018) 'Talking before the dead', *SubStance*, 47(1), pp. 64–79.

Mack, N., Kirkendale, S., Omullo, P., Ratlhagana, O., Masaki, M., Siguntu, P. *et al.* (2013) 'Implementing good participatory practice guidelines in the FEM-PrEP preexposure prophylaxis trial for HIV prevention among African women: A focus on local stakeholder involvement', *Open Access Journal of Clinical Trials*, October (5), pp. 127–135. Available at: https://doi.org/10.2147/OAJCT.S45717

Prasad, A. (2022) 'Anti-science misinformation and conspiracies: COVID–19, post-truth, and science and technology studies (STS)', *Science, Technology and Society*, 27(1), pp. 88–112. Available at: https://doi.org/10.1177/09717218211003413

Rosengarten, M. (2021) 'An unfinished history: A story of ongoing events and mutating HIV problems', in Bernays, S., Bourne, A., Kippax, S., Aggleton, P. and Parker, R. (eds) *Remaking HIV Prevention in the 21st Century: The Promise of TasP, U=U and PrEP*. Social Aspects of HIV series. Cham: Springer International Publishing, pp. 289–302. Available at: https://doi.org/10.1007/978-3-030-69819-5_21

Roy, A. (2020) 'Arundhati Roy: "The pandemic is a portal" ', *Financial Times*, 3 April. Available at: www.ft.com/content/10d8f5e8-74eb-11ea-95fe-fcd274e920ca

Savransky, M. (2014) 'Of recalcitrant subjects', *Culture, Theory and Critique*, 55(1), pp. 96–113. Available at: https://doi.org/10.1080/14735784.2013.821767

Savransky, M. (2018) 'The social and its problems: On the problematic of sociology', in Marres, N., Guggenheim, M. and Wilkie, A. (eds) *Inventing the Social*. Manchester, UK: Mattering Press, pp. 212–233.

Serres, M. (1997) *The Troubadour of Knowledge*. 3rd edition. Translated by Sheila Glaser and William Paulson. Ann Arbor: The University of Michigan Press.

Stengers, I. (2018) *Another Science Is Possible: A Manifesto for Slow Science*. Translated by Stephen Muecke. Cambridge, Medford, MA: Polity Press.

Subbaraman, N. (2021) 'This COVID-vaccine designer is tackling vaccine hesitancy –in churches and on Twitter', *Nature*, 590(7846), pp. 377. Available at: https://doi.org/10.1038/d41586-021-00338-y

Washington, H.A. (2008) *Medical Apartheid: The Dark History of the Medical Experimentation on Black Americans from Colonial Times to the Present*. New York: Anchor Books.

Whitehead, A.N. (1929) *The Function of Reason*. Princeton, NJ: Princeton University Press.

24

How to do social research with... sewing

Kat Jungnickel

Stitch. Thread. Unpick. Unravel. Seam. Interface. Piece. Cut. Fold. Pin. Press. Gather.

We use a surprising number of sewing terms in everyday language. They are particularly present in the doing of social research. We unpick concepts, thread ideas through arguments and stitch theory together with methods. We combine materials, and fold and press data into shape. We are trained to look for patterns, find holes in arguments and try to mend them. Language matters as much as the clothes that cover our bodies. Both are cultural, social, gendered and political. They hold memories and make meaning. They shape how we interact, respond, know each other and ourselves. They materialise class, race, gender and environmental norms and beliefs as well as offering means to protest and resist them. Yet, these words, and the many methods they describe, can become so familiar in their underpinning of everyday practice that we cease to notice them. As many researchers in sociology and science and technology studies (STS) have pointed out, paying attention to mundane and everyday objects and practices can cast new light on conventional or accepted socio-political norms and beliefs and raise questions about things we take for granted.

This chapter is not about paying closer attention to linguistic practice. It's also not just about clothing studies, though they are both implicit in the following sections. Instead, I focus on the doing of social research on, with and through sewing. Because of the nature of this book, I attempt to convey in words the potential of sewing as a method for getting up close to lives lived in the past and discuss what happens when we make and wear research. I have previously discussed this in terms of 'making things to make sense of things' (Jungnickel, 2018), whereby the use of practice research enables close ethnographic encounters with the past and helps to surface overlooked or hidden things into rich, embodied and affectual presents. Here I focus on what I call 'speculative sewing', which is the stitching together of data, theory, methods and fabric into three-dimensional arguments (Jungnickel, 2023b). I aim to describe how the process thickens data by rendering lesser-known research stories visible and knowable. If methods, as Law and Urry (2011) argue, don't just describe reality, they also make it, then clothes too can be investigated for their world-making potential. After all, as Haraway reminds us, it 'matters what matters we use to think other matters with' (2016, p. 12).

Getting Inventive with the Study of Inventions

My mother taught me to sew, and I developed these skills over time for personal use. I was initially nervous about bringing sewing into my social research. I was already known as a cycling sociologist, having merged my love of bicycles into my PhD and post-doctoral studies. Would I kill my passions if I brought (all of) my interests to work? Fortunately, the desire to sew was strong and I have since found that the stitching of my research and sewing skills have greatly benefited both and forged something altogether new.

For over a decade I have been exploring the critical and creative practice of speculative sewing in several projects about the socio-histories of wearable technology inventions. I have led teams of sewing social scientists on 'Bikes and Bloomers' about the history of inventive women's convertible cycle wear in late Victorian Britain and on 'Politics of Patents' which explores 200 years of inventors' attempts to disrupt, subvert or resist hegemonic norms via radical new forms of clothing. Both projects involve taking an inventive approach to the study of clothing inventions in global patent archives.

Patents are ideas in the form of legal documents (Figure 24.1). But they are much more. I think of them as ways of doing experimental time-travelling interviews. We can learn a lot about historic inventors, their concerns, skills and creative imaginings from their patent texts and images. They reveal some things easily and hold back on others, requiring us to take new approaches or ask different questions. Clothing patents not only include text and images, but they also provide step-by-step

Figure 24.1 Drawings from an 1895 clothing patent for a convertible cycling skirt (European Patent Office Espacenet).

instructions for future users to re-construct items of dress. As such, they invite us into the process of translating ideas (back) into matter. Of course, while not every great idea made its way into patent archives and there are many colonial, race, class and gendered biases that shape these records, they still provide insights into lesser-known inventors and socio-political issues of the time. Khan argues, for instance, that they 'provide a consistent source of objective information about the market-related activities of women during a period for which only limited data are available' (1996, p. 358).

Speculative sewing, or what I describe as the combination of research-ing, re-constructing and re-imagining clothing inventions, is a way of enter-ing into multidimensional dialogues. It combines theoretical engagement with ethnographic analysis and hands-on object-oriented practice. It is a method that challenges assumptions, expands skills and forces research-ers to question what is and isn't included in inventors' detailed instruc-tions. We render gaps visible, make sense of the mess, make decisions as we go along and reflect on these choices. Along with other feminist, queer and decolonial archive researchers, Swaby and Frank encourage 'experimentation as a form of dwelling and lingering in the archive to subvert linear notions of time and place' (2020, p. 124). They view it as a 'means to read, experience, feel and touch archives' (Swaby and Frank, 2020, p. 124). In the process of translating clothing inventions into interactive storytelling devices, we get up close and literally inside historic archive data.

Studying Clothing as a Social Scientist

Clothing of some kind touches *every* single body. It directly connects social life, technological change and the political world, and as such can be seen as central to ideas around the politics of identity and belonging, private and public space and agency. Bari writes evocatively about the intimacy of clothing: 'In clothes, we are connected to other people, and other places in complicated and unyielding ways' (2019, pp. 9–10).

There are many ways of studying clothing. Some use the lens of fashion, design and textiles to focus closely on the artefacts themselves, while others expand out to issues of sustainability and labour inequalities. I apply my 'sociological imagination' to explore clothing as a barometer of socio-political change: linking past problems to present issues, and personal lives to political systems and infrastructures. I look specifically to STS, sociology and cultural studies to frame a study of what we wear. Crane, for instance, argues that '[c]hanges in clothing, and the discourses surrounding clothing indicate shifts in social relationships and tensions between different social groups that present themselves in different ways in public space' (2000, p. 3). Parkins similarly argues that clothes 'either contest or reinforce existing arrangements of power and "flesh out" the meanings of citizenship' (2002, p. 2).

I study social change *in* and *through* clothing. This means I view clothing as a device, or a wearable technology, that enables, constrains and organises wearers in different ways in relation to socio-technical happenings and relations. Doing this involves making and wearing the clothes of others while researching their lives, influences and socio-cultural contexts. It's a perspective oriented to clothing's role in the public sphere. So, rather than looking at the surface of clothes, I get into the design embedded in its seams and stitches to better understand not only how and why someone invented it in the first place, but also how and where it might have been worn and how it worked. The latter is critical when studying convertible, multiple and hidden inventions that shift from one form into another (Jungnickel, 2023a).

This approach emphasises the role of bodies. Some researchers claim that clothes do not yield much information on their own. Entwistle (2015), for example, argues that clothes are not lifeless 'shells'. They hold traces of the people that made, lived in and shaped them. 'When dress is pulled apart from the body/self,' she writes, 'as it is in the costume museum, we grasp only a fragment, a partial snapshot of dress, and our understanding is thus limited' (2015, p. 10). Without bodies, clothes can only tell us so much. What they 'cannot tell us is how the garment was worn, how the garment moved when on a body, what it sounded like when it moved and how it felt to the wearer' (Entwistle, 2015, p. 10). In a similar vein, Miller reminds us that clothes 'are among our most personal possessions' and 'the main medium between our sense of our bodies and our sense of the external world' (2010, p. 23). He argues against investigating clothing only as a representation because it is also experienced; it mediates physical, socio-political and cultural interactions. 'A study of clothing,' he writes, 'should not be *cold*; it has to invoke the tactile, emotional, intimate world of feelings' (2010, p. 41, emphasis in original).

Making and Wearing Your Research

Clothes often make more sense on than off the body. This is especially important when historic clothing texts are more often written by critics than by wearers. Bendall (2019) discovered this in her research about 16th-century women's undergarments. Little data could be found, and what were available were 'notoriously prone to exaggeration and even malice' and revealed 'much more about male anxieties than information about what it was actually like to wear these garments' (2019, p. 366). Analysing text and images, and then making and wearing clothes adds extra textures and layers to the data. Bendall argues that 'materially reconstructing artifacts produces knowledge that cannot be gained by other means' (2019, p. 364).

Some research subjects demand this kind of engagement. Sometimes, the only way to understand data is in context. This is especially critical for clothing inventions like 1890s cycling costumes which convert from one form into another, such as a walking skirt into a cycling cape. There were occasions when my research teams could not make sense of an invention using text and line drawings alone. It wasn't until the patent was sewn into a full-sized garment, put on a body and various cord and button mechanisms were activated that we were able to grasp the inventor's intention. Similarly, I have experimented with demonstrating clothing inventions on hangers or laid out on tables, rather than getting dressed in them. It rarely works as well. Mechanisms get stuck or fail to work at all. Pieces slide off tables. Cords and ribbons tangle. Explaining an invention, with and on the body, using arms, hands, hips and legs, amplifies the liveliness of the ideas, thickens the dialogue between the present and the past and sparks engagement with different audiences.

Other researchers have found similar themes in their work. Connell and Nicosia cook with archival data in the process of updating recipes from 17th- and 18th-century recipe books. They argue that 'historical recipes belong in the modern kitchen – that they can and should be read and enacted as instructions, as well as studied as archival texts from a specific historical period' (2015, n.p.). 'After all', they argue, 'what are recipes if not primarily instructions for cooking?' (Connell and Nicosia, 2015, n.p.). Clothing patents are in many ways like recipes or historical manuals. They invite readers to try out the ideas, by making and wearing the inventions.

Critically, the aim of speculative sewing is not to create perfect historical replicas. This was neither my skill set nor interest. Similarly, Connell and Nicosia in their historical cooking project were not committed to 'recreating the experience of early modern cooking' and focused instead on a 'desire to taste the past' (2015, n.p.). In my experience, re-constructing historic clothing offers new ways into the research, a chance to spend time with the inventor through their invention, reflect on the making process and experience their dynamic artefacts in multisensory, hands-on bodily practice. ·

An Example: Appreciating a Boring Buttonhole

Buttonholes are pretty boring. They are easy to overlook and underappreciated in everyday life. Most commonly we know them as small, reinforced holes in fabric that allow a button to be passed through and secure two or more layers together. Buttonholes, and their accompanying buttons, are a fastening technique that has been around since at least the 13th century and most likely before. Unlike hems or zippers (or even buttons), button-holes rarely malfunction. Yet, their apparent simplicity belies the critical importance they bring to clothes and offer to social researchers. I suggest by way of an example of speculative sewing in practice that boring but-tonholes, and sewing more generally, can offer time-travelling portals to fascinating socio-political worlds.

Chances are you rarely look at buttonholes carefully unless there's something wrong with them (or you are attempting to mend or make one). STS scholars have argued that it is only when things break down or need repair that we come to recognise and appreciate the critical role they play in our lives. Star (1999) has done much to advocate the study of mundane things by pointing out that it is not the things themselves that are 'bor-ing', but how we tend to look at them. Doors, sewers, seatbelts, onions, Velcro and water pumps are just a few examples of things studied by STS researchers that attend to the idea that seemingly unremarkable artefacts and systems make explicit the familiar and taken-for-granted ways in which people make sense of and operate in everyday life (see, for example, Hawkins, 2005; Michael, 2006).

Buttonholes can be added to this list. They are easy to ignore when getting dressed, yet they can lead to embarrassing incidents when they fail or buttons get fastened in the wrong order. They can also be tricky to make and mend. Buttonholes are technically specific. They must be sewn in the right place, and evenly stitched at a certain width to secure the hole in the fabric and at just the right length to match a button. They're even more interesting when the reason for including them in clothing doesn't involve a button at all. As we discovered, buttonholes can be hacked to do something altogether different. In one 1890s convertible cycling skirt, buttonholes formed part of a larger infrastructural system of waxed cords, stitched channels and weights. Together, these elements made up a pul-ley system concealed in seams and hems that hoisted heavy layered skirts safely up and out of the way of the bicycle wheels. It enabled the wearer to secretly switch from socially acceptable fashions to safe and comfortable sportswear as needed.

Figure 24.2 Speculatively sewing historical clothing inventions (photograph by author).

Figure 24.2 documents this experience. A camera affixed to the ceiling of the office took images every 30 seconds for weeks as part of an ethnographic experiment. This image serendipitously captures my delight, and relief, at the end of a long day when I had finally worked out the point and purpose of hidden buttonholes in the invention. What was quick to read in the patent text took far longer to reproduce. It was more complex than initially expected. I had never spent this long thinking about a buttonhole before. I was forced to see it afresh and to answer questions about its use that I had not even thought to ask at the start. As I toiled, I reflected on how the inventor might have been thinking similar things, and possibly experiencing many of the same failures, in the process of inventing a convertible cycling skirt. What emerged in the process of this example of speculative sewing was a newfound appreciation of a boring buttonhole. I came to understand it as part of a complex socio-technical system for early women cyclists to claim active and independent public lives. I appreciated how the inventor worked with all the materials and skills she had to hand,

Figure 24.3 A reconstructed 1895 convertible cycle skirt with material raised up and out of the way of the wheels (photograph by author).

expanding and re-configuring even the humble buttonhole in her attempt to work around restrictions to women's freedom of movement in Victorian society (Figure 24.3).

Conclusion

Central to ethnographic research is the desire to gain a deep and thick understanding of the cultures and practices of a specific group. This is even more important, and challenging, when your subjects of study lived over a century ago and there are few traces of them in conventional records. Data on early inventors, especially women and marginalised people, tend to be fragmented and sparse. This requires us to become inventive with our methods. Historic patent archives are one source of data where we can learn about what interested, restricted or concerned (some) people enough to tackle a problem with their own hands and sewing skills. Speculative sewing renders these socio-political issues in multidimensional material forms that we can analyse from different perspectives. In this way it offers a multisensory glimpse of the many struggles early inventors faced and some of the ingenious methods they used to overcome them. Doing social research with sewing may not be appropriate for everyone or for all research subjects. What I hope to have conveyed is how applying a social science lens to existing skills and interests can add value to the craft of research. Also, by paying attention to boring and mundane things we might ask new questions about things we take for granted.

Acknowledgements

'Politics of Patents' (POP) is funded by a Horizon 2020 European Research Council consolidator grant (#819458). 'Bikes and Bloomers' was supported by an Economic and Social Research Council Knowledge Exchange grant (ES/K008048/1).

References

Bari, S. (2019) *Dressed: The Secret Life of Clothes*. London: Jonathan Cape.

Bendall, S. (2019) 'The case of the "French Vardinggale": A methodological approach to reconstructing and understanding ephemeral garments', *Fashion Theory*, 23(3), pp. 363–399.

Connell, A. and Nicosia, M. (2015) 'Cooking in the archives: Bringing early modern manuscript recipes into a twenty-first-century kitchen', *Archive Journal*. Available at: www.archivejournal.net/notes/cooking-in-the-archives-bringing-early-modern-manuscript-recipes-into-a-twenty-first-century-kitchen/

Crane, D. (2000) *Fashion and Its Social Agendas: Class, Gender and Identity in Clothing*. Chicago, IL, London: University of Chicago Press.

Entwistle, J. (2015) *The Fashioned Body: Fashion, Dress and Modern Social Theory*. 2nd edition. Cambridge: Polity.

Haraway, D. (2016) *Staying with the Trouble: Making Kin in the Chthulucene*. Durham, NC: Duke University Press.

Hawkins, G. (2005) *The Ethics of Waste*. Oxford: Rowman & Littlefield Publishers Inc.

Jungnickel, K. (2018) 'Making things to make sense of things: DIY as practice and research', in Sayers, J. (ed.) *The Routledge Companion to Media Studies and Digital Humanities*. London, New York: Routledge, pp. 491–502.

Jungnickel, K. (2023a) 'Convertible, multiple and hidden: The inventive lives of women's sport and activewear 1890–1940', *The Sociological Review*, Online First 1 March.

Jungnickel, K. (2023b) 'Speculative sewing: Researching, reconstructing and re-imagining clothing as technoscience', *Social Studies of Science*, 53(1), pp. 146–162.

Khan, Z.B. (1996) 'Married women's property laws and female commercial activity: Evidence from United States patent records, 1790-1895', *The Journal of Economic History*, 56(2), pp. 356-388.

Law, J. and Urry, J. (2011) 'Enacting the social', *Economy and Society*, 33(3), pp. 390-410.

Michael, M. (2006) *Technoscience and Everyday Life: The Complex Simplicities of the Mundane*. London: Open University Press.

Miller, D. (2010) *Stuff*. Cambridge: Polity.

Parkins, W. (ed.) (2002) *Fashioning the Body Politic: Dress, Gender, Citizenship*. Oxford, New York: Berg.

Star, S.L. (1999) 'The ethnography of infrastructure', *American Behavioral Scientist*, 43(3), pp. 377-391.

Swaby, N.A. and Frank, F. (2020) 'Archival experiments, notes and (dis)orientations', *Feminist Review*, 125, pp. 4-16.

25

How to do social research with... wax

Louise Rondel

Setting the Scene

On a tour of one of the UK's depilatory wax manufacturers, we finish the visit in the warehouse where my tour guide, the Managing Director of the company, points to the pallets of goods stacked from floor to ceiling. Providing an inventory of what is stored there, he lists the contents of the boxes and sacks and their countries of origin or the places to where they are being shipped: resins from Portugal, hydrocarbon resins from the Netherlands, paraffin waxes from China, France, and Taiwan, and palm oil from Malaysia alongside finished and packaged waxes destined for the UK, Korea, Romania, France, America, and Italy.

(Fieldnotes, October 2019)

A factory depot on an industrial estate may seem an odd place for an examination of beauty and 'femininity'.[1] Certainly, in this massive warehouse, standing amongst the pallets of raw materials and finished products and moving out of the way of a forklift, I was bemused as to how I had got there. My project had started out about women's relationship with beauty work and the reasons why they choose particular treatments. I had expected my fieldwork to take place in beauty salons, not in draughty warehouses next to a motorway junction. Yet the more time I spent with customers in salons interviewing them about their beauty practices (where hair removal was nearly always mentioned)

---

[1]Femininity appears in inverted commas throughout to recognise that this is but one version of 'femininity' and that it is socially, culturally and materially constructed.

Figure 25.1 In the warehouse: Raw materials for blending depilatory wax (photograph by Louise Rondel).

and observing beauty therapists whilst they worked (where depilatory waxing was one of the, if not *the*, most popular treatments),[2] I became increasingly interested in the materials necessary for the realisation of beauty work. I came to question the role played by the wax, other beauty products and their constitutive petroleum-based ingredients in the production of 'femininity' in the salon. Thus, I began to examine how wax *effects* – that is to say, puts into motion – this particular version of 'femininity'. It was wanting to explore what wax is and thus *what wax does* which prompted me to leave the beauty salon and explains why I ended up in the factory depot.

---

[2]This is perhaps unsurprising given, as other work in critical beauty studies has shown, '[e]ven a small amount of hair growth may be understood as a threat to femininity' (Toerien and Wilkinson, 2003, p. 88).

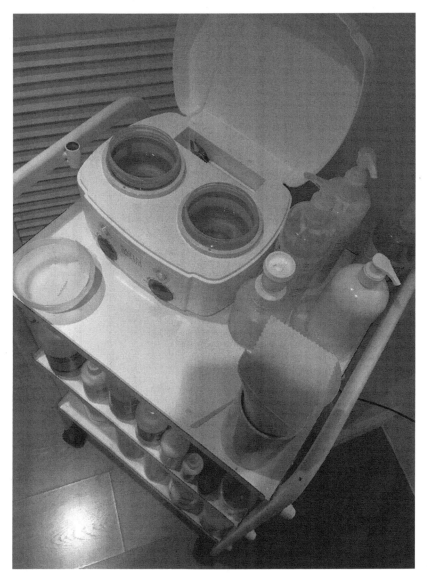

Figure 25.2 In the salon: The beauty therapist's work station (photograph by Louise Rondel).

Beauty Matters

To 'do social research with wax', I closely attend to the material itself, to what it is, how it behaves, who works with it and how it impacts on those with whom it comes into contact. In this, wax is considered 'vibrant matter'; a thing which 'has efficacy, can *do* things, has sufficient coherence to make a difference, produce effects, alter the course of events' (Bennett, 2010, p. viii, original emphasis); which has the 'capacity to prompt certain actions' (Hawkins, 2009, p. 193). This focus on wax as lively matter underscores the material dynamics entangled in the production of a 'feminine' appearance in the salon as it prompts particular practices and formations and, ultimately, makes hairlessness possible. Interrelatedly, 'doing social research with wax' highlights how this 'femininity' is inseparable from the long-term and unevenly distributed health impacts of the labour of beauty work as the beauty therapists 'co-emerge with the materials that we mine, manufacture, and mobilise' (Litvintseva, 2019, p. 154). As such, 'doing social research with wax' allowed me to explore not only how the wax's active materiality effects a particular hairless version of 'femininity', but it also permitted me to address broader concerns about how beauty products, oil dependence, labour practices, uneven health impacts, environmental injustices and 'femininity' are entangled.

In the following, I begin with my guided tour of the wax manufacturers to closely examine what the wax consists of and, in particular, the petro-products which afford it particular 'performance characteristics' (personal correspondence with wax manufacturers, November 2019). These characteristics – malleable, meltable, spreadable, viscous, viscid, colourful ('feminine'), pleasant-smelling ('feminine') – enable the wax to remove 'unfeminine' hair. In the second section, I continue this investigation by returning to the salon. Here, I attend to the beauty therapists' engagement with the wax and other tools and beauty products exploring how these are (at times literally) incorporated. In each section, I take a different methodological approach connected through putting wax-as-material and its effectuations at the centre of my inquiry. In the first section, I draw on the explanations of people working in the wax manufacturing trade, but find wax's active role overshadowed by an emphasis on how the products have been developed to respond to customer demand. Having already spent time in beauty salons and experienced the wax 'in action', I am left questioning the straightforward demand–supply narratives put forward by the manufacturers. In the second section, I return to the salon to consider the beauty therapists' relationships with the wax by asking them to tell me about what they are doing as they perform treatments. Unlike the explanations of those manufacturing wax, these *in situ* observational interviews make explicit wax's lively materiality, the role it plays in the therapists' working lives and how it serves to actively effect 'femininity'. These interviews also draw attention to the (potentially[3]) toxic and long-term health impacts of carrying out beauty work. I consider these not as consequences of the production of 'femininity', but rather as inseparable from it, for the very petro-products which provide the particular 'performance characteristics' of different beauty products also permeate the salon environment and bodies working therein in more insidious ways.

Meeting Demand?

Having spent the early part of my fieldwork in beauty salons, I became increasingly interested in the wax itself, where it comes from, and how it is made and so I arranged a visit to a wax manufacturer. At the beginning of my guided tour of the factory, I am invited into the boardroom and seated opposite a glass-fronted cabinet whose shelves are filled with the impressive range of products made by the company. Here, the Managing Director starts my visit by talking me through the uptake of waxing in the UK since the 1980s, describing how the preferences and treatments have changed and how the products have been innovated in order to respond to the different trends. As he explains it, a series of linear developments appears: propelled by various cultural factors, it has become normal for ever-increasing parts of women's bodies to be hairless and so the manufacturers have responded to this demand by blending different ingredients in different quantities, resulting in waxes with different properties, which act in different ways, and which thus can be used on different areas of the body. For example, he describes how the soft and sticky waxes of the 1970s

---

[3]It is important here to emphasise the *potential* toxicity of these products as although nobody and nowhere is free from toxins (Alaimo, 2008, p. 260), the ways in which these impact us vary enormously.

were fine for waxing the lower legs as here you have the shin bone and calf muscle which provide some traction against which to pull. But, he continues, these early waxes were unsuitable for the softer, fleshier and more sensitive areas of the thighs. And so, as full-leg and bikini-line and then Brazilian[4] and Hollywood[5] waxing became increasingly popular, it seems that, in response, waxes with different properties were developed so that this demand for extended hairlessness could be met (fieldnotes, October 2019).

In developing waxes to (seemingly) meet this demand, oil-derived ingredients feature heavily. In the warehouse, we are surrounded by pallets stacked from floor to ceiling and piled high with sacks of hydrocarbon resins, boxes of paraffin waxes and drums of white oil. In an email correspondence, the Quality Assurance Manager of another wax manufacturer explains how, amongst others, petro-products are used in depilatory wax to provide colour, fragrance and other properties (personal correspondence, November 2019). For example, he tells me that white oil (*Paraffinum liquidum*) – a by-product of the petroleum refining process whose 'major global producers' are Petro-Canada and Exxon – is 'fairly commonly used in depilatory products' (personal correspondence, November 2019). In addition, for hot waxes which need to 'remain malleable enough to be removed without the need for cloth waxing strips', polymers are added in order 'to provide these performance characteristics' (personal correspondence, November 2019). Most straightforwardly, these by-products give the wax particular ways of performing which, in turn, allow the wax to meet the demand for 'feminine' hairlessness – hairlessness which has been, according to my tour guide, largely driven by changing fashions and the increased availability of pornography (fieldnotes, October 2019).

In these explanations, it seems as if the developments in wax are straightforwardly reacting to consumer demands propelled by various socio-cultural factors. The wax seems muted, far from an active participant in the making of 'feminine' hairlessness. Yet I am left wondering about the role of the wax itself, for as formulas are developed which change what

---

[4] An intimate form of waxing where all the pubic and anal hair is removed except for a thin strip on the mons pubis.

[5] An intimate form of waxing where all the pubic and anal hair is removed.

wax is, the possibilities of what it can do (i.e., the hair it can remove and the body parts which can be hairless) are expanded. As I am sitting in the boardroom, I compare the neatly-packaged wax in the display cabinet to the fieldwork I had conducted in the beauty salons where I had experienced the hot, sticky, viscous, malleable wax at work. Despite the straightforward explanations of my tour guide, I question if the wax is merely meeting the demand for 'feminine' hairlessness? If perhaps 'feminine' hairlessness is, in fact, predicated on the wax and its petro-derived 'performance characteristics'? If these, in fact, are serving to effect 'feminine' hairlessness? What else is the wax engendering here and how is this imbricated in the production of 'femininity'? And I return to the salon with a keener attention to what the wax is and so to what it can do.

'It's All About How It Acts'

Unlike the explanations of those manufacturing wax where the product appears to be only responding to consumer demand, subordinate to the logic of demand–supply, spending time in the beauty salon and observing beauty therapists at work drew my attention to its liveliness. Returning to the beauty salon and asking the therapists to tell me about what they were doing as they worked put into relief how wax has its own ways of moving, stopping, sticking, not-sticking, spreading, cooling and ultimately removing hair. As one therapist describes to me as she carries out a leg and bikini waxing treatment, 'for me, it's all about how it acts', precisely explaining 'what I know from working with this' whilst using the spreading spatula to twirl the perfect amount of wax at the perfect temperature before deftly applying a swatch of the perfect width and length to the client's leg (fieldnotes, October 2019). Thus, as they work with it to produce 'feminine' bodies, narrating their work reveals how the wax brings about the beauty therapists' bodily movements and dispositions as the materially-informed skill of waxing becomes incorporated (as well as shaping their own bodies in less obvious and more pernicious ways). For those working with it in the salon, then, the wax's 'performance characteristics' – how it moves, sticks, heats up, cools down, is removed – become integrated into their bodily-spatial repertoire. In combination with how the wax itself acts, this is an acquisition of an embodied set of skills which further entrenches increased 'feminine' hairlessness, for as the beauty therapists are able to perform an ever-wider range of services, in part engendered by the wax, ever more services in turn become possible.

Focusing on the materiality of the wax and other beauty products (many of which also rely on petroleum-derived compounds for their 'performance characteristics') shows how these shape the beauty therapists' bodies in more insidious and (potentially) toxic ways too. Performing the depilatory treatments, the beauty therapist is continuously in motion. Negotiating and managing the wax and other products, the tools and the client's body, she[6] repeats the movements of bending over the treatment bed, applying the wax, smoothing the strip and ripping it off. Occupational health and social science research has shown some of the harmful bodily impacts of carrying out beauty treatments. For instance, there are reports into musculoskeletal issues and joint pain from long hours of standing and performing repetitive actions (de Gennaro *et al.*, 2014) and risk of injury from contact with hot wax and sharp tools or from thrashing customers undergoing painful waxing treatments (Herzig, 2009, p. 258). Thus, at the same time as skill becomes incorporated, these work practices painfully become ingrained in the salon workers' skin, muscles and joints. Although the wax itself might not be toxic, occupational health studies into beauty salon work have reported on concerns around exposure to Volatile Organic Compounds, phthalates and numerous other pollutants emitted from a cocktail of products used in hair and beauty treatments (Zota and Shamasunder, 2017). This research has pointed to how these salon exposures (potentially) give rise to a suite of health impacts: skin allergies, respiratory disorders, cancers, endocrine disruption, reproductive harms and impaired development in foetuses and children. Moreover, if, as Naomi Wolf has famously argued, beauty work has become women's 'third shift', working to limit their power and undo the gains of feminism (2002, p. 25), then it is crucial to attend to Miliann Kang's response that Wolf's position 'ignore[s] the many women who do not do their own beauty work ... *[who] pass off sizable portions of the third shift onto the shoulders of less-privileged women*' (2010, p. 15, emphasis added). Indeed, the research into the

---

[6]The beauty industry has a highly feminised workforce: in the UK, '94% of people working in beauty are female' (National Hair and Beauty Federations, 2019, n.p.).

health impacts of salon work has highlighted that this (potential) toxicity is most heavily borne by the largely female workforce and within this, by racialised and otherwise marginalised women. An attention to the materiality of the wax and other products, to the petro-products which constitute them, and to what they are and so *what they do* is one way of bringing these asymmetrical impacts to the fore. These, I argue, are not merely the consequences of working with these products and the notion of 'femininity' underpinning this work. Rather, attending to the wax (amongst other products) and what it does shows that these (potentially) toxic effects are fully entangled with 'femininity' as produced in the salon. The very compounds which enable the products to perform in particular ways are those which also give rise to these (potential) harms, ultimately making this version of 'femininity' possible.

Conclusion

'Doing social research with wax' has put into relief how the hairless version of 'femininity' produced in the salon is not only socio-culturally impelled but has significant material contingencies and is permeated by petro-products. I have argued that, by affording the wax particular 'performance characteristics', oil by-products make extended hair removal possible and so effect and entrench 'femininity' as hairless. 'Doing social research with wax' has further drawn attention to the significant bodily impacts on those who work with the wax and other beauty products as they make their living. These impacts include the development of the embodied skill of waxing which also serves to effect 'feminine' hairlessness as well as the more pernicious incorporation of the products, a (potentially) toxic burden most heavily borne by the disadvantaged women who perform the 'third shift' of beauty work. This (at times literal) incorporation of the products also works to effect 'femininity' as the impacts are inseparable from how the materials act.

But 'how to do social research with wax'? Underpinning this examination of the production of 'femininity', the associated petro-derived products and the unequal impacts of beauty work is the insistence that wax is a lively (or deadly) material. In other words, I take wax as an active participant in the social world with the ability to effect particular practices and formations and, concomitantly, to shape bodies and make 'femininity'. Methodologically, this has involved a focus on *what wax is* and so *what wax does*. This enabled me to question the straightforward demand–supply explanations whereby those working in wax manufacturing posit the developments in wax as merely a response to consumer demand for 'feminine' hairlessness. Instead, considering the wax's petro-afforded properties and examining how it acts in practice show that the hairless version of 'femininity' is equally prompted by the material. Leaving the factory and returning to the salon, the wax as an active participant most clearly comes into view, especially when asking the beauty therapists to tell me about what they are doing as they do it. Through these *in situ* narrations, not only their relationship with the wax and other beauty products but, entwined with this, '*how it acts*' and how it becomes incorporated are put into relief. Thinking through these alongside occupational health research which also emphasises the materiality of the products and their emissions, the (potential) toxicity of the work and its uneven distribution (inseparable from this production of 'femininity') are underscored. To 'do social research with wax', then, I have closely attended to what wax *is* and so what it *does*, and so to how it is worked with, to what it affords and effects, to the different (and potentially toxic) ways it is incorporated, and to how all of this is entangled to produce a particular version of 'femininity'.

References

Alaimo, S. (2008) 'Trans-corporeal feminisms and the ethical space of nature', in Alaimo, S. and Hekman, S. (eds) *Material Feminisms*. Bloomington, Indianapolis: Indiana University Press.

Bennett, J. (2010) *Vibrant Matter: A Political Ecology of Things*. Durham, NC, London: Duke University Press.

De Gennaro, G., de Gennaro, L., Mazzone, A., Porcelli, F. and Tutino, M. (2014) 'Indoor air quality in hair salons: Screening of volatile organic compounds and indicators based on health risk assessment', *Atmospheric Environment*, 83, pp. 119–126.

Hawkins, G. (2009) 'The politics of bottled water: Assembling bottled water as brand, waste, and oil', *Journal of Cultural Economy*, 2(1–2), pp. 183–195.

Herzig, R. (2009) 'The political economy of choice: Genital modification and the global cosmetic services industry', *Australian Feminist Studies*, 24(60), pp. 251–263.

Kang, M. (2010) *The Managed Hand: Race, Gender, and The Body in Beauty Service Work*. Berkeley, Los Angeles, London: University of California Press.

Litvintseva, S. (2019) 'Asbestos: Inside and outside, toxic and haptic', *Environmental Humanities*, 11(1), pp. 152–173.

National Hair and Beauty Federations (2019) '2019 Industry statistics for hairdressing, barbering, and beauty'. Available at: www.nhbf.co.uk/documents/hair-and-beauty-industry-statistics/ (Accessed: 23 February 2021).

Toerien, M. and Wilkinson, S. (2003) 'Gender and body hair: Constructing the feminine woman', *Women's Studies International Forum*, 26(4), pp. 333–344.

Wolf, N. (2002) *The Beauty Myth: How Images of Beauty Are Used against Women*. New York: HarperCollins.

Zota, A.R. and Shamasunder, B. (2017) 'The environmental injustice of beauty: Framing chemical exposures from beauty products as a health disparities concern', *American Journal of Obstetrics, and Gynecology*, 271(4), pp. 418–423.

26

How to do social research with... WhatsApp soapie

Yasmin Gunaratnam, Phoebe Kisubi Mbasalaki and Sara Matchett

Scene

Scene 1: Action!
   What happened to Tanya?
   TEXT MESSAGES READING:
   Has any1 seen Tanya?
   What really happened to Tanya?

A phone buzzes. The screen lights up. A text message. 'What happened to Tanya?' The question arrives embedded in a sequence of short textual narratives, photographs and video clips. Together, the various stories gather into scenes in a WhatsApp soapie or soap opera. Our soapie[1] was made towards the end of 2019, using participatory theatre and Performance as Research (PaR) methods with a group of 13 street-based sex workers in Cape Town. The soapie was part of a bigger trans-regional project on decolonising gender inequalities.[2] In centring bodies and emotions, PaR resists 'unhelpful dichotomies and fixed binaries which separate embodiment and intuition from intellectual practices, emotional experiences and ways of knowing' (Kershaw and Nicholson, 2011, p. 2).

   Before we describe our object, you should know that PaR has grown in use in post-apartheid South Africa (the apartheid regime ran between

---

[1] The idea to make the soapie was inspired by Sanlam's (a South African insurance company) WhatsApp drama series, *Uk'shona Kwelanga* (Sanlam, n.d.).
[2] The WhatsApp soapie was part of a five-year collaborative research project between the Centre for Theatre, Dance and Performance Studies (CTDPS), the African Gender Institute (AGI) at the University of Cape Town, and the non-governmental organisation (NGO), the Sex Workers Education and Advocacy Task Force (SWEAT). The wider research consortium GlobalGrace (Global Gender and Cultures of Equality), involved six countries (South Africa, Brazil, Bangladesh, Mexico, the Philippines and the United Kingdom).

1948 and 1994), mostly through work in university theatre and perfor-mance departments. PaR tries to convey the interanimation of thought and the experiencing body. Recognising a thinking, sensually appreciat-ing self was important to us because of the potential for the method to lure and be receptive to what can be difficult to put into words. Or, where the concepts and vocabulary to signify sidelined experiences are depleted, lacking or lost; a structure known as 'epistemic injustice' (Fricker, 2007).

The techniques that we used in developing our soapie come from Forum Theatre (Boal, 1985), a form of participatory theatre where audi-ences are invited to come up with possible solutions or alternatives to challenges presented in a theatre piece. In Forum Theatre, actors perform a scene, featuring an oppressed protagonist. The scene must end unre-solved, leaving the protagonist with their problems. It is then performed a second time and the audience is invited to pause the scene when they dis-agree with the protagonist's choices. The spectator (or 'spect-actor') who stalls the action then intervenes to try to change the outcome. They do this by replacing the protagonist and exploring other options. In workshop-ping our soapie scenes, there was no 'outside' audience. The sex workers were their own audience.

To make a soapie like ours requires a smart phone with audio-visual recording and editing functions. You will also need a group of perform-ers; knowledge of theatre (especially theatre of the oppressed techniques) and/or a script writer; and locations in which you can film in safety. We created a closed group of about 30 people to send our soapie to, using the WhatsApp broadcast list function. The group consisted of members of the theatre group, employees of our NGO partner, the Sex Worker Education and Advocacy Taskforce (SWEAT), global partners on the GlobalGrace project and other allies. Why work with a closed group? Because sex work is still criminalised and stigmatised in South Africa. We felt that a larger public audience would endanger the sex workers.

A Scene

The scene, then, is our object. A scene is a framing device, a dramaturgi-cal apparatus and a 'problem space' (Lury, 2021), in which conundrums unfold and stories are told and re-/enacted. A problem space, as Celia Lury describes it, is characterised by givens, goals and operators. '"Givens" are the facts or information that describe the problem', Lury explains (2021, p. 2), '"goals" are the desired end state of the problem – what the knower wants to know; and "operators" are the actions to be performed in reaching the desired goals'. As Lury makes clear, problems are dynamic. They are a becoming; unfolding with a method.

A scene as a sequence of action is not necessarily something we are aware of. Yet scenes are valuable sociologically and methodologically because they assert some form and timescale onto the material and/or imagined flows between givens, goals and operators. If you are up for a more psychoanalytic framing of that last point, a scene is a problem space of play in which external realities meet inner worlds of make-believe, to be messed around and experimented with: presence/absence, real/imaginary. For Gail Lewis (2017, p. 4), there is a potency and creative potential in this tension between presence and absence, in its prising open of a shifting space of 'coming into being differently'.

With 'coming into being differently' in the circumstances of post-apartheid South Africa, we invariably bump into 'seen' as a homophone of scene, holding other meanings and doing other work. The scene as 'seen' enters into discussions of 'presencing' in black feminist and anti-colonial writing and in theatre and performance studies (Lewis, 2017; Mbembe, n.d.). What it means for the lives of sex workers to be dramatised into appearance emerged in two registers of 'presencing' in our soapie: presence and sensing. These registers are mobile, resonating differently within the live scenes as they were workshopped and recorded in Cape Town and in how they journeyed outwards as visual, aural and typographic performances through WhatsApp. So, our object is layered in its movements, sensuality, times and scales. When in circulation it might afford a proximity to, as much as an uprooting from, the performed contexts.

As you move through our scenes, we encourage you to take some questions with you. *Who* is legitimised, however thinly, to have presence and *how* are they allowed to be present? Might presence have an uneven distribution for those who have to live under the radar in post-apartheid South Africa, and who might also face other hostilities such as Afrophobia and anti-migrant hatreds (see Matchett and Okech, 2015)? And what about Édouard Glissant's honouring of the right to opacity (Diawara, 2009)? Could dissimulation and opacity as survival and insurgency be compromised by the presencing energies and technologies of our methods? How can givens, goals and operators, as problems, appear and move around within and outside a scene?

Scene 2: Workshopping

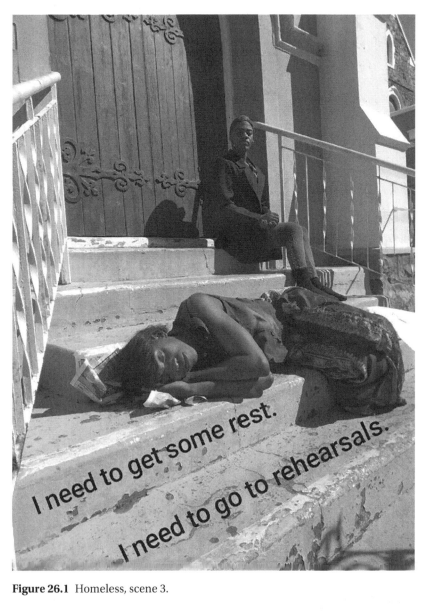

Figure 26.1 Homeless, scene 3.

The scenes in our soapie were created in scriptwriting workshops, led by scriptwriter Chase Rhys. The workshops were an offshoot of the first of five larger training modules for our participants, covering: 'Participatory Theatre/Theatre of the Oppressed'; 'Physical Theatre'; 'Voice as Material/ Poetry Making'; 'Public Art and Mask Work'; and 'Arts Administration and Fundraising'. Each module culminated in a live performance; each an experiment with different ways of making theatre. The first performance – *Intando Yam: My Choice* was staged in August 2019 and directed by Delia Meyer, a Forum Theatre practitioner.

Serendipitously, the episodic nature of *Intando Yam*, which included image sculptures, offered an obvious transition into creating the soapie. Once the group had translated their scenes into the language of WhatsApp, they began to workshop and rehearse them. Scenes were then filmed on a mobile phone. The completed scenes were given to Phoebe Kisubi Mbasalaki, who set up a WhatsApp group and posted one or two scenes per day over a two-week period.

Figure 26.1 is an example of a technique of sculpting/moulding the body into still images or tableaux to re-run and explore real-life situations, as well as more abstracted ideas such as relationships, emotions and attitudes. Working in silence, participants shape their own or each other's bodies, using only touch to convey and investigate ideas, sensations and emotions. They might move an arm or legs, adjust a head, soften or straighten out a posture. The images are then dynamised into action. The relays between stillness and movement of these adjustments can produce questions and new circumstances, manipulating and questioning the original framing of a problem, tugging it into different settings. As the scene moves, something unexpected can appear. How you curate, pace the send out of soapie scenes, how you splice text, image and sound, will further shape how a problem makes an appearance.

In producing images like this, the very absence of spoken language can help to transport experience into a mutable material form (the body as image), allowing it to be re-worked to tweak/transform the original problem. And as an image travels within the soapie, the live sensuous presence of the performer/participant in relation to themselves and to others that the workshops cultivated is left behind. What you could do differently with our object is to include more behind-the-scenes narratives, not so much in the hope of a faithful transposition of the left behind, but more in the spirit of what Fred Moten imagines as a 'a political radiophonics' (2017, p. 19), in which some of the imperfect life of the production of an image accompanies its journeys, encouraging more ambivalent readings.

Let's move on and show you another soapie scene and how you might use our object with behind-the-scenes stories to animate the flux and evaporations between method and problem. In the following section, we dropped ourselves into thinking and writing by exchanging WhatsApp voice notes, across the UK and South Africa. Transposing collaborative aurality into sociological writing is another provocation and use of our object.

Scene 3: Voice Notes

A voice note (20 seconds): Client Scene
I'm just not comfortable to do this (pause). I don't like this guy at all. I just need money, so it really hurts my feelings to do this. I'm sorry ... I'm just not happy, not at all.

This voice note extract was the first in a three-part scene. If the first note set up a protagonist and a problem, as many conventional Northern story plotlines do, the second note traced a moral reasoning. 'I mean what can I do to get money? Our clients are not this bad ... yes, I would rather fake a smile and do what's important. It will work. I know it will. I need the money'. The closing scene seems to peel back a resolution 'The only way for me to be happy and excited to do this is to take poppers. Yes, now (sound of a deep inhale and exhale) is the time for me to give the good selves. I'm excited about doing it ... sex work is work (hearty laugh, turning into a cackle)'.

As Delia Meyer told us in a voice note (of nearly 14 minutes), in the early stages of performing these scenes, one of the sex workers as a 'spect-actor' intervened with an alternative scenario. 'Hang on', Delia remembers the spect-actor saying, 'In that scene you are representing the client in a bad light ... the client actually pays our bills ... he is not your enemy'. And so, the sex-problem and the scene were deliberated and re-made. In the new composite version, Delia felt the client was 'softer' and 'gentler', with this more emotionally ambivalent rendition of sex work inciting another 'agitator', as 'the actions to be performed in reaching the desired goals' (Lury, 2021, p. 2). In the space of the new scene, the group came to discuss the reality of sex work, which can mean working with up to five clients in one night. 'What was pointed out was that it becomes very impactful and intense to be engaging with, in this sex act so many times in one night', Delia explained. An option in resolving this problem came from another sex worker who drew attention to their use of 'poppers'. (Poppers in South African slang are liquids in the alkyl nitrite family that intensify sexual pleasure.) The entwining of bodily and emotional labour in sex work can be hidden in conventional accounts. But with the theatrical inhale and exhale and the cackle of the voice-note, there is an intrusion/irruption of these types of work into sex.

Voice notes in PaR smudge the boundaries between event (speaking) and object (voice note), data and analysis. If the soapie was an experiment for the sex workers in manifesting something of the physical and economic complexity of their lives, the WhatsApp format risks trivialisation, even erasure. Participatory theatre via the mobile phone is an especially circumscribed venue in South Africa. The politics of bodily spacing and segregation are never far from the surface. With a voice note, tonal patterns, breath, pulse and pacing, as sonic qualities, can cut across histories of distance/separation, endorse or enlarge them. And once opened for the first time, the impact of a voice note can never be experienced in the same way again. Insofar as we might try to capture our experience as listeners and researchers in written fieldnotes, transcripts or voice notes themselves, we are already in the realm of sifting, sorting and flattening the sensory downpour into a narrative, complicating reflexive practices (see Froggett and Hollway, 2010 on 'scenic composition').

Scene 4: What Have We Done?

In this closing scene, we draw close to the ragged slashes of Minh-ha's (1986/1987, p. 9) refrain, 'I am like you/I am different'.

Here, we pause and note an inclination in Euro-narrative encodings of Africa: the tendency to catastrophise and tell miserable stories about those who bear the brunt of living with the ongoingness of colonial and settler-colonial injustices. Our soapie certainly resounded with scenes of everyday violations. But there were also playful, comedic stories, touching on what filmmaker and academic Frances Negrón-Muntaner (2020) terms 'decolonial joy', as those overflowing pleasures when we are able to experience a time in which coloniality is not defining. For us, decolonial joy was a lateral mist in the last soapie scene where the theatre group bursts into a South African protest song 'Senzenina', sung in *a capella* with a rhythmic, assertive stamping and shuffling of feet. The refrain – 'Senzenina' – translates from Xhosa and Zulu as 'What have we done?' 'Senzenina' is a renowned anti-apartheid and protest song (it is also sung at funerals). The idea to close the soapie with 'Senzenina' came from the theatre group who expanded its anti-colonial messaging. The defiant tones in which the performer sang and moved runs counter to a social system that criminalises and dehumanises sex workers. It is their defiance that gets in the way of an easy empathy in which otherness can be pulled into existing universal notions of humanity, equality or citizenship. To get a sense of these different registers of the closing scene, the receiver/listener/viewer does not need to be knowledgeable about the history of 'Senzenina', or of the lives of the sex workers. Rather, the uncertain expansiveness of the scene can become an opening through which to feel unequal violent inheritances: the scale of the distances of the 'I am like you/I am different' couplet.

What puzzles and unsettles us about our object is what lies in these scales of distance brought together by a soapie scene. Researchers and participants can never be sure of what is being lured or drawn down through a screen and how this can come to matter once a scene is made and sent out. Soapie scenes created in peripheralised regions with marginalised groups are especially fragile methodological and ethical objects. There are dangers of a doubling of objectification, as those usually objectified are enfolded and compressed into a portable object, released into digital economies where recorded experience is routinely skimmed and selectively mined (Han, 2021).

Rather than being a standalone methodological object and process, for us the soapie scene remains primarily an ambivalent ethical agitator. It is best used with other methods to reflect critically on and assess research relationships, tools and processes. As researchers we pass on our touchstone question and agitator, to be returned to throughout cycles of research.

'Senzenina'. What have we done?

References

Boal, A. (1985) *The Theatre of the Oppressed*. Translated by Charles A. McBride. New York: Theatre Communications Group.

Diawara, M. (2009) *Édouard Glissant: One World in Relation*. Directed by Manthia Diawara. French with English subtitles. New York: K'a Yéléma Productions.

Fricker, M. (2007) *Epistemic Injustice: Power and the Ethics of Knowing*. Oxford: Oxford University Press.

Froggett, L. and Hollway, W. (2010) 'Psychosocial research analysis and scenic understanding', *Psychoanalysis, Culture and Society*, 15(3), pp. 281–301.

Han, B-C. (2021) 'I practice philosophy as art', *ArtReview*, 2 December. Available at: https://artreview.com/byung-chul-han-i-practise-philosophy-as-art/

Kershaw, B. and Nicholson, H. (eds) (2011) *Research Methods in Theatre and Performance*. Edinburgh: Edinburgh University Press.

Lewis, G. (2017) 'Questions of presence', *Feminist Review*, 117, pp. 1–19.

Lury, C. (2021) *Problem Spaces: How and Why Methodology Matters*. Cambridge: Polity.

Matchett, S. and Okech, A. (2015) 'Uhambo: Pieces of a dream: Waiting in the ambiguity of liminality', in Fleishman, M. (ed.) *Performing Migrancy and Mobility in Africa: Cape of Flows*. London, New York: Palgrave Macmillan, pp. 110–124.

Mbembe, A. (n.d.) 'Decolonizing knowledge and the question of the archive'. Available at: https://wiser.wits.ac.za/system/files/Achille%20Mbembe%20-%20Decolonizing%20Knowledge%20and%20the%20Question%20of%20the%20Archive.pdf (Accessed: 23 May 2022).

Minh-ha, T. (1986/1987) 'Introduction', *Discourse*, 6, p. 9.

Moten, F. (2017) *Black and Blur: Consent Not to Be a Single Being*. Durham, NC, London: Duke University Press.

Negrón-Muntaner, F. (2020) 'Decolonial joy: Theorising from the art of valor y cambio', in Clisby, S., Johnson, M. and Turner, J. (eds) *Theorising Cultures of Equality*. London: Routledge, pp. 171–194.

Sanlam (n.d.) *Uk'shona Kwelanga*. Cape Town: Sanlam. Available at: www.sanlam.co.za/brandshowreel/Pages/ukshona-kwelanga.aspx

Index